THE
FOUNDATIONS
OF
SOCIAL ORDER

Studies in the Creeds and
Councils of the Early Church

by

Rousas John Rushdoony

ROSS HOUSE BOOKS
VALLECITO, CALIFORNIA 95251

Library of Congress Catalog Card Number: 68-25836

ISBN:1-879998-12-2

Printed in the United States of America

To Dorothy, with love

Other books by
Rousas John Rushdoony

Institutes of Biblical Law
Law & Society
Systematic Theology
God's Plan for Victory
Romans & Galatians
The Politics of Guilt and Pity
Christianity and the State
Salvation and Godly Rule
The Messianic Character of American Education
Roots of Reconstruction
The One and the Many
Revolt Against Maturity
By What Standard?
Law & Liberty

For a complete listing of available books
by Rousas John Rushdoony and other
Christian Reconstructionists, contact:

ROSS HOUSE BOOKS
PO Box 67
Vallecito, CA 95251

This publication is made possible
by the tithes and offerings
of the members of Nicene Covenant Church
and Pastor Ellsworth McIntyre, founder of
Grace Community Day Care & Schools,
4405 Outer Dr., Naples, Florida 34112.

TABLE OF CONTENTS

1998 Preface

by R. J. Rushdoony

In all my writings, I have sought to show the relationship between faith, theology, ideas, and life. In four of my books, my concern has been with the relationship between faith and history. In *The Foundations of Social Order* (1968), I dealt with the creeds and councils of the early church, how they reshaped men and nations, and their relevance to our time. In *The One and the Many* (1971), it was the inseparable connection of the doctrine of the Trinity with the problem of the one and the many that was my focus. This was, of course, written from the presuppositions of Cornelius Van Til's philosophy of religion. Earlier, in *This Independent Republic* (1964) and *The Nature of the American System* (1965), I had applied these ideas to American history. In the latter work, the section "The Religion of Humanity," dealt with the present great enemy of Christianity.

The loss of sound theology in the church has led to the decay of Christian faith and life. The modern era has seen the growing irrelevance of Christian faith and doctrine to the world in general. Its presence is very real, but its influence increasingly weak and minor. The relationship of the Rev. Billy Graham to American presidents aptly illustrates that fact.

Now the creeds and councils of the early church, in hammering out definitions of doctrines were also laying down the foundations of Christendom with them. Harold J. Berman, in *Law and Revolution*, demonstrated how the doctrine of Christ's atonement reshaped law and society, and how the present decline of that doctrine is leading to the death of Western civilization. In every area of faith and doctrine, like studies are necessary.

1

The abstraction of doctrine and theology from life has been one of the great disasters in the life of the church. Richard Weaver saw clearly that *Ideas Have Consequences*. To abstract Biblical faith from life to the classroom, and to limit its relevance to the private realm, is one of the great evils of the modern church. The Biblical prophets could not imagine such a departure. God being totally God and Lord over all things, no sphere of life or thought can be outside His government and authority.

Christianity cannot be reduced to the level of a pagan mystery religion, basically concerned with life after death, and with things personal here. The foundations of social order are indeed in the here and now, but in our faith and life, in what we believe concerning things ultimate. As men have turned from the Christian gospel, they have constructed a social gospel, and as they have surrendered God's law for antinomianism, they have supplanted God's law-word and they have turned to man's word, pietism, and pious gush. Church music now often celebrates man's feelings rather than the Holy Trinity.

This is the way of decline and death, and it must give way, and present indications tell us so, to a restoration of God's sovereignty, grace and undiluted word. The foundation of true social order can only be in the triune God and His enscriptured truth and word.

Rousas John Rushdoony
Chalcedon, August 12, 1998

Chapter One

The Apostles' Creed
and Creedalism

It has become popular in recent years for churches to profess that they are creedless and that their membership is an "open" and "living" one. One sect has made heavy use of the phrase, "No Creed but Christ." Every denial of creedalism is either based on hypocrisy or on ignorance. The word creed comes from the Latin *credo, I believe*. A creed is any formula or confession of faith by the members of a church. There is no church that does not require some form of assent as a condition of membership, if nothing more than a desire to join a particular church. Implicit in every such assent is a creed. Thus, a community church which simply asks prospective members if they wish to join has implicit in its question, in prior sessions with these catechumens, a denial of orthodox Christianity, an insistence on the individual's right to believe as he wills as long as he is sincerely dedicated to human betterment, and a general assent to the tenets of humanism. This particular church's vaunted creedlessness is in practice a hard and intolerant dogmatism, savagely hostile to Christian creedalism in the name of humanistic creedalism.

A creed is more than a church's standard. In most cases, a church's standard involves a far more intensive affirmation than does the creed. The requirements of the clergy, church officers, and church law may be far more detailed, and far more extensive and intensive than a creed permits. But the creed is the door to the house of faith. It is the minimal statement of belief. And it is *personal*: "I believe," *credo*. It is more than the church's faith: it is the believer's faith. A congregation recites or sings it, but they cannot say, "We believe," but "I believe." The creed is the door to the house

3

of faith, and it is intensely personal. The individual affirms every article of
the creed, from God as the Father Almighty and the Creator, to the
forgiveness of sins and the resurrection of the body, as his personal faith. It
is this point which separates Western Christianity from the Eastern
Church. The first personal plural, "we," is the Greek usage.[1] The Western
Churches have followed the Latin formula, "I believe." Significantly, Latin
Christianity and the Western Churches have seen a long series of reforms
to the present day, many summons to the faithful or by the faithful to
return to the faith, because the faith of the believer rather than the faith of
the church has had confessional priority.

The Apostles' Creed is, of course, not a creed written by the apostles but
an early ante-Nicene confession of faith summarizing the apostolic
preaching. Leith has observed that "The Creed does have a legitimate claim
to its title on the basis of the fact that all of its articles are to be found in the
theological formulas that were current around A. D. 100."[2] Schaff wrote:

> All the facts and doctrines which it contains, are in entire agreement
> with the New Testament....
>
> The rationalistic opposition to the Apostles' Creed and its use in the
> churches is therefore an indirect attack upon the New Testament
> itself.[3]

It is of interest to contrast various texts of the Apostles' Creed. The Old
Roman Form is given by Rufinus in Latin, c. A. D. 390, and by Marcellus
in Greek, c. 336-341:

> I believe in GOD THE FATHER Almighty.
> And in JESUS CHRIST, His only Son, our Lord;
> Who was born by the Holy Ghost of the Virgin Mary;
> Was crucified under Pontius Pilate and was buried;
> The third day he rose from the dead;
> He ascended into heaven; and sitteth on the right hand of the Father;
> From thence he shall come to judge the quick and the dead.
> And in the HOLY GHOST;
> The Holy Church;
> The forgiveness of sins;
> The resurrection of the body (flesh).[4]

The Received Form, or Textus Receptus, was adopted c. 700. It reads, with
the additions to the Old Roman Form added by Schaff in parentheses to
indicate them:

---

1. John J. Moment, *We Believe* (New York: Macmillan, 1942), 91.
2. John H. Leith, *Creeds of the Church* (Chicago: Aldine, 1963), 22.
3. Philip Schaff, *The Creeds of Christendom*, I (New York: Harper, 1887, 1919), 20.
See also Schaff, *History of the Christian Church*, II, (New York: Scribner's, 1884, revised edition), 528-537.
4. Schaff, *Creeds*, I, 21f.

I believe in GOD THE FATHER Almighty.
  (Maker of heaven and earth).
And in JESUS CHRIST, his only Son, our Lord;
Who was *(conceived)* by the Holy Ghost, born of the virgin Mary;
(Suffered) under Pontius Pilate, was crucified *(dead)*, and buried
    (He descended into Hell [Hades]);
The third day he rose from the dead;
He ascended into heaven; and sitteth on the right hand of *(God)* the
    Father *(Almighty)*;
From thence he shall come to judge the quick and the dead.
(I believe) in the HOLY GHOST;
The Holy *(Catholic)* Church
    (The communion of saints);
The forgiveness of sins;
The resurrection of the body (flesh);
    (And the life everlasting).[5]

An early English form of the creed, dated well before the Norman
Conquest and in official church use, is of considerable interest, in that the
translation reflects a clear understanding of some articles, such as the
communion of saints.

I beleue in God the Father Almightye, maker of heauen and earth.
And I beleue in the Sauiour Christ his onely begotten Sonne our
    Lorde,
who was conceaued of the Holy Ghost, and borne of Marye the
    virgyne,
suffred vnder the Pontish Pilate, on the crosse hanged, he was dead,
    and buryed, and he down descended to hel.
And he arose from death on the thyrd daye.
And he went vp to heauen, and sitteth now at the right hand of God
    Almightie the Father.
From thence he will come to judge both the quicke and the deade.
    And I beleue on the Holy Ghost.
And the holy Congregation.
And of the saintes the societie.
And sins forgeuenesse.
And of the flesh the again-rising.
And the euerlasting life.[6]

The Apostles' Creed is unlike all other creeds of other religions, whether
humanist, Buddhist, Moslem, Hindu, or otherwise. The faith of all other
religions is in *a body of ideas or claims concerning reality*. It may be a belief
in the ultimacy of man, or the ultimacy of nothingness, in the office of a
man (Mohammed as prophet), or an ultimate dualism or monism, but, in
any event, it demands a belief in certain ideas or claims. The Apostles'
Creed is radically different: it offers a synopsis of history, created by God

---

[5.] *Ibid.*

[6.] E. Thomson, editor, *Select Monuments of the Doctrine and Worship of the Catholic
Church in England Before the Norman Conquest* (John Russell Smith, 1875), 85f.

the Father Almighty, requiring salvation by Jesus Christ, His only begotten Son, who entered, lived, died, and was resurrected in history, and is now the Lord and Judge of history. His holy congregation is operative in history, which culminates in the general resurrection and everlasting life. The whole creed therefore is *a declaration concerning history.*

Nothing then can be more alien to the creed, and to Biblical faith, than the dialectical separation of faith and history. To contrast the Jesus of faith and the Jesus of history is to talk the language of paganism, not of Christianity. To affirm the inspiration of the Bible but to deny its historical infallibility is to renounce the Bible for dialecticism. Biblical Christianity is a declaration concerning what God has done in history, but it also makes clear that He is the Creator, the transcendental, ontological, and triune God Who cannot be reduced to history: He is its "maker."

Implicit in this declaration that God the Father Almighty is maker of heaven and earth is the claim of God to be the law-giver, determiner, and sustainer of heaven and earth and of all history. He is its maker, and it is totally subject therefore to Him. An assertion of the doctrine of creation is also an assertion of the doctrines of sovereignty and of the eternal decree, of predestination.

Not only a theology, but an eschatology, or doctrine of last things, which renounces history, or sees it as defeat, is faithless to Christianity. God is maker of heaven and earth, not Satan. History culminates in God's plan and triumph, not in Satan's victory. To the extent that any eschatology involves the victory of evil in history, to that extent it surrenders and retreats from history. Currently, one of the major sins besetting evangelical Christianity is eschatology which denies the evangel and denies history.

The Creed thus has vast implications concerning history because of its declaration that God is the creator of all things. This declaration immediately makes God the source of all ethics, of all morality, and of all law. In all non-Christian systems, the source of ethics and of law is the state; it is the *polis*, the empire, or the kingdom. There is no understanding the gulf between Aristotle and Plato, for example, and Christianity, apart from this fact, and the gulf cannot be legitimately bridged. Either God is the true source of morality and law, or the state is. If God is the true source, then the Word of God must be harkened to by church, state, school, and every sphere of life as the one authoritative source of morality and law. As institutions and orders declare law, they must do it ministerially, as administrators under God. The Word of God therefore speaks to every sphere, including church and state, and the Word of God is over the church and corrects and disciplines the church.

It is significant, and it was inescapable, that, as the early church formulated the creeds, the councils that announced the creeds also announced canons, or canon law, to govern the church and believers, and to declare God's law to the state. It was impossible for creedalism to develop without a parallel development of canon law. As the creeds progressively formulated the reality of God's sovereign power and Christ's role as priest, prophet, and king over man and history, the councils simultaneously brought life under the canons of the faith, under Biblical law and morality. The vitality and relevance of canon law has declined as Biblical creedalism has declined, and as statist law and ethics have progressively governed the church.

Tertullian ridiculed the political source of law in Rome. In effect, it made men the ultimate gods, in that, not only did the senate create laws, it also created gods:

> To say a word about the origin of laws of the kind to which we now refer, there was an old decree that no god should be consecrated by the emperor till first approved by the senate. Marcus Aemilius had experience of this in reference to his god Alburnus. And this, too, makes for our case, that among you divinity is allotted at the judgment of human beings. Unless gods give satisfaction to men, there will be no deification for them: the god will have to propitiate the man.[7]

True law, it was held, came from the triune God, and its claims are universal. All men know the law, because at creation it was inscribed on the tables of man's heart, and thus all men are subjects of the law and rebel in terms of it. Irenaeus declared that the Ten Commandments simply restated what creation had originally implanted:

> They (the Jews) had therefore a law, a course of discipline, and a prophecy of future things. For God at the first, indeed, warning them by means of natural precepts, which from the beginning He had implanted in mankind, that is, by means of the Decalogue (which, if any one does not observe, he has no salvation), did then demand nothing more of them.[8]

Christianity not only formulated a canon law, but, in terms of Christian faith, it reformulated civil law. As a result, as Percival has noted, canon law and civil law as the West knows it had their rise at about the same period.[9]

---

7. Tertullian, "Apology," 5, in *Ante-Nicene Fathers*, XI. *Writings of Tertullian*, I (Edinburgh: T. & T. Clark, 1872), 63.
8. Irenaeus, "Against Heresies," in *Ante-Nicene Fathers*, V, *Irenaeus*, I, Bk. IV, chapt. XV, i, 419.
9. Henry R. Percival, "An Excursus on the History of the Roman Law and its Relation to the Canon Law," in Percival, *The Seven Ecumenical Councils, their Canons and Decrees*, in *Nicene and Post-Nicene Fathers*, Second Series, vol. XIV, XXIX.

Because God is the creator, He is also the redeemer. Schaff's observations here are especially pertinent:

> As to creation: Irenaeus and Tertullian most firmly rejected the hylozoic and demiurgic views of paganism and Gnosticism, and taught, according to the book of Genesis, that God made the world, including matter, not, of course, out of any material, but out of nothing, or, to express it positively, out of his free, almighty will, by his word. This free will of God, a will of love, is the supreme, absolutely unconditioned, and all-conditioning cause and final reason of all existence, precluding every idea of physical force or of emanation. Every creature, since it proceeds from the good and holy God, is in itself, as to its essence, good. Evil, therefore, is not an original and substantial entity, but a corruption of nature, and hence can be destroyed by the power of redemption. Without a correct doctrine of creation there can be no true doctrine of redemption, as all the Gnostic systems show.[10]

The last sentence is particularly relevant. All the early creeds of the church begin by declaring God to be the creator: this is the starting point of all that follows.

The creed begins, "I believe," but, as we have seen, it is not an affirmation of certain ideas and concepts but *an assent to history* as God created it, redeems it, and governs it. Non-Biblical creedalism is active: it involves the individual's decision concerning a set of ideas and concepts. Biblical creedalism is an assent to God's creation, redemption, and government; it is passive because it affirms an act of redemption by the triune God of which man is simply the recipient by grace. But this passivity is the ground of true activity: man under God moves now in terms of true law, in terms of the canon of Scripture, to exercise dominion over the earth in the name of the triune God. Christian creedalism is thus basic to Western activism, constitutionalism, and hope concerning history.

[10.] Schaff, *Church History*, II, 540.

Chapter Two

Nicea:
History versus Imagination

As against Biblical Christianity, all other religions seek to impose an idea on history and to realize it, or to make it real. Humanism holds to a faith in man, in brotherhood and equality. The real world and history give no evidence of anything trustworthy in man, nor any evidence of brotherhood and equality. It is the purpose of humanism to achieve these goals and to convert history to them. The essence of Islam is a political order, and the purpose of Moslems is properly the achievement of this "rule of God" in and through a political order. The role of Mohammed was religious precisely because it was political to the core, and non-Christian religions are primarily political and are derived from the concept of a divine political order, an order which is itself the source of morality and religion. Buddhism holds to an ultimate and proximate relativism; since nothingness is ultimate, and all things are relative, the "way" is equally the contempt of life and the political control of life without regard for good and evil, i.e., the political contempt of life. In all non-Biblical faiths, the essence of religion is the attempt of man's imagination to impose a pattern or ideal upon history. There is, as a result, a marked hostility towards history. History as it comes from the hand of God has a pre-ordained meaning and direction, and it moves to a purpose neither decreed by man nor conducive to man's sin. As a result, man is in revolt against history. Man pits against history the imagination of his fallen heart.

A major example of this war against history is Gnosticism. Gnosticism attempted to destroy the enemy, Biblical Christianity, from within. It offered a place to Christ in its systems, but only to negate Christ. Thus,

9

Scott noted, "The Gnostics taught three Gods: the Absolute, who revealed himself by means of Christ, the Demiurge, the maker of the world, and the world itself."[1] The significance of this "trinity" is readily apparent: the Absolute and the Demiurge are opposites which negate one another, so that the world, or, more properly man, stands forth as the one true god. No exclusive divinity was allowed to Jesus; instead, His deity was made a deity common to all men ideally. Thus, Marcus, a Gnostic, and "a slightly older contemporary of Irenaeus," parodied the Christian creed in his circle of followers. The Marcosian Creed is cited by Irenaeus:

> In baptism they say over them:
> Into the name of the unknown Father of the universe;
> Into Truth, the Mother of all;
> Into Him who came down upon Jesus;
> Into union;
> And redemption;
> And communion in the powers.[2]

The purpose of this creed was simply to open up divinity to man; it "affirmed" the Father, but only as the "unknown," and the Holy Ghost, but only as the source of deity for all, and Jesus, but only as one among many men who gain divinity. For the Marcosians, salvation was knowledge: "for they affirm that the inner and spiritual man is redeemed by means of knowledge, and that they, having acquired the knowledge of all things, stand thenceforth in need of nothing else. This, then, is the true knowledge."[3] This knowledge was not knowledge of God's revelation in Scripture; it was essentially self-knowledge. The Marcosian knowledge led believers to say, "For I derive from Him who is pre-existent, and I come again to my own place whence I went forth."[4] Man's true knowledge and salvation is thus to assent to his imagination and declare himself divine.

Usually, however, Gnosticism did not content itself with formulating creeds. Creeds too obviously revealed its departure from and hostility to the Christian faith. It was much more effective to affirm the Apostles' Creed and to reinterpret it in terms of Gnosticism. This, from Gnosticism on through neo-orthodoxy, has been a favored method of heresy. Gnosticism was in essence humanism, the glorification of man. In humanism, man makes himself ultimate by undercutting the ultimacy of God. The vaguer the doctrines of the Father, Son, and Holy Ghost were

---

[1.] Hugh M. Scott, *Origin and Development of Nicene Theology* (Chicago: Chicago Theological Seminary Press, 1896), 95n.

[2.] F. J. Badcock, *The History of the Creeds* (Second edition: London: SPCK, 1938), 28ff. Irenaeus cites this creed in *Against Heresies*, Bk I, XXI, 3; on the Marcosians, see BK. I, xiii-xii, in *Ante-Nicene Christian Library*, vol. V, *The Writings of Ireanaeus*, I, 51-86.

[3.] Irenaeus, *Against Heresies*, BK. I, xxi,4; in Irenaeus, I, 83.

[4.] *Ibid.*, Bk. I, xxi, 5; in I, 84.

made, the more clearly man emerged as the sovereign, and man's order as the ultimate order.

In Arianism and semi-Arianism this humanism spoke in the church using the language of the Apostles' Creed but reinterpreting the words to give a new context to them. The subversive purpose of Arianism has been cited by Singer:

> Arianism was not so much the product of an unwise and misguided attempt to use classical philosophy to explain Biblical doctrines, as it was a deliberate effort to interpret Christianity in philosophical terms and to convert it into a kind of religious philosophy. The ultimate origins of this heresy are to be found mainly in Platonism and the philosophy of Philo, but some scholars profess to see some strains of Aristotle in it as well.[5]

The three main points of Arianism were, *first*, Christ was a created being; *second*, He was not eternally existent; and, *third*, Christ was not of the same essence with the Father. The orthodox faith insisted that Christ was first, begotten, not made; second, begotten before all worlds, and, *third*, Christ is of the same essence with the Father,

Arius, a presbyter of Alexandria, stated his position in his *Thalia*:

> God Himself then, in His own nature, is ineffable by all men. Equal or like Himself He alone has none, or one in glory. And Ingenerate we call Him, because of Him who is generate by nature. We praise Him as without beginning because of Him who has a beginning. And adore Him as everlasting, because of Him who in time has come to be. The Unbegun made the Son a beginning of things originated; and advanced Him as a Son to Himself by adoption. He has nothing proper to God in proper subsistence. For He is not equal, no, nor one in essence with Him. Wise is God, for He is the teacher of Wisdom. There is full proof that God is invisible to all beings; both to things which are through the Son, and to the Son He is invisible. I will say it expressly, how by the Son is seen the Invisible; by that power by which God sees, and in His own measure, the Son endures to see the Father, as is lawful. Thus there is a Triad, not in equal glories. Not intermingling with each other are their subsistences. One more glorious than the other in their glories unto immensity. Foreign from the Son in essence is the Father, for He is without beginning. Understand that the Monad was; but the Dyad was not, before it was in existence. It follows at once that, though the Son was not, the Father was God. Hence the Son, not being (for He existed at the will of the Father), is God Only-Begotten, and He is alien from either. Wisdom existed as Wisdom by the will of the Wise God. Hence He is conceived in numberless conceptions: Spirit, Power, Wisdom, God's glory, Truth, and Light. One equal to the Son, the Superior is able to beget; but one more excellent, or superior, or greater, He is not able.

---

5. C. Gregg Singer, "Arianism," in Edwin H. Palmer, General Editor, *The Encyclopedia of Christianity*, I (Wilmington, Delaware: The National Foundation for Christian Education, 1964), 392.

At God's will the Son is what and whatsoever He is. And when and since He was, from that time He has subsisted from God. He, being a strong God, praises in His degree the Superior. To speak in brief, God is ineffable to His Son. For He is to Himself what He is, that is, unspeakable. So that nothing which is called comprehensible does the Son know to speak about; for it is impossible for Him to investigate the Father, who is by Himself. For the Son does not know His own essence, for, being Son, he really existed, at the will of the Father. What argument then allows, that He who is from the Father should know His own parent by comprehension? For it is plain that for that which hath a beginning to conceive how the Unbegun is, or to grasp the ideas, is not possible.[6]

To analyze Arius' Thalia, *first*, this statement in effect not only eliminates Christ but God as well. God is unknowable even to Christ, who is the greatest of all creatures. A god who is so unknowable and who cannot reveal himself is thus an irrelevant god because of his radial incoherence. Despite all the fulsome glorification of God by Arius, in effect both here and in his Letter to Bishop Alexander, Arius is eliminating God except as a limiting concept. Dead or alive, Arius' god is irrelevant.

Second, Christ is eliminated by Arius. Although called the greatest of creatures, He is still a creature. Arius' Jesus cannot know God and therefore cannot reveal Him. And, although Arius' Jesus or Son cannot be surpassed, i.e., his god cannot create a superior one, still he can create one equal to the Son. The door is thus thrown wide open to other sons of god to rank equally high with god, and, because of their timeliness in history, rank higher than Jesus with men. Thus, not only is God the Father eliminated, but God the Son. And because there can by definition be none other equal to God, God the Holy Spirit is eliminated. And this unknowable and unrevealed god being irrelevant, man stands essentially alone as his own god.

Third, the Bible is also eliminated. An incoherent god cannot reveal himself. A revelation either in Christ or in the Bible is ruled out. How can a god be declared when by definition he is beyond self-declaration, either in his son or his word? Aruis' god, like man, lacks full self-consciousness; his own being is full of brute factuality and replete with chaos in effect, "For He is to Himself what He is, that is, unspeakable."

Fourth, the Biblical answer to the problem of the one and the many is denied. In the triune God, one God, three persons, there is an equal ultimacy of the one and the many. Unity and particularity are equally important. Arius restated the pagan emphasis on unity, and that unity was the empire. Everywhere, pagan statism found Arianism to be an ideal doctrine, and for a few centuries Arianism flourished in Europe as the

[6] Athanasius, "De Synodis," in Part II, in Philip Schaff and Henry Wace, *Nicene and Post-Nicene Fathers*, Series II, vol. IV (Eerdmans edition), 457f.

established faith. In the name of Christianity, Arianism established anti-Christianity. By professing Arian "Christianity," rulers could outlaw or oppose orthodox Christianity as subversive.

Fifth, as is now apparent, Arianism was humanism and statism. It was a popular faith with rulers, in that it made possible the continuation of the pagan exaltation of the state as the divine-human order and politics as the way of salvation. The emperor, Constantine the Great, with his essentially Roman concern for religion, turned soon to Arianism for support. One of his wins, a bronze follis of about A. D. 307-308, has on the obverse side, the head Of Constantine, and, on the reverse side, the sun-god.[7] For the empire, the door was open to Jesus as the great creature of God, but also open to many other divine creatures, all serving to unify the Roman Empire as the divine-human order. The Arian bishops were thus inescapably statist in their orientation and faith. For them, the empire was God's true order, and the emperor God's present manifestation and power on earth.

At the Council of Nicea, A. D. 325, the battle was waged over the key words, *homoousion* (being of one essence, i.e., with the Father), and *homoiousion* (of like essence), the semi-Arian compromise designed to give a semblance of orthodoxy while essentially destroying orthodoxy. Gibbon treated the difference between the positions with contempt. His hatred of orthodoxy is clearly unconcealed. In a well-known footnote, Gibbon observed, "I cannot forbear reminding the reader that the difference between the *Homoousion* and *Homoiousion* is almost invisible to the nicest theological eye."[8] It is impossible to dismiss this as ignorance: Gibbon knew what was at stake, and his allegiance was to statism as man's hope.

The triumph of orthodoxy at Nicea had tremendous importance. Schaff observed:

> The council of Nicaea is the most important event of the fourth century, and its bloodless intellectual victory over a dangerous error is of far greater consequence to the progress of true civilization, than all the bloody victories of Constantine and his successors.[9]

Leith's comments are also important:

> Theologically, the assertion that the Son is only like God undermined the Christian community's conviction about the finality of Jesus Christ. The claim that he was like God presupposed some standard to determine whether he was like God and the extent to which he was like God. It furthermore left open the possibility that someone else

---

7. Fred Reinfeld and Burton Hobson, *Ancient Coins* (New York: Sterling, 1964), 47, plate 104.
8. Edward Gibbon, *The Decline and Fall of the Roman Empire*, I, (New York: Modern Library), 719n.
9. Philip Schaff, *History of the Christian Church*, III, 631.

more like God might appear. Christianity would be only one of many possible religions. If God himself is incarnate in Jesus Christ, then this is the final Word. There is nothing further to be said.

The cultural significance of the Nicene theology is revealed in the disposition of the political Imperialists to be Arians. Imperialism as a political strategy was more compatible with the notion that Jesus Christ is something less than the full and absolute Word of God.[10]

The Nicene Creed, in its original form, according to Eusebius of Caesarea, reads:

We believe in one GOD, the Father Almighty, Creator of all things visible and invisible; and in one Lord JESUS CHRIST, the Son of GOD, only-begotten of the Father, that is, of the substance of the Father, GOD of GOD, begotten, not made, being of the same substance with the Father, by whom all things were made in heaven and in earth, who for us men and for our salvation came down from heaven, was incarnate, was made man, suffered, rose again the third day, ascended into the heavens, and He will come to judge the living and the dead. And in the Holy Ghost. Those who say, There was a time when He was not, and He was not before He was begotten, and He was made of nothing (He was created), or who say that He is of another hypostasis, or of another substance (than the Father), or that the Son of God is created, that He is mutable, or subject to change, the Catholic Church anathematizes.[11]

Since this was an ecumenical council, the Greek reading, "we believe," was used, but the Western version was changed to "I believe." Subsequent councils and usage led to a clearer formulation at points, and to the standard reading of the Creed in Western usage:

I believe in one God the Father Almighty, Maker of heaven and earth, And of all things visible and invisible:

And in one Lord Jesus Christ, the only-begotten Son of God; Begotten of His Father before all worlds, God of God, Light of Light, Very God of very God; Begotten, not made; Being of one substance with the Father; By whom all things were made: Who for us men and for our salvation came down from heaven, And was incarnate by the Holy Ghost of the Virgin Mary, And was made man: And was crucified also for us under Pontius Pilate; He suffered and was buried: And the third day he rose again according to the Scriptures: And ascended into heaven, And sitteth on the right hand of the Father: And he shall come again, with glory, to judge both the quick and the dead; Whose kingdom shall have no end.

---

10. John H. Leith, *Creeds of the Church* (Chicago: Aldine Publishing Co., 1963), 29.
11. Charles Joseph Hefele, *A History of the Christian Councils, from the Original Documents, to the Close of the Council of Nicaea, A. D. 325* (Second edition, revised. Edinburgh: T. & T. Clark, 1872), 294f. See Athanasius, *op. cit.*, 75. "Council of Nicaea," and Theodoret, "The Ecclesiastical History," I, ii, in *Nicene and Post Nicene Fathers*, Series II, vol.III, 50.

And I believe in the Holy Ghost, The Lord and Giver of Life, Who proceedeth from the Father and the Son; Who with the Father and the Son together is worshipped and glorified; Who spake by the Prophets: And I believe in one Catholic and Apostolic Church: I acknowledge one Baptism for the remission of sins: And I look for the Resurrection of the dead: And the Life of the world to come. Amen.

As is readily apparent, the Nicene Creed is an expansion of the Apostles' Creed and a defense of the Apostles' Creed from misuse by re-interpretation. In its present form, it incorporates the work of subsequent councils, including Chalcedon.

The most important later addition is the *Filioque* clause, the procession of the Holy Ghost from the Son. The lingering elements of subordinationism were thereby eliminated in the West; the clause was rejected in the East. By means of this clause, the full equality of the Father and of the Son was declared; the Trinity is one God, three persons, with no subordination of one person to another in substance or being, but only in terms of economy or operation.

Arius, after Nicea, regained power through political influence. On his recall, Alexander, Primate of Alexandria, in tears prostrated himself in the sacrarium, praying, "If Arius comes tomorrow to the church, take me away, and let me not perish with the guilty. But if Thou pittiest Thy Church, as Thou dost pity it, take Arius away, lest when he enters heresy enter with him." The next morning, on his triumphant procession to the church to be formally and publicly reconciled on imperial authority, Arius stopped and left the procession suddenly because of gastric pain. After waiting some time, his followers investigated and found that the old man Arius had collapsed in blood and fallen headlong into the open latrine. The orthodox party triumphantly recalled the words concerning Judas' death, who "falling headlong, burst asunder in the midst" and died (Acts 1:18). Arius' manner of death was used by the orthodox to discomfit the heretics and encourage the saints, and it was declared an act of God. The heretics preferred to forget it, and modern heretics have eliminated this and like events from history books as "irrelevant." It was, however, a providential conclusion to the great intellectual and spiritual battle of Nicea.

Chapter Three

Constantinople Against the Hatred of Certainty

An interview with an actor, Robert Walker, Jr., produced a very interesting comment:

> After a film, Walker retreats to his new Malibu home with his wife Ellie, a former June Taylor dancer he married in 1961, and their two children, Michael, 4, and David, 3. "We have a 'beachy' home," Walker says. "We're beach people — sun, sand, and scuba. But if this house ever takes us over, ties us down ... well, we'll burn it down."[1]

Granted that this actor's statement may well reveal him to be a poseur, but the fact that he found it a merit to pose as one dedicated to a hatred of roots is significant. Everything associated with roots and certainty is today despised by the self-styled new elite. Marriage, morality, family, law, order, certainty, and above all, Christianity, are hated with a passion. Man's freedom is to avoid all certainty except himself; the quest for certainty is seen as the quest for death. Life for these men means uncertainty and rootlessness. One student radical has remarked, "I hate people who *know* anything." The hatred of certainty is a major passion of existentialist man.

This hatred of roots and of certainty is basic to revolutionary activity. The revolutionist destroys things of value precisely because they have a value apart from him. Only what he decrees can stand. The revolutionist destroys roots, values, and laws because they speak of certainty, and he is at war with certainty. This is the basis of revolutionary destruction. It

---

[1.] Jack Ryan, "Robert Walker, Jr. The Sorrow Behind The Smile" in *Valley Times* Family Weekly, January 22, 1967(San Fernando Valley, California) 10.

seems senseless to those who fail to realize that destruction is basic to revolutionary faith.

This hatred of certainty was a major factor in the Roman Empire and its anti-Christianity, and it was a major aspect of the infiltrating humanism then and now. The humanistic parties did everything possible to bring uncertainty to the faith, to render vague the doctrines of God the Father, God the Son, and God the Holy Ghost, to cloud with uncertainty the doctrines of creation, salvation, and judgment. The hatred for doctrinal certainty was intense and dedicated. But this hatred of certainty is a pretense and a mask for the advancement of a new certainty, not God but man. It is part of the quest for a humanistic certainty.

A man, thus, who is ready to burn down a house if it ties him down says in effect that there can be no responsibility binding him except his desire to indulge himself. If his marriage or family ties him down, he will also "burn it down." His freedom is to be irresponsible to every God-given responsibility as a way of asserting his independence and his own godhood.

It was this hatred of Biblical certainty that the early councils had to war against. The ecumenical councils of the early church were in their purpose and nature very different from the modern councils and ecumenical efforts of the church. *First,* the early councils had as their primary purpose the defense and establishment *of truth, not unity.* Unity had to be established on the foundation of truth, not truth as a product of unity. *The councils came together for the purpose of conflict, the battle of truth against error,* and any unity on other than the whole truth of Scripture was anathema. *Second,* the concern of the councils was primarily *the faith, not the church.* Institutionally, the church suffered because of the conflict, but theologically it flourished and ensured its survival and growth. The modern ecumenical movement, and modern councils, are thus in purpose and work in direct contrast to the early councils: their concern is with unity, and with the institution, not the faith primarily.

The early church came to Nicea already battle-scarred from the struggle with the enemies without and within, struggles with the Empire and with the heretics. The fathers went to Nicea with the marks of battle — arms made useless by the application of red-hot irons to the nerves, crippled and maimed of body. "Some had the right eye dug out, others had lost the right arm."[2] The Post-Nicene battle was similar but more subtle. Now the Empire was an ostensible ally, but it was usually an ally of the heretics within the church against the orthodox faith.

Arianism was, according to Schaff, *first,* "deistic and rationalistic," whereas "Athanasianism" was "theistic and supernaturalistic." Arianism

---

[2.] Theodoret, "Ecclesiastical History," Bk I, vi, in *Nicene and Post-Nicene Fathers,* series II, vol. III, 43.

proceeded from human reason, Athanasianism from divine revelation."
Second, "Arianism associated itself with the secular political power and the
court party; it represented the imperiopapal principle" and it persecuted
the church and denied to it an area of independence from the Empire,
whereas the orthodox party was concerned with the integrity of the faith.[3]

The Second Ecumenical Council, the First Council of Constantinople,
met in A. D. 381 to meet the continuing challenge of humanists who were
attempting to erode the certainties of the faith. The men who gathered had
suffered severely at the hands of apostate churchmen in league with the
Empire. The Council's Synodical Letter of 382 cites these sufferings in
brief:

> Our persecutions are but of yesterday. The sound of them still rings
> in the ears alike of those who suffered them and of those whose love
> made the sufferers' pain their own. It was but a day or two ago, so to
> speak, that some released from chains in foreign lands returned to
> their own churches through manifold afflictions; of others who had
> died in exile the relics were brought home; others again, even after
> their return from exile, found the passion of the heretics still at the
> boiling heat, and, slain by them with stones as was the blessed
> Stephen, met with a sadder fate in their own than in a stranger's land.
> Others, worn away with various cruelties, still bear in their bodies the
> scars of their wounds and the marks of Christ. Who could tell the tale
> of fines, of disenfranchisements, of individual confiscations, of
> intrigues, of outrages, of prisons? In truth all kinds of tribulation were
> wrought out beyond number in us, perhaps because we were paying
> the penalty of sins, perhaps because the merciful God was trying us by
> means of the multitude of our sufferings. For these all thanks to God,
> who by means of such afflictions trained his servants and, according
> to the multitude of his mercies, brought us again to refreshment. We
> indeed needed long leisure, time, and toil to restore the church once
> more, that so, like physicians healing the body after long sickness and
> expelling its disease by gradual treatment, we might bring her back to
> her ancient health of true religion. It is true that on the whole we seem
> to have been delivered from the violence of our persecutions and to
> be just now recovering the churches which have for a long time been
> the prey of the heretics. But wolves are troublesome to us who,
> though they have been driven from the fold, yet harry the flock up
> and down the glades, daring to hold rival assemblies, stirring seditions
> among the people, and shrinking from nothing which can do damage
> to the churches.[4]

This is not the language of conciliation. The foundation of Constantinople's ecumenism was not smoothing out differences and building
bridges to the opposition but, on the basis of the uncompromising faith, to
drive out the enemy and to allow him no entrance save conversion. The

---

[3.] Schaff, *History of the Christian Church,* III, 643f.
[4.] *Decrees and Canons of the Seven Ecumenical Councils,* 188.

enemies were plainly termed "wolves"; they had to become lambs before they could be approached peaceably.

The Synodical Letter summarized the theological work of the Council:

> This is the faith which ought to be sufficient for you, for us, for all who wrest not the word of the true faith; for it is the ancient faith; it is the faith of our baptism; it is the faith that teaches us to believe in the name of the Father, of the Son, and of the Holy Ghost. According to this faith there is one Godhead, Power and Substance of the Father and of the Son and of the Holy Ghost; the dignity being equal, and the majesty being equal in three perfect hypostases, i.e., three perfect persons. Thus there is no room for the heresy of Sabellius by the confusion of the hypostases, i.e., the destruction of the personalities; thus the blasphemy of the Eunomians, of the Arians, and of the Pneumatomachi is nullified, which divides the substance, the nature, and the godhead, and superinduces on the uncreated consubstantial and co-eternal Trinity a nature posterior, created and of a different substance. We moreover, preserve unperverted the doctrine of the incarnation of the Lord, holding the tradition that the dispensation of the flesh is neither soulless nor mindless nor imperfect; and knowing full well that God's Word was perfect before the ages, and became perfect man in the last days for our salvation.[5]

The statement summarizes both the enemies of the faith and the word of the Council. The word "tradition" is used by the Synodical Letter in the sense of the Biblical faith.

The *first* heresy cited by the Council as excluded by the expanded creed was "the heresy of Sabellius," or Monarchianism. Sabellianism had Gnostic and Judaizing tendencies. It held to a strict monotheism or unitarianism as against trinitarianism. Sabellianism denied any distinction between the Father and the Son; there was but one person.[6] God is the monad, the original substance, inoperative and unproductive until it develops. The Father is "Wordless," i.e., cannot beget the Son, since God is by definition wisdomless and wordless, i.e., basically an unconscious original substance. He is the silent God. The universe as well as the Son are products of a dilation or expansion in God's substance and, at the end, this substance contracts, so that the creation disappears.[7] Thus, if the monad becomes a dyad or a triad, it is simply the one original substance that has expanded, and the expansion is temporary and transitory. Sabellianism was thus basically pantheism, and its god simply the abstract substance which evolves itself into the world of reality. "Some of the fathers traced the

---

[5.] *Ibid.*, 189.
[6.] Athanasius, "Four Discourses Against the Arians," III, iv, and "Statement of Faith," ii, in *Nicene and Post-Nicene Fathers*, IV, 395, 84.
[7.] Athanasius, "Four Discourses Against the Arians," IV, 13, 14, in *ibid.*, 437f.

doctrine of Sabellius to the Stoic system."[8] Sabellianism and the related Marcellians were condemned by the Council in Canon I.

Constantinople emphasized the reality of the Trinity, of one God and three Persons. Instead of an abstract concept of original substance, the Council affirmed the very personal God. Instead of a silent God, the Council declared the God of revelation. The universe, instead of being an expansion of "god," is His creation who is "one God, the Father All Governing, creator of heaven and earth, of all things visible and invisible."

The *second* heresy countered at Constantinople was the newer forms of Arianism, Eunomianism for one. Eunomius, leader, founder, and bishop of a sect of Arians, in effect denied the divinity of the Word, of God the Son. In the name of exalting the Father, Eunomianism denied divinity to the Son, but the Father it claimed to worship was an incoherent god who could not express himself. Eunomianism was thus a practical denial of the Father and the Son. The Son for Eunomius was only a creature, and God was simply a remote substance. Canon I of the Council condemned the Eunomians, and the Photinians (followers of Marcellus' disciple Photinus, who held that Jesus was a mere man.[9]) The Constantinoplitan Creed, an expansion of the Nicene, made it emphatically clear that Jesus Christ is truly God.

The *third* kind of heresy condemned was that of the Semi-Arians, Macedonians, or Pneumatomachi. The Pneumatomachi (from *pneuma,* spirit, and *machomai,* to speak evil against) were followers of Macedonius, bishop of Constantinople, who declared the Holy Ghost to be only a creature. With regard to the Son, the Semi-arians and Macedonius avoided calling Him either consubstantial with the Father or very God, and also avoided calling Him a creature. The denial of the deity of the Holy Ghost was a denial of any immanence in God. Thus, even if the Macedonians had been orthodox in their doctrines of the Father and the Son (which they were not nor could be, for the doctrine of the Trinity is a unified whole), they would still have left God irrelevant because unrelated to the world. God would have been the "wholly other" who could not truly reveal himself to man or operate in the universe. This absolutely transcendent god would also be a hidden god, a god without revelation and wholly cut off from man. He would thus be irrelevant except as a limiting concept, and the practical consequence of such a God is that there is no god but man.

The Pneumatomachi held that not only was the Holy Ghost a creature, but he was also an emanation from Jesus Christ, himself a creature. It was a part of the Arian creed that the Holy Ghost was a created being. To

---

[8.] John M'Clintock and James Strong, *Cyclopaedia of Biblical, Theological, and Ecclesiastical Literature,* IX, "Sabellius," (New York: Harper, 1849), 203.

[9.] *Decrees and Canons* of the *Seven Councils,* 172ff.

render Christ and the Spirit emanations was to open the way to making man an emanation, since the uniqueness was denied in favor of an inherent process, emanation. The resemblance to Gnosticism was obvious. Athanasius, who named the Pneumatomachi, also called them *Tropici,* because of their figurative interpretations of Scripture. Since God was for them hidden, there was no word from God and the Bible could thus contain only hints, figures suggestive of God but never a true revelation.

To Nicea's "I believe in the Holy Ghost," Constantinople added "The Lord and life-giver, Who proceeds from the Father, Who is worshipped and glorified together with the Father and the Son, Who spoke through the prophets." The Holy Ghost is thus clearly God, the third Person of the trinity.

Fourth, Constantinople condemned in Canon 1, and its creed, the Apollinarians. Apollinaris had, in attempting to expound Nicene doctrine, emphasized Christ's deity but partially denied His true humanity. Apollinaris thus was more than half way into Arianism, because his position was in effect a denial of the incarnation. Moreover, Apollinaris believed that a complete human nature in Christ would have implied sinfulness, which was in essence the pagan belief that creatureliness or finitude is sin, whereas the Biblical faith sees man as a creature, originally created wholly good. Not finitude but the moral transgression of God's law is sin. If finitude be seen as sin, then salvation of necessity is logically deification. However well-meaning the intentions of Apollinaris may have been, his presuppositions were Hellenic and anti-Christian. The statement of Nicea concerning Christ's incarnation was thus expanded to make emphatic the reality of the incarnation.

Fifth, Constantinople added to its declaration of the consubstantiality of the Trinity its Canon V, a confession of "the unity of the Godhead of the Father, and of the Son, and of the Holy Ghost."[10] Subordinationism was thus condemned, and the unity of the Godhead affirmed.

A comparison of the Creed of Nicea (Creed of 318 Fathers) with the expanded creed of 150 Fathers of Constantinople is of interest. Leith's version of Nicea reads (the Greek text being translated, and hence the plural pronoun):

> We believe in one God, the Father All Governing *(pantokratora),* creator *(poieten)* of all things visible and invisible;
>
> And in one Lord Jesus Christ, the Son of God, begotten of the Father as only begotten, that is, from the essence (reality) of the Father *(ek tes ousias tou patros),* God from God, Light from Light, true God from true God, begotten not created *(poiethenta),* of the same essence

---

10. *Decrees and Canons of the Councils,* 181f.

(reality) as the Father *(homoousion to patri)*, through whom all things came into being, both in heaven and in earth; Who for us men and for our salvation came down and was incarnate, becoming human *(enanthropesanta)*. He suffered and the third day he rose, and ascended into the heavens. And he will come to judge both the living and the dead.

And (we believe) in the Holy Spirit.

But, those who say, Once he was not, or he was not before his generation, or he came to be out of nothing, or who assert that he, the Son of God, is a different *hypostasis* or *ousia*, or that he is a creature, or changeable, or mutable, the Catholic and Apostolic Church anathematizes them.

The expanded Creed of Constantinople reads:

We believe in one God, the Father All Governing *(pantokratora)*, creator *(poieten)* of heaven and earth, of all things visible and invisible;

And in one Lord Jesus Christ, the only-begotten Son of God, begotten from the Father before all time (pro *panton ton aionon)*, Light from Light, true God from true God, begotten not created *(poiethenta)*, of the same essence (reality) as the Father *(homoousion to patri)*, through Whom all things came into being, Who for us men and because of our salvation came down from heaven, and was incarnate by the Holy Spirit and the Virgin Mary and became human *(enanthropesanta)*. He was crucified for us under Pontius Pilate, and suffered and was buried, and rose on the third day, according to the Scriptures, and ascended to heaven, and sits on the right hand of the Father, and will come again with glory to judge the living and dead. His Kingdom shall have no end *(telos)*.

And in the Holy Spirit, the Lord and life-giver, Who proceeds from the Father, Who is worshiped and glorified together with the Father and Son, Who spoke through the prophets; and in one, holy, catholic and apostolic Church. We confess one baptism for the remission of sins. We look forward to the resurrection of the dead and the life of the world to come. Amen.[11]

The original form of the Nicene Creed concludes with an anathema. Canon I of Constantinople I did the same thing. The modern distaste for anathemas is a disavowal of the faith. No man can affirm a faith if he affirms its opposite, nor can he defend a faith without waging war against its enemies. No unbeliever or heretic can be converted unless he be first recognized as an unbeliever rather than a brother under the skin. The anathemas are thus basic to creedalism.

Constantinople in A. D. 381 spelled out the certainties of the faith against attempts by humanism to render it uncertain. Humanism is again dedicated to the same desire, as always, to reduce Scripture to a maze of

---

[11.] Leith, *Creeds of the Church*, 30f., 33.

uncertainties, myths, figures, and symbols. Its purpose is to "free" man from Biblical faith, to burn down the house of faith so that man may be totally rootless and godless. But the flight from God's certainty is futile, in that every fiber of man's being, having been created by God, witnesses to God (Rom. 1: 18-25). The actor Walker said, "But if this house ever takes us over, ties us down ... well, we'll burn it down." His plan is futile. No man can burn down God's creation. Existentialist man is a myth, and the only burning existentialist man shall know is God's burning.

Chapter Four

Te Deum Laudamus

The early church was not without its able leaders, but it is an error to ascribe too great a role to the church fathers. Despite their heroic role, the best of them were not free from theological errors due to the lingering effects of pagan philosophies. Similarly, the various heresies brought open paganism into the very life of the church, and pagan practices and beliefs abounded. That the early church represented a confused picture and "a mixed multitude" is readily apparent. But the fact remains that a solid core of orthodoxy was also there. The growing collapse of humanism made the alternative, orthodox Christianity, all the more, not merely an alternative, but man's only hope. As against the vague myths of paganism and heresy, and the studied uncertainties of humanism, the hard, certain realities of Biblical faith were a joyful alternative even in the face of persecutions. A hymn of the church which gave exuberant expression to the triumphant nature of the orthodox faith was the *Te Deum Laudamus*. The *Te Deum* reflects the creedal faith very clearly. It is the church's song of triumph in the face of heresy and unbelief; it echoes the battles against Gnosticism, Arianism, and other heresies and celebrates the victory of orthodoxy and its joyful faith in the triune God.

The roots of the *Te Deum* are in the Greek hymn, *Gloria patri*, and in various hymns of praise. *The Apostolic Constitutions (c. 357?)* contains elements of the *Te Deum*.[1] The *Te Deum* goes back to the Codex Alexandrinus of the Bible, a portion of the hymn being five lines

---

[1] Apostolic Constitution, VII; xxvi, especially VII, xlvii; VIII, v; VIII, xii; VIII, xxxvii; in *Ante-Nicene Christian Library.* vol. XVI, 188, 205, 214f, 230, 248.

incorporated from that text.[2] The present form of the hymn probably dates back to the fourth century A. D.

The text of the *Te Deum,* as it appears in *The Book of Common Prayer, is* as follows:

> We praise thee, O God: we acknowledge thee to be the Lord.
> All the earth doth worship thee: the Father everlasting.
> To thee all Angels cry aloud: the Heavens, and all the Powers therein;
> To thee Cherubim and Seraphim: continually do cry.
> Holy, Holy, Holy: Lord God of Sabaoth:
> Heaven and earth are full of the Majesty: of thy glory.
> The glorious company of the Apostles: praise thee.
> The goodly fellowship of the Prophets: praise thee.
> The noble army of Martyrs: praise thee.
> The holy Church throughout all the world: doth acknowledge thee;
> The Father: of an infinite Majesty;
> Thine adorable, true: and only Son;
> Also the Holy Ghost: the Comforter.
> Thou art the King of Glory: O Christ.
> Thou art the everlasting Son: of the Father.
> When thou tookest upon thee to deliver man: thou didst humble
>   thyself to be born of a Virgin.
> When thou hadst overcome the sharpness of death: thou didst open
>   the Kingdom of Heaven to all believers.
> Thou sittest at the right hand of God: in the glory of the Father.
> We believe that thou shalt come: to be our judge.
> We therefore pray thee, help thy servants: whom thou hast redeemed
>   with thy precious blood.
> Make them to be numbered with thy Saints: in glory everlasting.
> O Lord, save thy people: and bless thine heritage.
> Govern them: and lift them up for ever.
> Day by day: we magnify thee;
> And we worship thy Name: ever, world without end.
> Vouchsafe, O Lord: to keep us this day without sin.
> O Lord, have mercy upon us: have mercy upon us.
> O Lord, let thy mercy be upon us: as our trust is in thee.
> O Lord, in thee have I trusted: let me never be confounded.

Proctor, in his study of the prayer book, cited an excellent summary of this hymn's contents:

> Comber observes that this ancient hymn contains, — *first,* an act of praise offered to God by us, and by all creatures, as well in earth as in heaven: *secondly,* a confession of faith; declaring, (1) the general consent unto it, (2) the particulars of it, concerning every person in the Trinity, and more largely concerning the Son, as to His divinity, His humanity, and particularly His incarnation, His death, His present glory, and His return to judgment: *thirdly,* a supplication grounded upon it — (1) for all His people, that they may be preserved here and saved hereafter; (2) for ourselves, who daily praise Him, that

2. Schaff, *History of the Christian Church,* III, 592n-593n.

we may be kept from future sin, and be pardoned for what is past, because we trust in Him.[3]

This summary is an excellent one and points to the character of the hymn. The *Te Deum* sings with the fierce joy and exuberant confidence of orthodox faith in the early church. Several important characteristics are clearly in evidence. *First*, it is the orthodox faith which the *Te Deum* clearly affirms. The popularity of the hymn was an indication of the popular roots of the orthodox faith: it was the faith of vast numbers of humble believers and of simple pastors. The vague uncertainties of Arianism and other heresies could appeal to the wilful, the rebellious, and the humanistic elements in the church, but to the humble believers talk about God as the monad and Christ as an emanation was insubstantial nonsense when compared to the hard, clear realities celebrated by the *Te Deum*.

Second, although the Christians were a minority in and out of the Empire, they sang the *Te Deum* in the confident joy that the true believer is always in the vast majority in God's universe: "All the earth doth worship thee ... the Heavens, and all the Powers therein; ... Heaven and earth are full of the Majesty of thy glory." The *Te Deum* echoes the faith of Psalm 19:1; "The heavens declare the glory of God; and the firmament sheweth his handiwork." People who believe that the opposition, however entrenched and numerically and politically strong, is merely a temporary cloud in God's universe, will not be readily discouraged or deflected in their steady movement towards power and dominion. The enemy had only a silent god; the orthodox party had the self-revealing God. The enemy had the power of Caesar behind it; the orthodox believers had the power of the triune God behind them. Caesar's overlord was their God and Savior. And this God, having died for them, would do yet more and care for them. They could therefore sing with joy, "Thou art the King of Glory, O Christ."

Third, with this confident faith, the orthodox believers could make the amazing prayer, "let me never be confounded," the culmination of the *Te Deum*. For the pagans, the gods and history forever confounded men. The lot of man was a sorry one, and the processes of the universe confounded, confused, and shamed man with frustration, defeat, decay, and death. It is customary for humanists to portray pagan antiquity as a golden age, a time of joy and of human self-realization and dignity; the portrait represents mythology. Pagan man held to a basically pessimistic outlook. It was a "you can't win" philosophy. *Fate* destined man to an ultimately dark and shadowed end, and man's todays were clouded by life's basic hostility to man. It was no less true of the barbarians that for them life was basically

---

[3.] Francis Proctor, *A History of the Book of Common Prayer* (London: Macmillan, 1875), 225. The reference to Comber is to *Companion to the Temple*, I, 96; *Short Discourses upon the Common Prayer*, 53.

frustrating. Vida Scudder cited a revealing passage in Bede as illustrative of the different world of Christianity:

> "For it is no wonder," says Bede of S. Cuthbert, "that the very creature should obey his wishes who so faithfully obeyed the great Author of all creatures. But we for the most part have lost our dominion over the creation that has been subjected to us, because we neglect to obey the Lord and Creator of all things." The creation that has been subject to us! How strangely had this quiet incidental phrase fallen on Pagan ears![4]

To be a Christian means, the orthodox party saw, restoration into Adam's dominion and kingship over the earth. Such a faith makes for a magnificent confidence in the face of all things. According to Bede, King Edwin's advisers in A. D. 627 urged adoption of Christianity for the pragmatic reason that it "contains something more certain" than their paganism and therefore "it seems justly to deserve to be followed."[5] It was no small factor in the appeal of orthodox Christianity that it offered "something more certain," and that this something was a gospel, good news, and the word of victory. Life had a way of confounding men, great and small, and a faith which could be confident in its prayer against confounding was clearly a commanding one.

The *Te Deum* was here as elsewhere clearly reflecting Scripture. Psalm 22:5 reads, "They cried unto thee, and were delivered: they trusted in thee, and were not confounded." In another psalm, David prayed, "Let not them that wait on thee, O Lord GOD of hosts, be ashamed for my sake: let not those that seek thee be confounded for my sake, O God of Israel" (Ps. 69:6). In numerous psalms, the confounding of the ungodly is called for (Ps. 35:4; 40:14; 70:2; 71:13, 14; 83:17; 97:7). The assurance of the orthodox believers in praying, "let me never be confounded," was grounded moreover in Paul's declaration, "But God hath chosen the foolish things of the world to confound the wise; and God hath chosen the weak things of the world to confound the things which are mighty" (1 Cor. 1:27). The confidence of the *Te Deum* is thus firmly grounded: God will not only spare His chosen ones from confounding, but He purposes to use them to confound the powers of this world!

Fourth, the mighty agent of this confounding of the ungodly is "the King of Glory," the Second Person of the Trinity, Jesus Christ. He is the great Judge and man's savior and present help. He is the incarnate one, who experienced all things man experiences, including "the sharpness of death."

The *Te Deum*, thus, is a triumphant expression also of orthodox Christian creedalism. Arius' *Thalia* had been sung by the Alexandrian

---

[4.] Vida D. Scudder, "Introduction," to the Venerable Bede, *The Ecclesiastical History of the English Nation* (London: Dent [Everyman], 1910), xix.

[5.] Bede, *Ecclesiastical History*, ch. XIII, 91.

dock-hands and others, and had enjoyed a brief popularity, but only as a means of mocking the orthodox believers. Except for its critical and mocking use, it had no meaning, certainly not as a song of faith. The *Te Deum*, however, is a song of faith, of confident and triumphant faith in the triune God who governs all history. The creedal controversies were not merely theological debates whose scope was restricted to the intellectuals of the church. The development and great popularity of the *Te Deum* illustrate the vitality of the creedal theology in the everyday life of the early church. This was both fed by the creedal controversies and also made possible the intellectualism which undergirded the orthodox fathers. The church which produced and supported the fathers was a battle-tested church which sang of certain victory in and through Christ the King: *Te Deum laudamus.*

Chapter Five

The Power and the Glory

Two ancient doxologies from the earliest era of the church continue in use to this day. These are the *Gloria in Excelsis,* the *doxologia major,* and the *Gloria Patri, the doxologia minor.* The *Gloria in Excelsis,* in the English form, declares,

> Glory be to God on high, and on earth, peace, good-will towards men. We praise Thee, we bless Thee, we worship Thee, we glorify Thee, we give thanks to Thee for Thy great glory, O Lord God, heavenly King, God the Father Almighty. O Lord, the only-begotten Son Jesus Christ; O Lord God, Lamb of God, Son of the Father, that takest away the sins of the world, have mercy on us. Thou that takest away the sins of the world, receive our prayer. Thou that sittest at the right hand of God the Father, have mercy on us. For Thou only art holy; Thou only art the Lord; Thou only, O Christ, with the Holy Ghost, art most high in the glory of God the Father. Amen.

The *Gloria Patri,* in the Western form, declares,

> Glory be to the Father, and to the Son, and to the Holy Ghost; As it was in the beginning, is now, and ever shall be: world without end. Amen.

The *glory* means the manifestation of the divine nature. In Christian doctrine, in terms of Biblical theology, the power and the glory are ascribed only to the triune God. In history, however, men who have gained world power, or great imperial power, have at the same time claimed the glory for themselves. They have ascribed to themselves divine powers and declared themselves to be the visible manifestation of the divine glory. St. Luke recorded one such incident in Acts 12:21-23. King Herod claimed "the glory" for himself and incurred the judgment of God.

Where the monarch claims to be the glory of God, it follows of course that his realm is therefore the Kingdom of God on earth. The Persian Empire clearly declared itself to be this kingdom and its ruler to be the possessor of the divine glory.[1]

In the Old Testament, the glory of God means, first, "the self-revealed character and being of God," and, second, "a physical phenomenon indicative of the divine presence."[2] The glory of God is also present where God has given power and authority, as unto Nebuchadnezzar (Dan. 2:37). St. Paul spoke of woman as "the glory of the man," i.e., "the woman making conspicuous the authority of the man" by her godly obedience.[3] According to Whitham,

> The "glory of God," ... must mean His essential and unchanging Godhead as revealed to man. And the familiar ascription 'Glory to God' would imply not only a right human praise, but the assigning to God of what He truly is, for nothing higher can be given Him. Similarly the true "glory" of man or nature must be that ideal condition, that final perfection, which exists as a real fact in the Divine mind. The glory of God is what He is essentially; the glory of created things is what they are meant by God to be, though not yet perfectly attained (Heb. 2:10, Rom. 8:18-21).[4]

The word glory also "carries with it ideas of 'light,' 'splendor,' and 'beauty'."[5] In terms of this, it is clear why long hair and a covered head is "power" (1 Cor. 11:10) and "glory" for a woman (1 Cor. 11: 15). It is the public witness to her acceptance of her ideal and destined role, and this acceptance and fulfillment of her God-ordained purpose is power and glory for her. This is confirmed by Robert Law, who called attention to the Biblical use of glory as meaning the "natural perfection" of the creature (1 Peter 1: 24; 1 Cor. 15:40, 41; 1 Cor. 11:15).[6]

The aspiration of apostate and fallen man has too often been the possession of the divine power and glory in some sense. That this claim was commonplace to pagan civilizations is well known, but it was and is common also to cultures claiming to be Christian. The conspicuous example is Byzantium. The imperial court was a religious institution

---

[1] F. W. Buckler, "Firdausi's *Shahnamah* and the *Genealogia Regni Dei*," *Journal of the American Oriental Society*, Supplement no. 1, September, 1935, 1-21.

[2] G. B. Gray, "Glory (in O.T)" in James Hastings, editor, *A Dictionary of the Bible*, II (New York: Charles Scribner's Sons, 1919 [1899]), 184.

[3] J. Massie, "Glory (N.T.)" in *ibid.*, II, 186.

[4] A. R. Whitham, "Glory," in James Hastings, editor, *A Dictionary of Christ and the Gospels*, I (New York: Charles Scribner's Sons, 1917 [1906]), 648.

[5] *Ibid.*, I, 649.

[6] Robert Law, "Glory," in James Hastings, editor, *Dictionary of the Apostolic Church*, I (New York: Charles Scribner's Sons, 1919 [1916]), 451.

centering on the divine power and glory of the emperor. Everything was done to suggest the glory of God in the person of the emperor. A bronze tree, gilded over, whose branches were filled with mechanical gilded birds which uttered cries according to their species, stood before the throne. The throne was surrounded by mechanical lions which roared and beat their tails, and the throne arose toward the ceiling while the mortals approaching the throne made their three obeisances to the emperor with their faces on the ground.[7] The golden tree was apparently to suggest the tree of life, whose life-giving power the emperor's favor dispensed.

In the modern world, the claimants to the power and the glory of God have been less dramatic and more pragmatic and practical. The divinity has been located in the people, in the masses, in democracy, so that "the people" are in theory the power and the glory. No transcendence is allowed, a total immanence is posited: the divine potency is inherent in the people. Thus, Mao Tse-Tung has said of the United States, Hitler, imperial Russia of the Tsars, imperial Japan, and other past and present powers, that they "are merely paper tigers. The reason is that they are divorced from the people."[8] The power is in the people. Therefore, "The army must become one with the people so that they may see it as their own army. Such an army will be invincible."[9] But the people cannot be allowed to exercise this power: they are guilty of "ultra-democracy" and "the petty bourgeoisie's individualistic aversion to discipline" if they think of it. It is actually counter-revolutionary to imagine that the people have the right to exercise their own "power," and war must be waged against such a belief:

> In the sphere of theory, destroy the roots of ultra-democracy. First, it should be pointed out that the danger of ultra-democracy lies in the fact that it damages or even completely wrecks the Party organization and weakens or even completely undermines the Party's fighting capacity, rendering the Party incapable of fulfilling its righting tasks and thereby causing the defeat of the revolution. Next, it should be pointed out that the source of ultra-democracy consists in the petty bourgeoisie's individualistic aversion to discipline. When this characteristic is brought into the Party, it develops into ultra-democratic ideas politically and organizationally. These ideas are utterly incompatible with the fighting tasks of the proletariat.[10]

In the Western countries, these same attempted seizures of the power and the glory, taking varying forms, are also present. The concept of "the

---

[7.] F. A. Wright, translator, *The Works of Liudprand of Cremona,* in "Antapodosis," (London: George Routledge & Sons, 1930), 207f.

[8.] Speech at the Moscow Meeting of Communist and Workers' Parties. November 18, 1957, in *Quotations From Chairman Mao Tse-Tung,* (Peking: Foreign Language Press, 1966), 75.

[9.] "On Protracted War," May, 1938, Selected Works, II, 186, in *ibid.,* 153.

[10.] "On Correcting Mistaken Ideas in the Party" (December 1929), *Selected Works,* Vol. I, 108, in *ibid.,* 163f.

democratic consensus" is a common one. An elite group is the interpreter and possessor of the people's glory in the form of an intellectual tradition. The consensus is not what the People as a majority wish or vote for but what the elite "know" they should wish. The consensus is Rousseau's general will, and the elite group is the incarnation of man's power and glory.[11]

When Jesus taught that prayer should include the ascription of the power and the glory to God ("For thine is the kingdom, and the power, and the glory, for ever. Amen." Matthew 6:13), He was underscoring all of Scripture, and all of His ministry. The ascription of the power and the glory to the triune God placed Christianity in conflict with not only the Roman Empire but every other realm it entered into.

The two doxologies were and are expressive of Biblical faith. The doxologies joyfully ascribe all the power and the glory to the triune God. They are thus expressive of Christian confidence in the face of a savagely hostile empire.

But they are also more. They express an implicit defiance of all counterclaims to the power and the glory. To declare in the face of the world that this sovereignty of God is the timeless reality: "As it was in the beginning, is now, and ever shall be: world without end. Amen," this was an amazing act. The doxologies thus represented both an amazing confidence and an unbounded faith concerning the certain victory of the triune God over the visible powers of history. They implicitly defy the world in the confidence that the God who makes atonement for men's sins is also their shield and defender, the Lord of time and eternity.

[11.] See R. J. Rushdoony, *The Messianic Character of American Education* (Nutley, New Jersey: The Craig Press, 1963), 253ff.

Chapter Six

Ephesus:
The Worship of Man
Condemned

Although the councils were convened by the emperors, one of the most obvious characteristics of the councils was their theological independence. The State was never permitted to dictate to the church, and the resolute independence of the orthodox theologians was beyond question. And, although later theological vitality passed to the West, the early preeminence of the East was marked.

One of the persistent humanistic demands of the church was for the worship of man. Emperor worship had been, of course, man worship, but, in a broader sense, all humanism is man worship, and this was the basic faith of antiquity. Some of the attacks on Christians sought to destroy Christianity's God-oriented faith by insisting that the church too was humanistic and worshipped a man, Jesus. Why then, it was held, should the church take a position of hostility to the Empire and to emperor worship?

In a Syriac document on the martyrdom of a deacon, Habib, the governor raised the issue, when Habib refused to offer Sacrifice to the official cult:

> The governor said: How is it that thou worshippest and honourest a man, but refusest to worship and honour Zeus there?
>
> Habib said: I worship not a man, because the Scripture teaches me, "Cursed is every one that putteth his trust in man": but God, who took upon Him a body and became a man, (Him) do I worship and glorify.[1]

---

1. "Martyrdom of Habib the Deacon," in *Ante-Nicene Christian Library*, vol. XX, *Syriac Documents*, p. 99f.

Every attempt was also made to insinuate man-worship into the church. With God the Son having become incarnate, it was a point of attack for the humanists to use Jesus Christ as the vehicle for man-worship. By several means, this humanism was insinuated into the church, but the basic strategy resolved itself into two forms. *First,* the deity of Jesus Christ could be denied, as Arianism did, and yet the worship of Christ could be insisted on. This meant plainly that a man Jesus was being worshipped, not God the Son. *Second,* it was held that Jesus was not literally God incarnate but a man who had effected a union of wills with God, so that he was one with God. For this position, Jesus was one with God, not by birth and nature, but by moral will, so that a deification of the creature had taken place.

The third ecumenical council, the Council of Ephesus in A. D. 431, had this issue of man-worship to deal with in the form of Nestorianism. Chrystal summarized under three heads the apostasy of Nestorius: *First,* the denial of the incarnation of God the Word; *second,* the worship of a human being, i.e., a man named Jesus; *third,* "degrading the Eucharist to the worship of bread and wine as Christ's humanity, and to the cannibalism of eating Christ's real flesh and drinking his real blood in the rite."[2]

At the heart of these errors was the fundamental error, man-worship and the denial of Christ's deity. According to Berkhof,

> Instead of blending the two natures into a single self-consciousness, Nestorianism places them alongside of each other with nothing more than a moral and sympathetic union between them. The man Christ was not God, but God-bearer, *theophorus,* a possessor of the Godhead. Christ is worshipped, not because He is God. but because God is in Him.[3]

For Nestorius, according to Landon; "the Word was, indeed, united to man, but was not *made man.* Christ was not born of the Virgin, and never suffered death."[4]

In 428 Nestorius had become patriarch of Constantinople. Nestorius had immediately tried to earn a reputation as a zealous defender of the faith by persecuting the previously condemned forms of Arianism and other heresies, while dealing very cordially with Pelagians. The church historian, Socrates Scholasticus, did not believe that Nestorius actually "denied the Divinity of Christ" but saw him as rather an ignorant and ambitious man "for being a man of natural fluency as a speaker, he was considered well educated, but in reality he was disgracefully illiterate."[5]

---

2. James Chrystal, *The Third World Council,* Ephesus, A. D. 431, vol. III (Jersey City, Chrystal, 1908), 91.
3. Louis Berkhof, *Reformed Dogmatics* (Grand Rapids: Eerdmans, 1937), 109.
4. Edward H. Landon, *A Manual of Councils of the Holy Catholic Church,* I (Edinburgh: John Grant, 1909, revised edition), 255.
5. Socrates Scholasticus, "Ecclesiastical History," VII, 32, in *Nicene and Post-Nicene Fathers,* Series Two, vol. II, 171.

Socrates may have been right, although it is unlikely, as to Nestorius' ignorance, but the fact remains that, whether through ignorance or intent, Nestorius was a humanist whose basic religious motive was man-worship. That he was also close to the throne, and an ambitious man, adds to his basically anthropocentric perspective.

The attitude of the council was one of total rejection of creature-worship, whether of the Perfect Man, Jesus, the Virgin Mary, and apostle, prophet, or saint. The principle of creature-worship was rejected in whole.[6] The shorter letter of Cyril, Bishop of Alexandria, to Nestorius stated the position of the Council:

> For it is not true that He was first born a common man out of the holy Virgin, and that then the Word descended upon Him, but being united to flesh in the womb itself, He is said to have undergone a birth in the flesh, because He claims as His own the birth of His own flesh. So we say that He both *"suffered"* and *"rose again,"* not that the Word of God suffered in His own [Divine] Nature either the stripes or the piercings of the nails or the other wounds, for His Divinity did not suffer, and that because It was without a body; but because that which had been made His own body suffered these indignities, He Himself is said furthermore, in that sense, to have suffered [those things] for us. For the unsuffering [Word] was in the suffering body. And in the same way also we understand that He died. For in His Nature, the Word of God is immortal and incorruptible, and He is Life and Life-Giver. But, because His own body, *"by the grace of God,"* as Paul says, tasted *"death for every man,"* He Himself is said to have suffered that death for us, not that it belongs to His [divine] Nature to experience death, for to say or to think that would be madness, but that, as I have just said, His flesh tasted death. So also again, because His flesh was raised, that resurrection is attributed to Him [the Word], not that He [the Word] fell under the power of corruption [God forbid]; but because His body was raised again.[7]

The distinction is a vital one: if Jesus Christ be reduced to a remarkable man who united Himself to God and became God in that sense, then the door is opened to the redivinization of this world, its orders, and the state. Then again emperors can become gods, and great men unite themselves with divinity to become the expression of God's will for their age. The approach to God then is through man; man works towards God, and the issue is not grace, God's condescension to man, but works, man's ascent to God. The issue at stake was the survival of Christianity. Cyril cited the difference precisely:

> For the Scripture hath said, not that the Word united a man's person to Himself, but that He "was made flesh." But "The Word was made flesh" means nothing other than that, like us, He took part of flesh

6. James Chrystal, *The Third World Council*, I, i. 1895.
7. *Ibid.*, 74-78, Chrystal's translation. In Percival, *Seven Ecumenical Councils*, 198.

and blood, and made a body like ours, His own, and came forth out of a woman, not having cast away his being as God, and His [former] birth out of God the Father, but He has remained, even since His taking of flesh, exactly what He was before. This, the doctrine of the exact faith, everywhere (the faith) sets forth and maintains.[8]

Nestorianism meant a total surrender of Christianity, and the Council of Ephesus was sharply aware of this. In spite of Nestorius' eminence, and the imperial favor, the Council anathematized Nestorius.

Prior to this action, Nestorius answered St. Cyril's letter and declared it to be insulting to him. He accused Cyril of holding "that the consubstantial Divinity is liable to suffering." Nestorius plainly denied the incarnation; making a distinction between the man who by moral union became one with God, and so became "the anointed One," and God:

> Everywhere the Scripture of God, when it makes mention of the Lord's incarnation, transmits to us *a birth* and a suffering *not of the Divinity*, but of the humanity of the Anointed One, so that the Holy Virgin is to be called by the more accurate appellation *"Bringer forth of the Anointed One,"* not *"Bringer Forth of God."*[9]

Nestorius used the term *incarnation* but only to deny it. Through a misunderstanding, and mistranslation, Ephesus has been seen as defending or making possible the worship of the Virgin Mary, when it actually condemned all creature worship. *Theotokos* has been translated as "Mother of God," and Nestorius has been perversely seen as opposing the exaltation of Mary. But *Theotokos*, as Chrystal point out, means "Bringer Forth of God," i.e., that the Virgin Mary brought forth God the Son in His incarnation. Nestorius would have made Mary simply the bringer forth of Christ, the Anointed One, a man who was to be worshipped as God.[10]

Instead of incarnation, Nestorius affirmed a *conjunction* (or *connection)* of God and man, and he accused his enemies of being Arians and Apollinarians, and, worse, heathens, while declaring his faith was the faith of the fathers and of Scripture.

> It is a thing right therefore and worthy of the Gospel transmissions to confess that the body is the temple of the Divinity of the Son, and a temple united by a certain lofty and divine conjunction, so that the Nature of the Divinity appropriates [to itself] the things of that body: but to charge therefore upon that expression, *"appropriation,"* the properties also of the flesh conjoined, I mean *birth* and suffering, and death, belongs truly, brother, to the erroneous opinions of the heathen, or the errors of Apollinaris who was smitten in mind, and of Arius, and of a mind sick with the other heresies, or rather with whatsoever is worse than those. For it will necessarily happen that

---

[8.] Chrystal, I, 97-105. Percival, 198.
[9.] Chrystal, I, 161.
[10.] *Ibid.,* I, vif.

such will be hurried away by the term *"appropriation,"* and on account of that *"appropriation"* they will make God the Word a partaker in sucking the breast, and a sharer in gradual growth and of the fear at the time of the suffering, and one who needed angelic aid. And I will be silent as to circumcision, and sacrifice, and sweatings, and hunger, and thirst; which things, inasmuch as they happened to His flesh for our sake are to be joined together to be worshipped. But these statements concerning the Divinity will be received as lies and will also become the cause of our just condemnation as slanderers. These are the traditions of the holy Fathers. These are the announcements of the Scriptures of God.[11]

Nestorius found it impossible to accept a literal incarnation. To believe that Mary had brought forth incarnate God and had suckled Him, and that this incarnate God had been circumcised, had grown, and had shared in humanity's trials, was to Nestorius offensive. To him, a moral union was the answer.

Nestorius' solution to the Christological challenge is a significant one, and genuinely humanistic. The initiative is reserved to man: God is passive, man is active. It is not God who reaches down to man in the incarnation, but man, who by his works reaches a point of progress and moral achievement whereby he is in union with God. History is determined, not by God but by man, by time, not by eternity.

Nestorius had deposed some orthodox clerics under charges of Manichaeanism, and he now accused Cyril of being influenced by these men and by the same doctrine.[12]

In the voting on Nestorius' Epistle to Cyril, the hostility of the Council to Nestorius was marked. They clearly recognized his denial of orthodoxy. As Chrystal noted, *"the very essence* of Christianity was involved, that is: 1. The truth of the Incarnation of the Word; and 2. *The question of serving a Man, a creature,* that is, the Man put on by the Word, contrary to the fundamental law laid down by Christ Himself in Matt. iv., 10, and Luke iv., 8."[13]

The Long Epistle of St. Cyril to Nestorius expressed the decision of the Council of Ephesus and was put into the Acts. After reviewing the creed, Cyril declared:

Following in all points the confessions of the Holy Fathers which they made (the Holy Ghost speaking in them), and following the scope of their opinions, and going, as it were, in the royal way, we confess that the Only Begotten Word of God, begotten of the same substance of the Father, True God from True God, Light from Light, through Whom all things were made, the things in heaven and the

11. *Ibid.,* I, 163-5.
12. *Ibid.,* I, 165f.
13. *Ibid.,* I, 177n.

things in the earth, coming down for our salvation, making himself of no reputation, was incarnate and made man; that is, taking flesh of the holy Virgin, and having made it his own from the womb, he subjected himself to birth for us, and came forth man from a woman, without casting off that which he was; but although he assumed flesh and blood, he remained what he was, God in essence and in truth. Neither do we say that his flesh was changed into the nature of divinity, nor that the ineffable nature of the Word of God was laid aside for the nature of flesh; for he is unchanged and absolutely unchangeable, being the same always, according to the Scriptures. For although visible and a child in swaddling clothes, and even in the bosom of his Virgin Mother, he filled all creation as God, and was a fellow-ruler with him who begat him, for the Godhead is without quantity and dimension, and cannot have limits.

Confessing the Word to be made one with the flesh according to substance, we adore one Son and Lord Jesus Christ: we do not divide the God from the man, nor separate him into parts, as though the two natures were mutually united in him only through a sharing of dignity and authority (for that is a novelty and nothing else), neither do we give separately to the Word of God the name Christ and the same name separately to a different one born of a woman; but we know only one Christ, the Word from the Father with his own Flesh.[14]

Cyril not only declared the reality of the incarnation, but he, with the Council's approval, declared the two natures to be in true union without confusion; this was asserted to be the orthodox faith. Thus, what was more formally defined at Chalcedon had been already the orthodox faith. Cyril went on to make it clear that Christ was not a deified man: "we do not say that the Word of God dwelt in him as in a common man born of the holy Virgin, lest Christ be thought of as a God-bearing man." Rather, "he became flesh," was truly incarnate, though without confusion of natures. It was "not as if a man had attained only such a conjunction with God as consists in a unity of dignity alone or of authority." The position of Nestorius made the worship of man the worship of God. "It is horrible to say in this connexion as follows: 'The assumed as well as the assuming have the name of God.' For the saying of this divides again Christ into two, and puts the man separately by himself and God by himself. For this saying denies openly the Unity according to which one is not worshipped in the other, nor does God exist together with the other; but Jesus Christ is considered as One, the Only-begotten Son, to be honoured with one adoration together with his own flesh."[15] The doctrine taught by Nestorius supposedly preserved God's being to Himself, but in actuality it made man God, because it made a man able to become God by act of will.

---

14. Percival: *Seven Ecumenical Councils,* 202. See Chrystal, I, 214-216.
15. *Ibid.,* 203.

The answer of Nestorius to the final summons of the Council was to shut the door in the face of the visiting bishops and then to preach even more bluntly his particular doctrines. Theodotus, Bishop of Ancyra, said that Nestorius declared, "that we must not assert nourishing by milk in regard to God, nor the birth out of a virgin. And so he often said here that we must not say that God is two months old or three months old."[16] For Nestorius, it was an impossibility for the passive "unmoved Mover" to become the active agent or to become incarnate. Man could become god, but God could not become man.

The Council, in reading the opinion of the church fathers, found the opinion of Nestorius clearly named as heresy. Thus, Gregory the Great of Nazianzus, in Epistle I to Cledonius, had written, "If anyone say that the Man had been formed and that then God put him on, be he condemned: for that is not a bringing forth of God [out of a woman] but an avoiding of being brought forth."[17] Nestorius had both made clear that Jesus was only man by nature, and also that Jesus was to be worshipped: "I worship him [the Man, that is, Christ's humanity] who is worn, for the sake of Him [God the Word] who wears. I bow to him who is seen, for the sake of Him [God the Word] who is hidden. God is unseparated from him [the Man] who appears. For that reason I do not separate the honor of the unseparated One. I separate the Natures, but I unite the bowing."[18] But the Council made it clear that only God could be worshipped; not even Christ's humanity could be worshipped but only His deity. The humanity of Christ is not nor ever can be deified. The two natures are without confusion, even in the unique incarnation. Nestorius held to "the unmixed conjoinment of the [Two] Natures. Let us worship the Man co-bowed to with the Almighty God in the divine conjoinment."[19] By moral union, Christ having become one with God through his moral excellency and works, Christ was therefore to be worshipped as God. The door was opened to any man or state who by moral excellence or works united himself with God to be worshipped as God. In the name of defending God's honor, Nestorius usurped God's worship for man.

When Hellenic humanism captured the church in the medieval period, this exaltation of man came to the fore in the church. Innocent III held that "the pope holds the place of the true God," and Marcellus in the Lateran Council, and with its full approval, called Julius "God on earth." Cardinal Bellarmine held that "the Pope can transubstantiate sin into duty, and duty into sin," thereby placing him above God and His law, also making man active and God passive.[20] Protestant modernism has similarly demoted

---

16. *Chrystal,* i, 409-412.
17. *Ibid.,* I, 440f.
18. *Ibid.,* I, 461.
19. *Ibid.,* I, 464.

Jesus to a Nestorian moral union with God and thereby exalted man (and itself) to a position of potential union with God and actual judgment (and thereby superiority) over God's word.

The Council then approved St. Cyril's Twelve Anathematisms Against Nestorius. The First Anathema or Chapter declared: "If anyone does not acknowledge that the Immanuel is really God, and that therefore the Holy Virgin was Bringer-Forth-of God, for she brought forth in a fleshly way the Word, Who had come out of God and been made flesh, let him be anathema." Nestorius issued a Counter Anathema I:

> If any says that He who is Emmanuel is God the Word, and not rather *God with us* [Matt. i., 231], that is, that He [God the Word] dwelt in that nature which is like ours, inasmuch as He was united to our *lump* [Rom. xi., 16] which he took from the Virgin Mary, and names the Holy Virgin, *Mother of God the Word*, and not rather of Him who is *Emmanuel*, and [asserts] that God the Word Himself was turned into flesh, which He took for the showing of His own Deity, that He might be *found in fashion as a Man* [Philip, ii., 81], let him be anathema.[21]

The *Second Anathema* stated, "If any one does not acknowledge that the Word [who came] out of God the Father has been united by His Substance to flesh, and that He is One Anointed within His own flesh, that is, that the same One is both God and Man together, let him be anathema." By way of answer, Nestorius tried to identify the orthodox position with Apollinarianism and Sabellianism, holding that it did "infinitely and uncircumscribedly coextend flesh to the Divine Nature," whereas Cyril and Ephesus had made clear that there was no confusion of the two natures. The discarnate God of Nestorius was not unlike the hidden god of the Arians: the total remoteness and impossibility of such a god made it inescapable that an actual god be sought for in and of this world. Nestorius denied, *first,* the incarnation, and, *second,* gave worship to the man Jesus directly, and to God the Word *indirectly only,* that is, *relatively,* as Chrystal has shown. Nestorius' Second Anathema read:

> If any one in that [merely external] conjunction of God the Word which was made to flesh, asserts that a change of the Divine Essence from place to place has been made, and that flesh is capable of containing His Divine Nature, and that It was united to flesh in birth; or, again, infinitely and uncircumscribedly coextends flesh to the Divine Nature to contain God, and says that the very same nature is both God and Man, let him be anathema.[22]

The orthodox doctrine held to the union without confusion of the two natures, a union by incarnation. Nestorius held to a moral union, with a

---

20. Chrystal, I, 510f.
21. Chrystal, I, 314-317, 321.
22. *Ibid.*, I, 318-321, 323.

strictly discarnate separation of the two natures, but a worship and therefore tacit deification of the human nature.

The *Third Anathema* of Cyril and the Council declared, "If any one separates the [two] Substances in the one Anointed after the union, and cojoins them in a *conjunction* alone of dignity, that is of authority, or power, and not rather in a coming together in a Nature Union, let him be anathema." The Nestorian position made Christ no different than the prophets by nature, but yet the recipient of worship from man and authority from God. Nestorius' Third Counter Anathema stated:

> If any one does not say that Christ is One by a [mere external] conjunction, who is also Emmanuel, [Emmanuel is explained in Counter Anathema I, to be a mere man], but that He is one by a Nature which is made up of each of the two Substances, that is, that of God the Word and that of the Man taken by Him, and does not at all confess that one [mere external] connection of a Son, which even now we preserve without any mingling [of the Two Natures], let him be anathema.[23]

To Nestorius, the central offense was the incarnation, and his hostility to it is marked.

The *Fourth Anathema* of Cyril declared:

> If anyone shall divide between two persons or subsistences those expressions which are contained in the Evangelical and Apostolical writings, or which have been said concerning Christ by the Saints, or by himself, and shall apply some to him as to a man separate from the Word of God, and shall apply others to the only Word of God in the Father, on the ground that they are fit to be applied to God: let him be anathema.[24]

This anathema was aimed at attacks against the two great Alexandrian theologians, Athanasius and Cyril, and against the attacks on the councils from Nicea to Ephesus, because of their approval of the doctrine of Economic Appropriation. This doctrine affirmed the two natures in true union without confusion. It forbade the ascription of certain acts to Christ's humanity and others to His deity, for such an ascription would assume an alternating consciousness and no true union. In that true union, "we must economically ascribe to Him, God the Word, all the human names and human expressions used of that Man in the New Testament, in order to guard against our being led, as were the Nestorians, to worship a mere creature, contrary to Matt. vi.,10."[25] In that the Divine is the infinitely superior and controlling nature in the incarnate son, we must *economically* ascribe to Him the activities and words of the whole, for, while God the Son was truly incarnate, the determination of all things

---

[23.] *Ibid.*, I, 322-325.
[24.] Percival, 211.
[25.] Chrystal, I, 326.

never passed from eternity to time, nor from God to man. Athanasius made this point in his arguments against the Arians. "For it was fitting that the redemption should take place through none other than Him who is the Lord by nature, lest, though created (i.e., as new creatures in Christ] by the Son, we should name another Lord, and fall into the Arian and Greek folly, serving the creature beyond the all-creating God."[26] It would be the "Greek folly," humanism, if man's salvation were primarily the work of Christ the Man. By the doctrine of Economic Appropriation, the ultimacy of God and His sovereignty and decree were maintained. Athanasius further stated:

> It became the Lord, in putting on human flesh, to put it on whole with the affections proper to it; that, as we say that the body was His own, so also we say that the affections of the body were proper to Him alone, though they did not touch Him according to His Godhead. If then the body had been another's, to him too had been the affections attributed; but if the flesh is the Word's (for the Word became flesh), of necessity then the affections also of the flesh are ascribed to Him, whose the flesh is. And to whom the affections are ascribed, such namely as to be condemned, to be scourged, to thirst, and the cross, and death, and the other infirmities of the body, of Him too is the triumph and the grace. For this cause then, consistently and fittingly such affections are ascribed not to another, but to the Lord; that the grace also may be from Him, and that we may become, not worshippers of any other, but truly devout towards God, because we invoke no originate thing, no ordinary man, but the natural and true Son from God, who has become man, yet is not the less Lord and God and Saviour.[27]

St. Cyril quoted this passage from Athanasius in defending his Twelfth Anathema. From Nicea on, it had been made clear that creature worship was intolerable to orthodoxy, and from the earliest beginnings of the church, worship of Christ as man was anathema. St. Epiphanius (in *Ancoratus*, sec. 50) declared bowing an act of religious service and therefore a prerogative of God; it cannot be given to man. "'And let them not vainly heap up blasphemies to themselves. For if the Son is a creature He is not to be bowed to .... For it is foolish to bow to a creature, and to do away the first commandment ....'"[28] Epiphanius, in writing on the *Ariomaniacs*, Heresy LXIX, section 31, accused the Arians of making an idol of Christ, in that Christ was for them a mere creature whom they made into a false god, a created god, when the only true God is the uncreated and triune God.

> Is then even the Sole-Born so judged among you, and do ye think so disgracefully in regard to Him who redeemed you, since indeed He

---

26. Athanasius, "Four Discourses Against the Arians," II, xv, 142 in *Nicene and Post-Nicene Fathers*, Series II, vol. IV, 356.

27. Athanasius, *ibid.*, Discourse III, chap. xxvi, sect. 32; 411.

28. James Chrystal: *Nicaea, A. D. 325*, vol. I (Jersey City: Chrystal, 1891), 240.

did redeem you? But ye are no longer of His fold, for ye deny your Saviour and Redeemer. For if He is not real God, then He is not to be bowed to: and if He is a creature, He is not God. And if He is not to be bowed to why then is He called God? Cease ye to work out the Babylonian nature again, for ye have set up the likeness and the image of Nebuchadnezzar, and have sounded that much talked of trumpet to gather the warriors, and with music and cymbals and stringed instrument ye have made the peoples to fall by means of your deceptive words, for ye have got them to serve an image rather than God and truth. And what other is real [God] as the Son of God is?[29]

Nestorius could not rightfully accuse the orthodox party of introducing an innovation. From the beginning, creature worship had been opposed, the unity without confusion upheld. In his answer, however, he persisted in ascribing Apollinarianism to Cyril and the Council, and in denying the incarnation. The Nestorian Counter Anathema IV read:

> If any one understands as though they belonged to (but) One Nature, those expressions in the Gospels and in the Apostolic Epistles which were written concerning Christ, who is of Two Natures, and tries to ascribe the sufferings of flesh as well as of Divinity also to the Word Himself of God, let him be anathema.[30]

The *Fifth Anathema* stated, "If any one dares to say that the Anointed One is an inspired man and not rather that He is really God, as [being the] One Son by [His Divine] Nature, forasmuch as the Word was made flesh, and like us shared blood and flesh, let him be anathema."[31] Nestorius' Counter Anathema V read: "If any one ventures to say that, even after the assumption of human nature, there is one Son of God, he who is so in nature, while he (since the assumption of flesh) is certainly Emmanuel; let him be anathema."[32] The implication again is that the alternative is between Nestorius' moral union or a Monophysite position.

The *Sixth Anathema* declared, "If any one dares to say that the Word Who came out of God the Father is God or Master of the Anointed One, and does not rather confess that the same One is both God and man together, forasmuch as *the Word has been made flesh* according to the Scriptures, let him be anathema."[33] The Sixth Nestorian Counter Anathema read:

> If anyone, after the Incarnation calls another than Christ the Word, and ventures to say that the form of a servant is equally with the Word of God without beginning and uncreated, and not rather that it is made by him as its natural Lord and Creator and God, and that he has

---

29. *Ibid.*, I, 241f.
30. Chrystal: *Ephesus*, I, 326n.
31. *Ibid.*, I, 327f.
32. Percival, 212.
33. Chrystal, I, 328f.

promised to raise it again in the words: "Destroy this temple, and in three day I will build it again"; let him be anathema.[34]

Nestorius here assumed that his opponents held to a transubstantiation of Christ's human nature into the substance of God the Word. Moreover, he assumed that the human nature came, not from the Virgin Mary, but directly from God and was without beginning and therefore uncreated flesh. For Nestorius there could be no primacy of God in the incarnation without a destruction of man; hence, he denied the incarnation in favor of conjunction or moral union to retain primacy for man. Cyril's Anathema VI and VII condemned, first, the Nestorian opinion that Christ was simply an inspired man, not God of God, and that Christ was simply energized by the Holy Spirit. Second, Cyril condemned the transfer of the glory of God the Word to Jesus as man. In the Seventh Anathema, Cyril declared, "If any one says that Jesus as [being] a [mere] Man, was [merely] energized by God the Word, and that the glory of the Sole-Born has been put about him [that mere Man] as being another besides [the Sole-Born Word] Himself, let him be anathema."[35] The Nestorian Counter Anathema VII read:

> If any one says that the man who was formed of the Virgin is the Only-begotten, who was born from the bosom of the Father, before the morning-star was (Ps. cix., 3), and does not rather confess that he has obtained the designation of Only-begotten on account of his connection with him who in nature is the *Only-begotten* of the Father; and besides, if any one calls another than the Emmanuel Christ; let him be anathema.[36]

The charge again is of the transubstantiation of the humanity of Christ into the deity. Nestorius read the doctrine of Economic Appropriation as transubstantiation. Nestorius had an implicit doctrine of economic appropriation of another sort. For him, *first*, God could not become incarnate. *Second*, all attributes appearing on the scene of time and history had to be economically appropriated therefore by man, since man is the primary agent in time and history. *Third*, it follows therefore that whatever of God appears on the human scene, in time and history, must be appropriated by man, because by definition it cannot be God incarnate, or God primarily, but God in moral union with man as the prime agent.

The *Eighth Anathema* of Cyril and the Council declared:

> If anyone shall dare to say that the assumed man ought to be worshipped together with God the Word, and glorified together with him, and recognized together with him as God, and yet as two different things, the one with the other (for this "Together with" is added [i.e., by the Nestorians] to convey this meaning); and shall not

---

34. Percival, 213.
35. Chrystal, I, 329f.
36. Percival, 213f.

rather with one adoration worship the Emmanuel and pay to him one glorification, as (it is written) "The Word was made flesh": let him be anathema.[37]

In worshipping the Son, we worship therefore not His humanity but His deity only. When we are forbidden to worship the humanity of God incarnate, it follows necessarily that all creature-worship, and bowing to any creature in worship, is absolutely forbidden. As a result, the Council was clearly opposed to the veneration of Mary and the saints and felt that it had erected a theological barrier to all creature-worship. The Nestorian Counter Anathema VIII stated:

> If any one says that the form of a servant should, for its own sake, that is, in reference to its own nature, be reverenced, and that it is the ruler of all things, and not rather that [merely] on account of its connection with the holy and in itself universally ruling nature of the Only-begotten, it is to be reverenced; let him be anathema.[38]

Here Nestorius ostensibly renounces creature-worship by declaring that those who say that the Christ is ruler of all things and to be worshipped are wrong; for Nestorius Christ is to be worshipped or reverenced, although a man, on account of His "connection" with God! Thus, Christ for Nestorius cannot be worshipped as God, but He can be worshipped as a man connected with God! As St. Cyril, in one of his works, observed: "God alone is free and absolute. For, so to speak, He demands tribute from all, and so to speak, receives worship as due from all. And if Christ be the end of the Law and the Prophets [Rom. x., 4], but is a [mere] inspired Man, may we not say that the end of the prophetic predictions has brought the crime of worshipping a man to us?"[39] This same subject was dealt with by the Fifth Ecumenical Council, A. D. 553, in its Anathema IX, which declared: "If any one says that the Anointed One is to be bowed to in Two Natures, by which two worships are brought in, one peculiar to God the Word, and another peculiar to the Man ... but will not bow to God the Word infleshed within His own flesh, with [but] one worship, as the Church of God has received from the beginning, let such a one be anathema."[40]

The *Ninth Anathema* declared:

> If any man shall say that the one Lord Jesus Christ was glorified by the Holy Ghost, so that he used through him a power not his own and from him received power against unclean spirits and power to work miracles before man and shall not rather confess that it was his own Spirit through which he worked these divine signs; let him be anathema. [41]

---

37. *Ibid.*, 214.
38. *Ibid.*
39. Chrystal, I, 334n.
40. *Ibid.*, I, 335n.
41. Percival, 214f.

The Counter Anathema IX of Nestorius read:

> If anyone says that the form of a servant is of like nature with the
> Holy Ghost, and not rather that it owes its union with the Word
> which has existed since the conception, to his mediation by which it
> works miraculous healings among men, and possesses the power of
> expelling demons; let him be anathema. [42]

Chrystal summarized the three views as to worshipping the humanity of
Christ very ably. For the Nestorians, "Both Natures in Christ are to be
worshipped, His Divinity absolutely, His Humanity relatively only. Each
Nature is separate, and yet the worship to both is to be united." The
Monophysites came to hold that "There is only One Nature in Christ since
the Union, that is, the Divine, and it alone is to be worshipped. But the
Orthodox reply that, *in fact*, however, Christ's human nature does remain,
and therefore, in worshipping all of Christ as God absolutely, the
One-Naturite was in fact a *Creature-Worshipper*." The orthodox held that
"One only of Christ's Two Natures is to be worshipped, that is, the
Divinity, and that absolutely. As an old writer puts it, 'There are Two
Natures in Christ — One Divine and to be bowed to, and one human and
not to be bowed to.'"[43] The issue with respect to the Holy Spirit was a
related one. Christ had declared, in John 16:14, 15, that "all things that the
Father hath are mine." The Holy Ghost therefore proceeded from the
Father as from the Son. For Nestorius therefore instead of God incarnate
working miracles by His own Spirit, a man works miracles through his
moral command over the Spirit. Cyril condemned the opinion that a
merely human Christ worked miracles and reserved that power to the
incarnate Son of God by His own Spirit.

In the *Tenth Anathema*, Cyril and the Council dealt with the work of
Christ as mediator and savior:

> Whoever shall say that it is not the divine Word himself, when he was
> made flesh and had become man as we are, but another than he, a man
> born of a woman, yet different from him, who is become our Great
> High Priest and Apostle; or if any man shall say that he offered
> himself in sacrifice for himself and not rather for us, whereas, being
> without sin, he had no need of offering or sacrifice: let him be
> anathema.

The Counter Anathema X of Nestorius read:

> If any one maintains that the Word, who is from the beginning, has
> become the high priest and apostle of our confession, and has offered
> himself for us, and does not rather say that it is the work of Emmanuel
> to be an apostle; and if any one in such a manner divides the sacrifice
> between him who united [the Word] and him who was united [the

---

42. *Ibid.*, 215.
43. Chrystal, I, 347n.

manhood] referring it to a common sonship, that is, not giving to God that which is God's, and to man that which is man's; let him be anathema.[44]

God the Word is our Mediator, not a mere man. To open the door as Nestorius did to man was to allow also any creature, saints, angels, or martyrs, to become mediators, and St. Cyril emphasized this in his *Five-Book Contradiction of the Blasphemies of Nestorius* (Bk. 111, sec. 103). Nestorius made mediation the work of man. Salvation thus became man's work, not God's Grace. The orthodox doctrine of Economic Appropriation reserved unto God the ultimacy, primacy, authority, and activity in all things. The Nestorian doctrine of Economic Appropriation reserved unto man the ultimacy, primacy, authority, and activity in all things, and to add insult to injury, claimed to do it in defense of God's glory. In the confessions of the Reformation, the long-subverted orthodox doctrine of mediation was restored and made central.

The *Eleventh Anathema* of Cyril and the Council declared:

> Whosoever shall not confess that the flesh of the Lord giveth life and that it pertains to the Word of God the Father as his very own, but shall pretend that it belongs to another person who is united to him (i.e., the Word) only according to honour, and who has served as a dwelling for the divinity; and shall not rather confess, as we say, that the flesh giveth life because it is that of the Word who giveth life to all: let him be anathema.

The Nestorian Counter Anathema XI read: "If any one maintains that the flesh which is united with God the Word is by the power of its own nature life-giving, whereas the Lord himself says, 'It is the Spirit that quickeneth; the flesh profiteth nothing' (St. John vi. 64), let him be anathema."[45] The reference here is to the sacrament of communion. St. Cyril had made it clear, in his teachings, that his position was not consubstantiation and transubstantiation, as they came to be called later. Moreover, in the elements it is not the substance of the deity of Christ which is received, nor is it the eating and drinking of Christ's real blood and flesh. The idolatry of worshipping Christ's deity or humanity in the elements was also barred. The Anathema condemned those who held that mere human flesh and blood can spiritually quicken any one, when it is the Word that quickens us in the Eucharist by His Life-giving Spirit. To receive mere flesh and blood, Cyril taught, spiritually quickens no one, and to eat flesh and to drink blood is cannibalism and wickedness.[46] The Nestorians held to a real presence of the human flesh and blood of Christ, although the Nestorians denied it. Cyril, however, did not accept that denial as valid.[47]

[44.] Percival, 216.
[45.] *Ibid.*, 217.
[46.] Chrystal, I, 407; cf. n. 606, 240-313.

The *Twelfth Anathema* of Cyril and the Council declared:

> Whoever shall not recognize that the Word of God suffered in the flesh, that he was crucified in the flesh, and that likewise in that same flesh he tasted death and that he is become the first-begotten of the dead, for, as he is God, he is the life and it is he that giveth life: let him be anathema.

The Nestorian Counter Anathema XII as usual declared its humanism in the name of preserving the dignity of God:

> If any one, in confessing the sufferings of the flesh, ascribe these also to the Word of God as to the flesh in which he appeared, and thus does not distinguish the dignity of the natures; let him be anathema.[48]

Here again it is the reality of the incarnation and the doctrine of Economic Appropriation which is at stake. Nestorius' Counter Anathema is aimed at these doctrines. Not only was the doctrine affirmed by the Third Council, but the Fourth Ecumenical Council gave sanction to the term *Economic Appropriation* by approving St. Cyril's "Epistle to John of Antioch," which read in part:

> And, moreover, we all confess that the Word of God is not liable to suffering, even though He Himself in all-wisely managing the mystery (of Redemption) is seen to ascribe to Himself the sufferings which happened to His own flesh. And for that very reason the all-wise Peter saith, *Christ then hath suffered for us in the flesh* [1 Peter iv., 1], and not in the Nature of the ineffable Divinity. For in order that He Himself may be believed to be the Saviour of all He refers the sufferings of His own flesh to Himself by Economic Appropriation. A thing implying that doctrine is what was predicted through the prophetic utterance, as from Himself, *I gave my back to scourges, and my cheeks to blows, and I turned not away my face from (the) spittings of shame* [Isaiah 50:6].[49]

Thus, while the deity did not in itself suffer, by Economic Appropriation, suffering is attributed to it.

Theodotus, Bishop of Ancrya, in reporting on Nestorius' answer to the final summons, had said, "I am indeed pained for my friend. Nevertheless I honor piety before any friendship."[50] The Council was not marked by personal hostility to Nestorius; it was marked by a concern for the orthodox faith, and Nestorius, by his arrogant dismissal of it, brought on his condemnation, "namely, that our Lord Jesus Christ, whom he has blasphemed, decrees by the Holy Synod that Nestorius be excluded from the episcopal dignity, and from all priestly communion."[51] The Council

---

47. *Ibid.*, I, 408n.
48. Percival, 217.
49. Chrystal, I, 409f, n.
50. *Ibid.*, 400f.
51. Percival, 218.

had been patient with the man though hostile to the heresy. Although the emperor favored Nestorius, he was finally excluded from office.

When the Council of Ephesus was convened, St. Augustine, Bishop of Hippo, was to have presided, but he died in the latter part of 430. The Council, however, accomplished something very important to Augustine: Pelagianism was condemned, or, in the words of the Synod Report, "Pelagians and Celestians," referring to Celestius, a follower of Pelagius, were condemned. Pelagius, a monk born in Britain, made salvation a matter of man's moral works, not of God's grace. Percival's comment is apt: "The only 'grace' which he would admit the existence of, was what we may call external grace, e.g., the example of Christ, the teaching of his ministers' and the like."[52] This was open humanism. Pelagius and Celestius had found refuge with Nestorius, bringing their heresies together. Earlier, the Bishop of Rome had seen no heresy in Nestorius, but the work of the orthodox theologians, led by Cyril, Augustine, and others, steadily alerted the church to these heresies. Canon IV of Ephesus stated, "If any of the clergy shall fall away, and publicly or privately presume to maintain the doctrines of Nestorius or Celestius, it is declared just by the Holy Synod that these also should be deposed."[53] Pelagianism had already been condemned in the West, and Ephesus therefore did not enter into the details of the issue as it did with Nestorianism. Moreover, Nestorius having been condemned, the heresies he sheltered were also struck down.

The two hundred bishops who met at Ephesus had done an important work. The Council was bitterly contested, and its history subsequently is a complex one of contested authority. Modern scholars have often been apologists for Nestorius. Chalcedon however confirmed Ephesus, and the false council of Ephesus of 449, the Robber Council, was condemned. At the Robber Council, many bishops were not allowed a voice in the meeting dominated by Eutyches' patron, Dioscurus of Alexandria, who induced the emperor Theodosius II to convoke the meeting. Dioscurus was supposedly Cyril's follower but in reality a Monophysite and a leader of that party. For the Monophysites, the divine was emphasized; they denied that there were two natures after the incarnation, and even the body of Christ was a divine body. The human attributes were all transferred to the "humanized Logos." In Schaff's words, Eutyches "asserted, therefore, on the one hand, the capability of suffering and death in the Logos-personality, and on the other hand, the deification of the human in Christ."[54] This was humanism in the name of anti-humanism. Humanity was absorbed into the Trinity in the name of God-centered religion! In the place of Economic Appropriation, the Monophysites held to the real absorption of humanity into divinity.

[52.] *Ibid.*, 229.
[53.] *Ibid.*
[54.] Philip Schaff, *History of the Christian Church* III, 737.

Dioscurus presided and ruled with the aid of violent monks and armed soldiers. The form of orthodoxy was maintained by adopting the twelve anathematisms of Cyril, whereas in reality another doctrine was affirmed. The two-nature (dyophysite) faith was condemned, and Flavianus, its champion, was condemned. The proconsul, Proclus, with armed soldiers and chains, entered to compel the bishops to sign. After severe violence, ninety-six of them did, with many severely wounded. Flavianus, Bishop of Constantinople, died within three days of the injuries he received. It was said that the monks kicked him savagely, and Dioscurus jumped on Flavianus as he lay upon the ground. The Robber Council gained a savage and impressive short-term victory, but it stood self-condemned by its disgraceful conduct. The victories of the true Council of Ephesus were hammered out in the arena of faith, of consistent theological thinking. The victories of the false council rested on violence and were short-lived. Within two years, Chalcedon had denounced them, but, before then, the opinion of all true Christians had condemned the Council of Robbers.[55]

The Ecumenical Council of Ephesus accomplished a very important and yet difficult task. It affirmed the reality of the incarnation and the primacy of God the Son in that incarnation. This subtle point was a crucial one. The humanists saw clearly how Christianity could be converted into humanism. *First*, the reality of the incarnation could be denied, as Nestorius denied it. *Second*, the incarnation could be affirmed but the humanity of Jesus Christ could be given priority over His divinity. If, in the incarnation, the humanity gained ascendancy and control over the divinity, then humanity would be introduced into a position of eternal power and determination over God. Time would then govern eternity, and man would rule over God. While nominally affirming a central doctrine of the faith, such a doctrine of the affirmation of the incarnation would actually be an affirmation of humanism, of man. By pressure against the faith at this point, the humanists would be ostensibly affirming the reality of the incarnation against orthodox mistreatment of it. The defense of the faith dealt obviously with an extremely subtle point, which, however crucial, would seem to the simple and unlearned to be merely theological hairsplitting. To this day, the doctrine of Economic Appropriation has remained an almost forgotten victory. It remains, however, a necessary victory. Against the renewed onslaughts of humanism, there can be no sure defense of the faith apart from the armor of Scripture and its defenders at Ephesus.

[55.] Contemporary churchmen are defending this council. See Albert C. Outler, "Theodosius' Horse: Reflections on the Predicament of the Church Historian," in *Church History*, XXXIV, 3, September 1965, 251-261.

Chapter Seven

The Council of Chalcedon: Foundation of Western Liberty

For several reasons, and especially because of the Council of Chalcedon, the year A. D. 451 is one of the most important dates of all history. Important as the Battle of Avarair was in stemming the westward march of dualistic thought and imperialism, Chalcedon, even more centrally, established the Christian foundation of Western culture and made possible the development of liberty. Chalcedon handed statism its major defeat in man's history.

The problem centered on the definition of the two natures of Christ and their union. Behind the problem stood the resurgence of Hellenic philosophy in Christian guise and the claims of the state to be the divine order on earth, to be the incarnation of divinity in history. The Hellenic faith held to a radically different concept of being than did Biblical faith. The Christian distinction between the uncreated being of God and the created being of man and the universe placed an infinite gulf between the two, a gulf unbridgeable by nature and bridged only by grace, by grace unto salvation and by grace permitting a union or community of life, not of substance. For the Greeks, as for non-Christian religions generally, all being is one undivided being; the differences in being are of degree, not of kind. In this great chain of being, it is a question of place on the scale or ladder of being, whereas for Christian faith the difference is one of divine and uncreated being as against created and mortal being.

In terms of this Greek perspective, salvation is not an act of grace but rather of self-deification. Moreover, the central institution in history becomes the state, because the state as the highest point of power in history manifests the nascent or incarnate divinity of being either in the body politic, the rulers, or in their offices. In various forms, this faith was the substructure of all pagan statism. Thus, the issue very literally was one between Christ and Caesar. At the beginning of the Christian era, the world was confronted with two epiphanies, in Bethlehem and in Rome. As Ethelbert Stauffer, in *Christ and the Caesars*, points out, Augustus saw himself as "the world's saviour who was to come." When, in the year 17 B.C., "a strange star shone in the heavens, he saw that the cosmic hour had come, and inaugurated a twelve-day Advent celebration, which was a plain proclamation of Virgil's message of joy: 'The turning-point of the ages has come'." The political order embodied and manifested the divinity inherent in being, and salvation was therefore in and through this high point of power, Caesar. "Salvation is to be found in none other save Augustus, and there is no other name given to men in which they can be saved."[1] Conflict between Christ and Caesar was thus inescapable.

Rome was quite willing to recognize the church and give it an approved status as a legitimate religion provided that the church recognized the superior jurisdiction of the state and the political order as the true and primary manifestation of the divine. As Francis Legge noted, "The officials of the Roman Empire in time of persecution sought to force the Christians to sacrifice, not to any of the heathen gods, but to the Genius of the Emperor and the Fortune of the City of Rome; and at all times the Christians' refusal was looked upon not as a religious but as a political offense."[2]

When the Empire became Christian, in a variety of forms the Roman statist theology reasserted itself. Indeed Christ was in some form divine, but, more than the Church, the Empire was held to be the voice of God. The recognition of the Church by the Empire was soon followed by the persecution of orthodoxy, as witness Athanasius, for espousing the divinity and supremacy of Christ. The problem was God or man, Christ or the state, who is man's saviour, and how is divinity incarnated?

The Council of Chalcedon met in 451 to deal with the issue as it came to focus at the critical point, in Christology. If the two natures of Christ were confused, it meant that the door was opened to the divinizing of human nature; man and the state were then potentially divine. If the human nature of Christ were reduced or denied, His role as man's incarnate savior was reduced or denied, and man's savior again became the state. If Christ's deity were reduced, then His saving power was nullified. If His humanity and

---

[1] Ethelbert Stauffer, *Christ and the Caesars*, (Philadelphia: Westminster Press, 1955), 81-89.

[2] Francis Legge, *Forerunners and Rivals of Christianity Front 330 B.C. to 330 A. D.*, Vol. I (New York: University Books, 1964 [1915]), xxiv.

deity were not in true union, the incarnation was then not real, and the distance between God and man remained as great as ever.

This was the *problem*. The *person* in this crisis was St. Leo, or Leo the Great, whose celebrated letter, "The Tome," defending the orthodox faith, carried the day. St. Leo, as the one pope whose theological abilities have been creative and have led the Church, was not lacking in the administrative abilities the office normally demands. Moreover, as Trevor Jalland has noted, "Leo was no heresy hunter."[3] His concern was pastoral: the defense of Christ's flock against evil, and the evil in this case was theological. Significantly, the Tome began with a severe rebuke to the highly revered Eutyches, elderly archimandrite of a monastery and popular figure, for presuming to be a leader in an area where he was a novice: "what more iniquitous than to hold blasphemous opinions, and not to give way to those who are wiser and more learned."

St. Leo insisted on the integrity of the incarnation, very man of very man, and very God of very God, two natures in union without confusion. Moreover, what Christ assumed in His incarnation was humanity, nature, not the sinful nature of fallen man but undeformed nature. "What was assumed from the Lord's mother was nature, not fault; nor does the wondrousness of the nativity of our Lord Jesus Christ, as born of a Virgin's womb, imply that his nature is unlike ours. For the selfsame who is very God, is also very man."

The response of the Council to the letter is well known. The cry was raised with loud applause, "That is the faith of the fathers! That is the faith of the apostles! So we all believe! So the orthodox believe! Anathema to him who believes otherwise! Through Leo, Peter has thus spoken. Even so did Cyril teach. That is the true faith."

The Definition or Formula of Chalcedon summarized the orthodox doctrine of Christ:

> Therefore, following the holy Fathers, we all with one accord teach men to acknowledge one and the same Son, our Lord Jesus Christ, at once complete in Godhead and complete in manhood, truly God and truly man, consisting also of a reasonable soul and body; of one substance with the Father as regards his Godhead, and at the same time of one substance with us as regards his manhood; like us in all respects, apart from sin; as regards his Godhead, begotten of the Father before the ages, but yet as regards his manhood begotten for us men and for our salvation, of Mary the Virgin, the Godbearer; one and the same Christ, Son, Lord, Only-begotten, recognized IN TWO NATURES, WITHOUT CONFUSION, WITHOUT CHANGE, WITHOUT DIVISION, WITHOUT SEPARATION; the distinction of natures being in no way annulled by the union, but rather the

---

[3.] Trevor Jalland, *The Life and Times of St. Leo the Great* (London: Society for Promoting Christian Knowledge, 1941), 420.

characteristics of each nature being preserved and coming together to form one person and subsistence, not as parted or separated into two persons, but one and the same Son and Only-begotten God the Word, Lord Jesus Christ; even as the prophets from earliest times spoke of him, and our Lord Jesus Christ himself taught us, and the creed of the Fathers has handed down to us.

This definition of the Fourth General or Ecumenical Council has remained as the touchstone of orthodoxy. Its influence on theology has been decisive. It is, for example, impossible to understand John Calvin apart from his fidelity to Chalcedon.

But the influence of Chalcedon in philosophy and politics has been no less great. Western culture has been largely a product of Chalcedon, and the continuing crises in both church and state reflect their departures from or rebellions against Chalcedon.

Chalcedon, *first* of all, separated Christian faith sharply from the Greek and pagan concepts of nature and being. It made clear that Christianity and all other religions and philosophies could not be brought together. The natural does not ascend to the divine or to the supernatural. The bridge is gulfed only by revelation and by the incarnation of Jesus Christ. Salvation therefore is not of man nor by means of man's politics, or by any other effort of man.

Second, by denying the confusion of the human and the divine, Chalcedon established a standard against that pagan stream of mysticism which sought precisely the union of the divine and human substances into one being. Such mysticism implicitly made irrelevant the work of Christ, and indeed His very person, in that every man became potentially his own Christ through mystical absorption into the Godhead. The Church was also of course made irrelevant by this mysticism. More than this, Chalcedon prevented human institutions from professing to be incarnations of the deity and able to unite the two worlds in their existence. The state was reduced to a human order, under God, and it was denied its age-old claim to divinity for the body politic, the ruler, or the offices.

Chalcedon thus placed a double roadblock against man's mystical pretensions. By asserting the unique incarnation, without confusion or change of the two natures, *first,* personal mysticism was barred, and, *second,* collective mysticism was barred also. Neither the person nor the state could, by its works, experience, or upward growth or evolution unite with and become absorbed into the Godhead. The uniqueness of the incarnation was a preventative, and the insistence that there was neither change of the two natures, or confusion of them in that unique incarnation meant that no church or state could validly claim that, as Christ's humanity, they had entered into His deity also. Had Chalcedon's definition not been made the test of orthodoxy, then humanism could have validly utilized the incarnation, with theological sanction, to introduce Christ's people, whether as church, state, school, or individuals, into this change of nature from humanity into divinity. To be a Christian in the fullest sense would have meant deification; participation in the sacrament of communion would have meant participation in more than the new humanity of Jesus Christ, together with the blessing of access in Him to God the Father. Instead, the sacrament would become participation in Christ's deity. Man would eat God to become God. Humanism and paganism would then triumph over Biblical Christianity.

As long as the old pagan view of being prevailed, the state could be the divine-human order. Divinity then became so greatly immanent or incarnate in the state that there was no appeal beyond the state. The state was, at least for its day, the final order. In this scheme of things, man was simply a political animal, a social animal: he was definable in terms of the group, the body politic. Man had no true transcendence nor any ground of appeal against the state. In this condition, liberty was nonexistent. *Permission from the state* to exercise certain areas of activities could exist, but not a *liberty apart from and beyond the state* grounded in man's creation by God.

The state, of course, refused to accept Chalcedon's body-blow with equanimity. The claims to divinity took more subtle and ostensibly Christian forms. One of the most critical of these struggles has been described by Gerhart B. Ladner. According to Ladner, the premise of iconoclasm was the claim of the Eastern Empire to be the true incarnation of the divine, the visible and manifest Kingdom of God on earth. "Not only because the images had such an important place in the Byzantine Church, theologically and liturgically, that an attack against them was ipso facto an attack against the Church but also and still more because, as we shall see, the emperors showed unmistakably that even in maintaining the belief in the supreme, supernatural government of Christ, they did not wish to permit on this earth any other but their own image or more exactly the imagery of their own imperial natural world." Leo III wrote to Pope Gregory II, "I am King and Priest." The eastern Empire was generally congenial to "the heresies which attacked the perfect unity or the entirety of the divine and the human nature in Christ (Arianism, Nestorianism, monophysitism, monotheletism); for the dissolution of this unity or the dimunition of the entirety of each nature, in narrowing the extension of Christ's government in the human world widened the extension of the emperor's rulership." By undercutting the incarnation and by confusing the two natures, these heresies, and their imperial proponents, again made possible the resurgence of "the view that the State is the highest visible form of life on the earth."[4]

The Western Empire also faced a similar struggle. Indeed, "vicarius Dei" was a title claimed by many Western emperors. Otto III saw himself as the successor of St. Paul and signed his letters with St. Paul's formula, calling himself "servus Jesu Christi." And, as Eugen Rosenstock-Huessy pointed out, Otto believed that "to him is entrusted the Dove of Inspiration," the Holy Ghost. Much later, Emperor Maximillian (1493-1518) planned in 1512 to become pope himself.[5]

But this attempt is not limited to the time of the Empires but is endemic to Western history, with empires and states warring against the liberty of Chalcedon, and the state seeking again to become the saving order. In Dostoyevsky's *The Brothers Karamazov*, the staretz declared, "Not the Church becoming State, but the State becoming Church, mark that well."[6]

In the Old Testament, priest and king were two separate offices in Israel. The attempt by King Uzziah to exercise priestly office brought upon him Divine judgment in the form of leprosy (2 Chron. 26). The two offices were not to have an immanent union but only a transcendental one. Because church and state are ordained by God as the ministries of grace and of justice, and because grace and justice both rest in the righteousness, holiness, and mercy of God their essential frame of reference is supernatural. They are united only in Christ, who declared to Pilate that His "kingdom is not of this world" (John 19:36), i.e., not derived from this world, but is rather an eternal and divine kingdom, derived from the triune God. Instead of an eternal kingdom, the pagan state seeks a purely historical kingdom, i.e., one derived entirely from history and manifesting only the divinity inherent in history.

To return to the Definition of Chalcedon. Cornelius Van Til, in *The Defense of the Faith,* has described the purpose of the Formula: to make known the meaning of the incarnation, and to preserve the integrity of the union. "Christ came to bring man back to God. To do this he was and had to be truly God." "It was the second person of the ontological trinity, who was in respect of his essence, fully equal with the Father, who therefore existed from all eternity with the Father, who in the incarnation assumed human nature." In the incarnation, Jesus Christ was truly man and truly God.

> The Creed of Chalcedon has expressed all this by saying that in Christ the divine and the human natures are so related as to be "two natures, without confusion, without change, without division, without separation." The former two adjectives safeguard against the idea that

4. Gerhart B. Ladner, "Origin and Significance of the Byzantine Iconoclastic Controversy" in Pontifical Institute of Mediaeval Studies, *Mediaeval Studies,* vol. II, 1940 (New York: Sheed and Ward, 1940), 127-149.
5. Eugen Rosenstock-Huessy, *Out of Revolution* (New York: William Morrow, 1938), 503ff, 437.
6. *Ibid.,* 91f.

the divine and the human are in any sense intermingled; the latter two adjectives assert the full reality of the union.[7]

This point is very important. Not only was the reality of the two natures "without confusion, without change" declared, but the reality of their union, "without division, without separation," similarly asserted. The attempt of statist theology to divinize nature was declared to be anathema, but so was the attempt of statist theology to diminish the reality of the incarnation. To the degree that the reality of the incarnation was diminished, to that degree the state again asserted its claim to total lordship over man and society as the savior and redeemer thereof.

Monophysite thinking, by diminishing the reality of Christ's humanity or destroying it, thereby left Christ's humanity an unreal thing, and the incarnation a vague and clouded fact. Jesus Christ as very man of very man was the new and last Adam (1 Cor. 16:45), and His Church is the new and redeemed humanity. Membership in Christ, as set forth in the communion elements, His body and blood, is membership in the new, redeemed humanity, the destined heirs of creation in Christ. The Christians were thus a *new race*, sometimes called "the third race," i.e., supplanting the old divisions of Jew and Gentile, Greek and barbarian, Roman and non-Roman. This note resounds through the liturgies of St. John Chrysostom and Basil the Great: "Adam is recalled, the curse is made void, Eve is set free, death is slain, and we are made alive. Wherefore, in hymns we cry aloud: Blessed art thou, O Christ our God." The liturgies speak "of the race of Christians." In a Proeortion of the Nativity of Christ, we read, "The Virgin, today, cometh into a cave to bring forth ineffably the Word that is before the ages. Dance, thou universe, on hearing the tidings: glorify with the Angels and the Shepherds him that willed to be beheld a little Child, the God before the ages."[8] "Dance, thou universe!" People who summoned the universe to dance in joy at the incarnation, who knew themselves to be God's new humanity, bound in Christ and His sacrament to a community of life with His divinity, were not ready to bow the knee to Caesar as Christ. Instead, they wanted a Christian state, church and state alike under Christ the King.

Monophysitism ostensibly exalted Christ by diminishing His humanity, but it simply endangered or destroyed the reality of the incarnation. It reduced the realm of the Church to the spiritual, which was left poorly related to the world, and again turned over the material world to Caesar. Nestorianism made Christ into a divinized man rather than incarnate God, and it thereby simply strengthened statist theology. Any subordinationist

---

[7.] Van Til, *Defense of the Faith* (Philadelphia: Presbyterian and Reformed Publishing Company, 1955), 32.

[8.] J.N.W.B. Robertson, editor, *The Divine Liturgies of John Chrysostom and Basil the Great* (London: David Nutt, 1894), 157, 195, 453f.

Christology, which gave to God the Son a reduced status in the Trinity, similarly reduced the church as Christ's body.

Statist theology rested on the primacy of nature as the voice and manifestation of God, and nature's high point of power in history is the state. Statist theology was ready to accommodate grace by giving it a subordinate role, by using grace to buttress nature. It created a nature-grace dialectic which was a revival of the Greek form-matter dialectic and thus implicitly anti-Christian. In such theology, Christ simply becomes a support to the state rather than Lord over church and state. George Huntston Williams points out that "Christ as *rex et sacerdos* is divinely King and only humanly a Priest."[9] The result was a political theology subordinating church to state.

But a true Christology is not dialectical but trinitarian. It rests, not on the dialectics of nature versus grace, but on the moral crisis, sin versus grace. Nature fallen is in need of redemption. Christ enters the world to establish a new humanity in whom He creates by His regenerating and sanctifying power a new nature, one in communion with Him. God has no war against nature, and His struggle is not against nature but against sin. In the redeemed humanity, Christ rules over all things, state and church included.

The modern dialectic is nature versus freedom, a further development of the older dialectical formula, form versus matter. In this new dialectic, accommodation gives way to hostility towards Christ. Statist theology no longer needs Him. As the manifest and incarnate power of man and nature, the state offers itself as man's true freedom, man's hope of grace, as it were, through whom paradise will be restored. The state thus claims to be also man's true church and man's true Christ. The roots of this claim are in pagan antiquity, but they run deeply through the medieval period also. Ernst H. Kantorowicz, describes the early mysticism of parliament:

> Before the close of Parliament in 1410, the Speaker of the Commons saw fit to compare the body politic of the realm with the Trinity: the king, the Lords spiritual and temporal, and the Commons jointly formed a trinity in unity and unity in trinity. On the same occasion the Speaker compared the procedures of Parliament with the celebration of a mass: the reading of the Epistle and the expounding of the Bible at the opening of Parliament resembled the initial prayers and ceremonies preceding the holy action: the king's promise to protect the Church and observe the laws compared with the sacrifice of the mass; finally, the adjournment of Parliament had its analogy in the *Ite, missa est,* the dismissal, and the *Deo gratias,* which concluded the holy action. Although these comparisons do not mean very much all by themselves, they nevertheless reflect the intellectual climate and

9. George H. Williams, *The Norman Anonymous of A. D. 1100,* Harvard Theological Studies XVIII (Cambridge: Harvard University Press, 1951), 127f.

show to what extent political thought in the. "high Gothic" age gravitated towards mysticizing the body politic of the realm.[10]

Later, as Kantorowicz points out, and as Cardinal Pole did at the time, Henry VIII "treated the Church as a simple *corpus politicum*, and therefore as part and parcel of the realm of England."[11] The modern conservative references to "God and country" preserve this older form of statist theology.

In its modern form, the statist theology goes further. It not only ignores Christ and the Church, it begins to deny their right to exist. A critical battleground is the issue of taxation. The modern state assumes the position of having a right to tax the church as a *corpus politicum*, and then magnanimously forgoes this right on the ground that the Church is a charitable or nonprofit institution. The hidden premise is that the Church is under the state and exists by permission. But the whole claim of Chalcedonian theology has been that the Church, directly under Christ the King, is an independent domain, even as the State is, and that the Church cannot be taxed because it has extraterritorial rights, as it were. It is a separate domain, with its own realm of law, and the State has no jurisdiction in that realm. As neither Church nor State are themselves Christ, neither can usurp sovereignty over Christ's realm: they can only exercise authority in the jurisdiction given them by Christ the King.

The long struggle of the Church to gain independence of jurisdiction and then to maintain it, although alien to our present purpose, needs to be restudied and stressed among Christians as they move rapidly into another phase of the struggle: the attempt of the new paganism to deny the Church any independent jurisdiction. There are supposedly Christian voices calling for the taxation of the churches. Significantly, these same persons deny Chalcedonian theology. For them Jesus Christ is not very God of very God and very man of very man, unchangeably, inseparably, unconfusedly united in the one only-begotten Son our Savior. The significant and determinative realm for them is not the supernatural, God, but the natural, man; not eternity but time. Thomas J. J. Altizer has stated openly the implicit principle of modernism: "'historicity' means a total immersion in historical time, an immersion that is totally isolated from any meaning or reality that might lie beyond us." This means for man "an absolute autonomy which finally encloses him within the concrete moment itself."[12]

---

[10]. Ernst H. Kantorowicz, *The King's Two Bodies, A Study in Mediaeval Political Theology* (Princeton: Princeton University Press, 1957), 227.

[11]. *Ibid.*, 229.

[12]. Thomas J. J. Altizer, *Mircea Eliade and the Dialectic of the Sacred* (Philadelphia: Westminster Press, 1963), 23, 26.

For Chalcedon, Jesus Christ, as the Second Person of the Trinity, reigned in heaven as the Creator and determiner of all things even when He walked the earth. As St. John declared, "the Word was God .... All things were made by him; and without him was not any thing made that was made" (John 1: 1, 3). In such a Christology time is governed by eternity, man by God. Statist theology however demands that time govern eternity, and man govern whatever god exists, or, better, be his own god. Any theology which weakens the Definition of Chalcedon weakens the primacy of the triune God over history, and any theology which denies Chalcedon must of necessity affirm history as the primary area of determination. Time then alone is the source of the historical, and the supernatural is denied. God the Son not only does not determine time and history, He is denied historicity because He demands reference to the ontological Trinity, to eternity, to be understood. The only Christ permitted is a totally human Christ, one totally immersed in time and exclusively and totally a product of history. This is "the historical Jesus" of higher criticism. "Demythologizing" criticism has a similar goal: to reduce Jesus to history, to a total meaning from within history. But the quest for the "historical" and "de-mythologized" Jesus is an impossibility. The Jesus of Scripture is only understandable in His every word and act in terms of the eternal decree and purpose of the triune God. The history of modern criticism is post Kantian history, a philosophical abstraction, not the real history of man the creature in a God-created world. The real Jesus of history is set forth in Scripture and defined by Chalcedon.

Significantly, modernism's characteristic message is the social gospel and social action. Modernism is the statist theology of contemporary man. Its gospel, its good news, is that the state has an answer to all man's problems. Whether it be a burden of body or soul, poverty, cultural deprivation, mental health, disease, ignorance, family problems, and all things else, the state has a program and a plan of salvation. The United Nations Charter, in its Preamble, also reflects this hope: "We the peoples of the United Nations determined to save ...." The U. N. is "determined to save," and its goal is a world "without distinction as to race, sex, language, or religion" in its social order (Charter IX, 55: 1, 1, 3; etc.). The goal of politics today is messianic: its purpose is paradise regained, a perfect world order by means of law and technology. Man's problem is not seen as sin but as a backward environment which science can correct. Statist theology sees all problems answered by statist action; the goal of all men of good will must therefore be social legislation. More power must be given to the state in order to realize the city of man.

The fathers at Chalcedon aimed their Definition against "persons undertaking to make void the preaching of the truth," and Chalcedon's purpose was "to exclude every device against the Truth." For them, everything was at stake in this question of the incarnation. If the reality of the union without confusion were denied, then not only the reality of salvation was gone, but also the reality of Christ's Kingship and law. The ecumenical councils issued "canons." Bright, in his *Notes on the Canons,* has pointed out that "The original sense, 'a straight rod' or 'line' determines all its religious applications, which begin with St. Paul's use of it for a prescribed sphere of apostolic work (2 Cor. x. 13, 15), or a regulative principle of Christian life (Gal. vi. 16)."[13] Christ the King has a canon, a regulative principle, a law, for church and state, and the denial of the reality of the incarnation was also the denial of this regulative principal and law. If Chalcedon's Definition were not true, then there was no canon. God, if He existed, was remote from man and unable to bridge the gap between Himself and man. The law given to Adam, Noah, and Moses presupposed the reality of the incarnation: the triune God who created is also the incarnate God who redeems and restores the world to His law and dominion. The meaning thus is clear: No Christ, no law. The canons issued by Chalcedon rested on the Definition of Chalcedon in that they presupposed the reality of the incarnation as defined and therefore the binding power of the law of Christ. A God who is not the creator is an alien to the universe: it is its own evolving law. A God who is truly the savior of the world is of necessity its creator: He has made it, and its only possible health is in its restoration to communion with Him. His law therefore is the only true regulative principle for the world.

There was, then, a legal issue at stake. In statist theology, for the rationalist, law is logic; for the empiricist, law is experience. In either case, it is basically a product of nature, man, and history. It is totally immanent and has no transcendental frame of reference. Statist theology has moved steadily into legal positivism, into an affirmation that the only true law is positive law, the law of the state. There is then no supreme court of appeal beyond the state. The universe becomes a closed universe, without a higher law or an absolute truth. Man is locked into the world and the relative "truth" of the state.

The fathers at Chalcedon, in noting the work of the Second Ecumenical Council, the First Council of Constantinople, in 381, referred to the formulation of the doctrine of the Holy Ghost as a bulwark "against those who were seeking to destroy his sovereignty." A similar defense was now at stake, for the unconfused, immutable, indivisible, inseparable union meant the sovereignty of Christ. Sovereignty, duty, and law are inseparably united. The source of law in any system is not only the locale of sovereignty but also the god of that system. God only is the true sovereign and the true source of law. Christian feudalism had no concept of human

---

[13.] In Percival, *Decrees and Canons of the Seven Ecumenical Councils,* 9.

sovereignty, and American federalism, as a Protestant revival of feudalism, began with an avoidance of the word sovereignty. Its proper application is to God alone. By defining Christ as very God of very God, in true but unconfused union with man and thus very man of very man, Chalcedon thereby declared Christ to be the one true source of a regulative principle, a canon, and therefore Christ's Word was instruction and law for man, for church, state, and every other order. By preserving the union from confusion, Chalcedon preserved the canon from becoming a potential realization of man. Christ as man, as the last Adam, kept the law perfectly, to manifest His perfect obedience as man to the law of God. Christ as God was and is the eternal source of the canon, being He by whom all things were made; "and without him was not any thing made that was made" (John 1:3). To have permitted belief in the confusion of the natures would have meant that man could become an aspect of his own God, aspire to be, in his union with Christ, his own lawmaker and co-creator. Humanity would have been introduced into deity, not in a community of life but in a community of substance. But, said the fathers, anything other than this Christ in perfect union without confusion is "another faith," and "the holy Ecumenical Synod defines that no one shall be suffered to bring forward a different faith, nor to write, nor to put together, nor to excogitate, nor to teach it to others."

Chalcedon made possible Western liberty. It is possible to speak of true liberty as a product of Christian faith, because antiquity saw the city-state or the imperial state as a religious entity, a visible manifestation of the divine order. As Fustel de Coulanges observed, "Every city was a sanctuary; every city might be called holy." The city represented a holy and divine order, and it had an "omnipotence" and an "absolute empire which it exercised over its members. In a society established on such principles, individual liberty could not exist. The citizen was subordinate in everything, and without any reserve, to the city; he belonged to it body and soul." Because the state embraced all of life, including worship, and because it was the manifestation or incarnation of the divine order, man had to submit to the state as his visible god. "There was nothing independent in man; his body belonged to the state, and was devoted to its defense."[14] Plato was not alone in holding, in his *Laws* that "children belong less to their parents than to the city."[15] This was usually the case. The unity of life was totally immanent, fully realized in the body politic. The state was the One, the unity of being. Because man's life was comprehended by the state, particularity was less an aspect of man than of the state, or of states. The one and the many were to be known only in terms of political units.

[14.] Fustel De Coulanges, *The Ancient City*, (Garden City, New York: Doubleday Anchor Books, 1936 [1864]), 141, 219f.
[15.] *Ibid.*, 221.

In Chalcedonian faith, the ultimate one and the many cannot be located in creation but only in the triune God, one God, three Persons, in whom the one and the many have equal ultimacy. Moreover, because Chalcedonian theology, by its doctrine of Christ, preserved the integrity of the Trinity, it upheld the Biblical answer to the problem of the one and the many. When unity and particularity (or individuality) are in their ultimate source transcendental and firmly grounded in the triune God, man's realization of unity and individuality is freed from the oppressive presence of the state as the realized order. In the Christian view, man's life is not comprehended by the state; it is comprehended only by the triune God. Man's unity is only truly realizable in God and His Kingdom; man's individuality is again only realizable in and through God. This means that man's eternal destiny is a predestined one and bound to the grace of the ultimate One and Many, the Trinity. But it also means that man's present life is freed from the predestination of the state. Man's self-realization is not in the state but in God. The meaning of this was not lost on the early church. Bishops and preachers rebuked emperor and state for daring to presume too much, for claiming authority which belonged to God only. Christianity was no sooner a recognized religion than its orthodox thinkers began to push back the claims of the state. The state was seen as the ministry of justice (Rom. 13: 1-8); it could not claim to be the ultimate or comprehending order. Man, as God's creature, transcended the state by virtue of his citizenship in God's eternal Kingdom. The ancient city, according to Coulanges, "governed the soul as well as the body of man" and, "infinitely more powerful than the states of our day, united in itself the double authority that we now see shared between the state and the church."[16] The state was the vehicle of the will of the gods if not their incarnation. The Church now undercut this claim by affirming that God had manifested through Christ the Son and the written word His canon of truth. In antiquity man had been bound to the state but "freed" from God. Orthodox Christianity freed man from the state by binding him to God, who is man's true ground of freedom and fulfillment. The source of this Christian liberty is trinitarianism, with its logical concomitant, Chalcedonian Christology. St. Leo insisted on this necessary relationship. Anti-trinitarianism meant also hostility to the true union. In Sermon XXIII, "On the Feast of the Nativity, III," St. Leo declared:

> But the Godhead, which is One in the Trinity of the Father, Son, and Holy Ghost, excludes all notion of inequality. For the eternity of the Trinity has nothing temporal, nothing dissimilar in nature: Its will is one, Its substance identical, Its power equal, and yet there are not three GODS, but one GOD; because it is a true and inseparable unity, where there can be no diversity. Thus in the whole and perfect nature

---

16. *Ibid.*, 224.

of true man was true GOD born, complete in what was His own, complete in what was ours.[17]

Again, in Sermon LXXV, "On Whitsuntide, I," St. Leo made clear that the error of Sabellius was to be avoided. The three Persons are a real Trinity:

> For in the Divine Trinity nothing is unlike or unequal, and all that can be thought concerning its substance admits of no diversity either in power or glory or eternity. And while in the property of each Person the Father is one, the Son is another, and the Holy Ghost is another, yet the Godhead is not distinct and different; for whilst the Son is the Only begotten of the Father, the Holy Spirit is the Spirit of the Father and the Son, not in the way that every creature is the creature of the Father and the Son, but as living and having power with Both, and eternally subsisting of That Which is the Father and the Son.[18]

The equal ultimacy of the one and the many and their locale in the Trinity was thus strictly safeguarded by St. Leo. It was further safeguarded by his insistence on creationism. In Sermon XXII, "On the Feast of the Nativity, II," St. Leo declared that God "created the universe out of nothing, and framed by His almighty methods the substance of the earth and sky into what forms and dimensions He willed."[19]

God, having created all things, governs them absolutely. St. Leo held, as Sermon LXVII reveals, "On the Passion, XVI," to "the unchangeable order of GOD'S eternal decrees, with Whom the things which are to be decided are already determined, and what will be is already accomplished."[20] God is thus the first cause in all history; man's causality is a secondary causality. The state thus is placed under God; initiative in history is withdrawn from man and the state and given to God; the incarnation is denied to the state and made unique in Jesus Christ and without confusion of natures. The center of history is beyond history, and the Christians are the new "chosen race" of God in Jesus Christ (Sermon XXXIII, 3, "On the Feast of the Epiphany, III").[21]

On the foundation of Chalcedon, the formulation of Biblical Christology, Western liberty has been built. Ignorance and neglect of Chalcedon has been basic to the decline of the Church. Strange voices in Christendom assert the necessity for Christian relevance, but the relevance they have in mind is not to Christ and His Kingdom but to the reviving pagan statist theology and the attempts by the pagan humanistic state to lead man into a paradise without God. But the reduction of man to the dimensions of the state, to the dimensions of time and history, is the

---

17. *Nicene and Post-Nicene Fathers,* Series Two, vol. XII, 133.
18. *Ibid.,* 190.
19. *Ibid.,* 132.
20. *Ibid.,* 178.
21. *Ibid.,* 145-147.

enslavement of man, not his liberation. Christendom needs to echo the decision of the fathers at Chalcedon, who, after declaring the Definition, stated, "this is the faith of the Apostles: by this we all stand: thus we all believe." The alternative is Christ or Caesar, liberty or slavery, God or man. Is salvation man's upward reach, or God's downward reach? Is it man's word or God's grace? Is God or the state man's savior? The answer of Chalcedon is emphatically for God and liberty.

Western liberty began when the claim of the state to be man's savior was denied. The state then, according to Scripture, was made the ministry of justice. But, wherever Christ ceases to be man's savior, there liberty perishes as the state again asserts its messianic claims. Man is in trouble, and history is the record of his attempt to find salvation. Man needs a savior, and the question is simply one of choice: Christ or the state? No man can choose the one without denying the other, and all attempts at compromise are a delusion.

Chapter Eight

The Athanasian Creed:
The One and the Many

Creeds in the early church were of two varieties, baptismal and conciliar. The baptismal creeds were affirmations of faith at baptism, creeds of entrance into the faith. The Apostles' Creed is the basic baptismal creed. Although other baptismal creeds preceded and followed the Apostles' Creed, in particular St. Ephiphanius' (c. 310-403) two creeds, the Apostles' Creed has remained as the basic creedal statement for converts.[1] Conciliar creeds were tests of orthodoxy and therefore usually had anathemas attached to them. The Nicene Creed, in its developed Constantinopolitan form, became the baptismal creed of the Eastern Church and is therefore both a conciliar and baptismal creed. As a result, the Athanasian Creed is not strictly a creed in either of these senses, since it is neither the work of a council nor a baptismal creed. Clarke has called it "not properly a creed at all, but a hymn on the Creed, like the *Te Deum*."[2] However, while not the work of a council, it is the product of the church's struggle against heresy, and it is a test of orthodoxy, so that it is closely related to the conciliar confessions and is properly a creed.

This creed bears the name of St. Athanasius, or Athanasius the Great, although it is definitely not his work. Since Athanasius was at Nicea the great champion of the orthodox doctrine of the Trinity, this creed affirming that doctrine bears his name, although it is more directly a result of St. Augustine's influence than that of Athanasius.

---

1. See Schaff, *Creeds of Christendom*, II, 32-38.
2. C. P. S. Clarke, *Short History of the Christian Church*, (London: Longmans, Green, 1929), 25f.

Athanasius (299-373), while not a reliable guide on the doctrine of the atonement, was a faithful champion of the trinitarian faith, and as early as Ephiphanius, is termed "the father of orthodoxy." His opposition to Arianism made him the target of political persecution, and he was exiled five times. During one exile of six years, he lived in the Egyptian desert with monks. Assassins were hired on one occasion to dispose of Athanasius. The statists named George of Cappadocia, an Arian bishop, to replace Athanasius. George took possession of his office with imperial troops and began to persecute savagely both the orthodox believers and to pillage the pagan temples. The pagans seized George, paraded him through the city tied on a camel, and then burned both George and the camel. According to Schaff, Arian legend made a saint of George and first made Athanasius into an enemy wizard, and then into a dragon whom "St. George" overcame.[3] Every kind of accusation was made against Athanasius; he was accused of murdering Arsenius, who was very much alive and in hiding; he was accused of raping a virgin who turned out to be a prostitute who had never before seen Athanasius and who failed in her task by identifying another man as Athanasius. His life for years was a troubled and hunted one. The creed rightfully honored him as the first great conciliar champion of trinitarianism. At first, the creed was simply called "the Catholic faith," and it gained the Athanasian title during the Arian controversy in Gaul, when the Athanasian origins of the controversy were invoked.

The Western tendencies towards subordinationism were invoked by the Arians to counteract orthodoxy. St. Augustine taught strongly against subordinationism and for the unity and equality of the Trinity, and this view, although first stressed in the East, came to have true roots in the West as a result of Augustine's work. This Latin faith the Athanasian Creed summarized. Augustine taught the procession of the Holy Ghost from the Father and the Son and the perfect essential unity of the hypostases. Schaff saw the Athanasian Creed as the expression in classic form of the Augustinian doctrine of the Trinity, "beyond which the orthodox development of the doctrine in the Roman and Evangelical churches to this day (1867) has made no advance."[4] This creed embodies passages from Augustine's work on the Trinity (A. D. 415) and from the Commonitorium of Vincentius of Lerinum, A. D. 434. The creed probably dates from around 450 or a little later; it is from Gaul, in the Augustinian school of thought. The influence of the Creed in Western Christianity has been very great. Luther regarded it as the weightiest and greatest work of the church since the time of the apostles. The Church of England dropped its compulsory use in 1867, and the Protestant Episcopal Church of

---

[3.] Schaff, *Church History*, III, 888n.
[4.] *Ibid.*, III, 690.

America, in the Convention of 1785 in Philadelphia dropped both the Nicene and Athanasian Creeds and struck out from the Apostles' Creed the clause, "He descended into hell." Pressures from the Archbishops of Canterbury and York brought in 1786 the restoration in America of all but the Athanasian Creed. The damnatory clauses were the reason for hostility. The Eastern Church has never formally accepted this creed, although there has been limited use of it.[5]

The Athanasian Creed, as it appears in the Lutheran liturgy, and in other churches, declares:

> Whoever will be saved, before all things it is necessary that he hold the catholic (i.e., universal, Christian) faith.
> Which faith except every one do keep whole and undefiled, with out doubt he shall perish everlastingly.
> And the catholic faith is this, that we worship one God in Trinity and Trinity in Unity.
> Neither confounding the Persons nor dividing the Substance.
> For there is one Person of the Father, another of the Son, and another of the Holy Ghost.
> But the Godhead of the Father, of the Son, and of the Holy Ghost is all one: the glory equal, the majesty coeternal.
> Such as the Father is, such is the Son, and such is the Holy Ghost.
> The Father uncreate, the Son uncreate, and the Holy Ghost uncreate.
> The Father incomprehensible, the Son incomprehensible, and the Holy Ghost incomprehensible.
> The Father eternal, the Son eternal, and the Holy Ghost eternal.
> As there are not three Uncreated nor three Incomprehensibles, but one Uncreated and one Incomprehensible.
> So likewise the Father is almighty, the Son almighty, and the Holy Ghost almighty.
> And yet they are not three Almighties, but one Almighty.
> So the Father is God, the Son is God, and the Holy Ghost is God.
> And yet they are not three Gods, but one God.
> So likewise the Father is Lord, the Son Lord, and the Holy Ghost Lord.
> And yet they are not three Lords, but one Lord.
> For like as we are compelled by the Christian verity to acknowledge every Person by Himself to be God and Lord.
> So we are forbidden by the catholic religion to say, There be three Gods or three Lords.
> The Father is made of none, neither created nor begotten.
> The Son is of the Father alone, not made nor created, but begotten.
> The Holy Ghost is of the Father and of the Son, neither made nor created nor begotten, but proceeding.
> So there is one Father, not three Fathers; one Son, not three Sons; one Holy Ghost, not three Holy Ghosts.
> And in this Trinity none is before or after other; none is greater or less than another;

---

5. Schaff, *Creeds of Christendom*, 35-42.

But the whole three Persons are coeternal together and coequal, so
that in all things, as is aforesaid, the Unity in Trinity and the
Trinity in Unity is to be worshipped.
He therefore, that will be saved must think thus of the Trinity.
Furthermore, it is necessary to everlasting salvation that he also
believes faithfully the incarnation of our Lord Jesus Christ.
For the right faith is that we believe and confess that our Lord Jesus
Christ, the Son of God, is God and Man;
God of the Substance of the Father, begotten before the worlds; and
Man of the substance of His mother, born in the world;
Perfect God and perfect Man, of a reasonable soul and human flesh
subsisting.
Equal to the Father as touching His Godhead and inferior to the
Father as touching His manhood;
Who, although He be God and Man, yet He is not two, but one
Christ:
One, not by conversion of the Godhead into flesh, but by taking the
manhood into God;
One altogether; not by confusion of Substance, but by unity of
Person.
For as the reasonable soul and flesh is one man, so God and Man is
one Christ;
Who suffered for our salvation; descended into hell; rose again the
third day from the dead;
He ascended into heaven; He sitteth on the right hand of the Father,
God Almighty; from whence He shall come to judge the quick
and the dead.
At whose coming all men shall rise again with their bodies and shall
give an account of their own works.
And they that have done good shall go into life everlasting-, and they
that have done evil, into everlasting fire.
This is the catholic faith; which except a man believe faithfully and
firmly, he cannot be saved.[6]

A reading of this creed makes obvious the reason for its unpopularity. It
is long, and people are impatient with long creeds; worship must be brief.
The other creeds have a beauty of phrase and a musical quality, whereas the
Athanasius is precisely and logically theological. The fact remains,
however, that this creed is extremely important and represents a major
victory of Western Christianity.

For Western Christianity, Biblical theology rests firmly on a trinitarian
foundation, without subordination. In theology, the attributes or
properties of God are divided into incommunicable and communicable.
The incommunicable attributes, which manifest God as God in His
transcendence are, *first,* aseity or independence, whereby God is absolute,
sufficient unto Himself. *Second,* the immutability of God means that, since

---

6. Schaff, *Creeds of Christendom,* II, 66ff., renders Substance as Essence also; incom-
prehensible as either unlimited or infinite; faithfully as rightly; and, in the concluding sentence, faithfully and firmly as truly and firmly.

God is absolute and therefore dependent on nothing besides Himself, He does not and cannot change. *Third,* God is infinite. With respect to the infinity of God, Van Til has pointed out:

> In relation to the question of time we speak of the *eternity* of God while with respect to space we speak of the *omnipresence* of God. By the term eternity we mean that there is no beginning or end or succession of moments in God's being or consciousness (Ps. 90:2; 2 Peter 3:8). This conception of eternity is of particular importance in Apologetics because it involves the whole question of the meaning of the temporal universe: it involves a definite philosophy of history. By the term omnipresence we mean that God is neither included in space nor absent from it. God is above all space and yet present in every part of it (1 Kings 8:27; Acts 17:27).[7]

The *fourth* incommunicable attribute of God is unity. As Van Til has pointed out, "We distinguish between the unity of singularity (singularitatis) and the unity of simplicity (simplicitatis). The unity of singularity has reference to numerical oneness. There is and can be only one God. The unity of simplicity signifies that God is in no sense composed of parts or aspects that existed prior to himself (Jer. 10:10; 1 John 1:5)."[8]

The communicable attributes of God are those which stress his immanence and are, *first,* spirituality; God is a Spirit (John 4:24); *second,* invisibility; *third,* omniscience.

The doctrine of the Trinity declares that the three persons are co-substantial: "not one is derived in his substance from either or both of the others. Yet there are three distinct persons in this unity; the diversity and the identity are equally underived."[9]

Augustine, in writing *On the Trinity,* emphasized the unity, equality, and equal ultimacy of the three persons of the Godhead:

> Wherefore let us hold this above all, that whatsoever is said of that most eminent and divine loftiness in respect to itself, is said in respect to substance, but that which is said in relation to anything, is not said in respect to substance, but relatively; and that the effect of the same substance in Father and Son and Holy Spirit is, that whatsoever is said of each in respect to themselves, is to be taken of them, not in the plural in sum, but in the singular. For as the Father is God, and the Son is God, and the Holy Spirit is God, which no one doubts to be said in respect to substance, yet we do not say that the very supreme Trinity itself is three Gods, but one God. So the Father is great, the Son great, and the Holy Spirit great; yet not three greats, but one great. For it is not written of the Father alone, as they perversely suppose, but of the Father and the Son and the Holy Spirit, "Thou art

---

7. Cornelius Van Til, *The Defense of the Faith* (Philadelphia: Presbyterian and Reformed Publishing Company, 1955), 26.
8. *Ibid.*
9. *Ibid.*, 28.

great: Thou art God alone" (Ps. 86:10). And the Father is good, the
Son good, and the Holy Spirit good; yet not three goods, but one
good, of whom it is said, "None is good, save one, that is God." For
the Lord Jesus, lest He should be understood as man only by him who
said, "Good Master," as addressing a man, does not therefore say,
There is none good, save the Father alone; but, "None is good, save
one, that is God" (Luke 18:18, 19). For the Father by Himself is
declared by the name of Father; but by the name of God, both
Himself and the Son and the Holy Spirit, because the Trinity is one
God. But position, and condition, and places, and times, are not said
to be in God properly, but metaphorically and through similitudes ....
So the Father is omnipotent, the Son omnipotent, and the Holy Spirit
is omnipotent; yet not three omnipotents, but one omnipotent: "For
of Him are all things, and through Him are all things, and in Him are
all things, to whom be glory" (Rom. 11:36). Whatever, therefore, is
spoken of God in respect to himself, is both spoken singly of each
person, that is, of the Father, and the Son, and the Holy Spirit; and
together of the Trinity itself, not plurally but in the singular. For
inasmuch as to God it is not one thing to be, and another thing to be
great, but to him it is the same thing to be, as it is to be great;
therefore, as we do not say three essences, so we do not say three
greatnesses, but one essence and one greatness. I say essence, which in
Greek is called *ousia*, and which we call more usually substance.[10]

The influence of this passage from *On the Trinity* (A. D. 400) on the
Athanasian Creed is quite apparent. Augustine made it clear that the only
subordination in the Trinity is economic and relative, not essential. The
three Persons of the Trinity are equally ultimate in their particularity as
well as their unity. Their individuality is real and their unity is real; they
are truly three Persons, one God. The name God is equally applicable to all
three Persons. It is an Arminian heresy to reserve the name of God to the
Father alone. This common usage makes Arminianism closer to Arianism
and Nestorianism than to orthodox Christianity. The Athanasian Creed
declares the attributes of God belong to all three Persons without
differences of any kind. "It is only the epithets 'ingenerate,' 'generated,' 'by
the Father,' and 'proceeding' that are connected respectively and
exclusively with the Father, the Son, and the Spirit."[11]

God then means the Father, the Son, and the Holy Ghost, and no two
Persons of the Trinity are greater together than a third, nor are all three
Persons together anything greater than each severally. As Augustine wrote:

We have said elsewhere that those things are predicated specially in
the Trinity as belonging severally to each person, which are
predicated relatively the one to the other, as Father and Son, and the
gift of both, the Holy Spirit; for the Father is not the Trinity, nor the

---

[10.] Augustine, "On the Trinity," Bk. V, chap. 8, section 9, in *Nicene and Post-Nicene
Fathers,* First Series, vol. III, 91f.
[11.] George Park Fisher, *History of Christian Doctrine* (New York: Charles Scribner's Sons, 1896), 147.

Son the Trinity, nor the gift the Trinity: but whenever each is singly spoken of in respect to themselves, then they are not spoken of as three in the plural number, but one, the Trinity itself, as the Father God, the Son God, and the Holy Spirit God; the Father good, the Son good, and Holy Spirit good; and the Father omnipotent, the Son omnipotent, and the Holy Spirit omnipotent; yet neither three Gods, nor three goods, nor three omnipotents, but One God, good, omnipotent, the Trinity itself; and whatsoever else is said of them not relatively in respect to each other, but individually in respect to themselves. For they are thus spoken of according to essence, since in them to be is the same as to be great, as to be good, as to be wise, and whatever else is said of each person individually therein, or of the Trinity itself, in respect to themselves. And that therefore they are called three persons, or three substances, not in order that any difference of essence may be understood, but that we may be able to answer by some one word, should any one ask what three, or what three things? And that there is so great an equality in that Trinity, that not only the Father is not greater than the Son, as regards divinity, but neither are the Father and Son together greater than the Holy Spirit; nor is each individual person, whichever it be of the three, less than the Trinity itself.[12]

The importance of this point with respect to the Trinity appears as we analyze the problem of the one and the many. As Van Til has pointed out, there is for the Christian a distinction between the Eternal One-and-Many and the temporal one and many. For non-Christian philosophies, no such distinction exists, since for them all being is one being. For Christian philosophy, as Van Til has shown, orthodox thinking holds that "the eternal one and many form a self-complete unity. God is absolute personality and therefore absolute individuality. He exists necessarily. He has no non-being over against himself in comparison with which he defines himself; he is internally self-defined."[13] For orthodox Christian thought, there is an equal ultimacy of the one and the many in the Trinity, that is, the oneness of things is as ultimate as the individuality and the particularity of things. The oneness of God is not more ultimate than His three Persons, nor His three Persons more ultimate than His oneness. To cite Van Til again, whose work has placed him squarely in the great tradition of Athanasius, Augustine, and Calvin, "Unity in God is no more fundamental than diversity, and diversity in God is no more fundamental than unity. The persons of the Trinity are mutually exhaustive of one another. The Son and the Spirit are ontologically on a par with the Father."[14] The Christian doctrine of the Trinity avoids the pitfalls of an abstract universal (or one) and abstract particulars, in that neither the universals, or oneness of things, is an abstraction from concrete particulars, nor are the particulars

---

12. *Ibid.*, Bk. VIII, preface; 115.
13. Van Til, *op. cit.*, 42.
14. *Ibid.*

merely abstractions from a *concrete universal.* "It is only in the Christian doctrine of the triune God, as we are bound to believe, that we really have a *concrete universal.* In God's being there are no particulars not related to the universal and there is nothing universal that is not fully expressed in the particulars."[15]

The temporal one and many are entirely God's creation; everything that is, is God's creation, and "non-being is the field of God's possible operation. Since non-being is nothing in itself for God, God had to create, if he wished to create at all 'out of nothing.'"[16] The temporal one and many thus are created by God, and He is the law of their creation. As a result, the temporal order must see a similar relationship between the one and the many as exists in the Eternal One-and-Many. Non-Christian philosophy veers from an emphasis on the one to the many, from, to state it politically, totalitarianism to anarchism, from an insistence that unity is truth to an insistence that individuality is the true order. It is thus in constant conflict: the state or man; the husband and wife as individuals, or marriage as an institution; the group or the person? Which represents true order? All non-Christian thought holds to the ultimacy of either the one or the many and as a result veers from totalitarianism to anarchism. It can only maintain a balance between the two dialectically, briefly and in a tension which collapses. Orthodox Christianity, by its doctrine of the Trinity, avoids this basic problem of philosophy. The state is not more important than the citizen, nor the citizen than the state; both are equally basic to God's order and equally established in His law. Marriage as an institution is under God and according to His word, but the man and wife are equally under God and protected by His law, so that marriage is not sacrificed to the individual desires, nor the individuals to an institution. Both are equally established by and live under God's law order. A philosophy which emphasizes the one or the universals will make individuals abstract and unreal against the concrete universal: the citizens are sacrificed to the state, and man and wife are nothing as against the institution of marriage. A philosophy which holds that the many are real, and universals are abstractions, will destroy the state to free the concrete particular, anarchist man, and deny that marriage as an institution has any valid claim over the desires and whims of man and woman.

Orthodox Christianity has always held to the full-orbed trinitarian faith, and the Athanasian Creed is the classic expression of this doctrine. Every heresy in the church has been subordinationist in some form or another. If, for example, by God, the Almighty Creator, the Father is meant exclusively, and the Son and the Spirit are seen as some kind of junior gods

---

15. *Ibid.,* 43.
16. *Ibid.*

at best, the consequence has been the priority of natural order to revealed order. Natural law (or positive law, as a later development) comes to a position of ascendancy over revealed law. The basic order is seen as the natural order, and the revealed order comes to be a kind of addition, a complement, to an already operative order. In such heresies, the state becomes man's basic order, and the church is peripheral and subordinate to the state, the basic order. The true vicar of God in such a situation is the state and its head, and the state comes to be man's saving order, the Kingdom of God on earth.

Such a theology becomes a form of the old imperial theology, and politics again becomes the source of ethics. In orthodox Christianity, ethics is derived from religion, from theology, but in paganism and in subordinationist heresies, ethics is derived from politics because man is governed by a political theology, i.e., the state is the functioning voice and agency of its god.

The Athanasian Creed, meticulously, thoroughly, precisely, and in Augustinian language, closed the door to subordinationism and rendered it a heresy. It was never an acceptable faith, but now it was declared: "Whosoever will be saved, before all things it is necessary that he hold to the catholic faith," i.e., this anti-subordinationist doctrine of the Trinity, for "This is the catholic faith; which except a man believe faithfully and firmly, he cannot be saved."

These damnatory phrases have been bitterly attacked by critics of the Athanasian Creed. It has been inferred that everyone below the level of St. Augustine is barred from heaven and consigned to hell for failing to understand the full-orbed doctrine of the Trinity. For so long, complicated, and philosophical a creed to become a test of faith, it is held, is to limit Christianity to a handful of orthodox intellectuals. The charge is totally groundless. The creed defines the orthodox doctrine of the Trinity; the humble believer is required to *believe* it, not to understand it in all its implications. The believer's obligation is to *accept* the faith, to *receive* it, not to become a learned expounder of it.

The critical point is this: if the trinitarianism affirmed by the Athanasian Creed be not affirmed, then another savior than Christ is affirmed, and no man can be saved who holds to another savior. Subordinationism was the instrument whereby the imperial doctrine of salvation was re-entering the church. Modern subordinationists hold to political salvation, and, in the subordinate area of religion, all good Buddhists, Moslems, Hindus, cannibals, and all others are held to be saved in terms of their own premises. The inevitable outcome of all subordinationism is another savior. This both Athanasius and St. Augustine realized. For them Christianity itself was at stake in the controversies of their day. Every approach to Arian unitarianism was an approach also to religious universalism. Christianity would cease to be Christianity and would become another one of the many syncretistic faiths of the day. Subordinationism makes God the Father, the Creator who has not fully or truly revealed Himself in Jesus Christ, the ultimate one and the universal. There is then no particular which is also ultimate: only final unity. Moreover, since this creating one is better operative in the created order than in revelation, then all religions better reveal him than does the Bible and Christ. All religions are thus given dignity and Christ is reduced to one among many natural strivings towards the final unity.

To "free" man from the orthodox doctrine of the Trinity is to "free" man from God. By this doctrine, God's sovereignty is maintained, and His eternal decree declared: time and history are determined by God. Without this doctrine, God again becomes the silent god of Arianism, an unconscious inchoate being who is silent because he cannot reveal himself. Such a god is only ultimate as the original being out of which all being evolves, not as the creator and determiner of all things. Out of such a god, good and evil have equally emerged and are thus equally ultimate. According to Augustine, in *De Libero Arbitrio*, Van Til points out,

> It was a great boon to him when the Manichees had told him in his youth that he could live as he pleased since he was not ultimately responsible for his deeds. There was an ultimate force of evil, something demonic, more comprehensive and more compelling than the will of man, that made men sin. But now as a Christian Augustine knows that he himself, that man, not some super-individual force is responsible for sin.[17]

The *forms* of this "liberation" vary, and Manichaeanism is but one of many forms. In every form, however, wherever the doctrine of the Trinity, as declared by Scripture and summarized in the Athanasian Creed, is denied, there a "death of God" philosophy is in process of formation.

It is therefore clearly "necessary" that "whosoever will be saved" hold to this orthodox Trinitarian faith, for "This is the catholic faith; which except a man believe faithfully and firmly, he cannot be saved."

---

17. Cornelius Van Til, *Christianity in Conflict*, vol. I, pt. III, Syllabus (Westminster Theological Seminary, Philadelphia, 1962), 123.

Chapter Nine

Constantinople II: The Fallacy of Simplicity

An ancient and persistent danger is the fallacy of simplicity. There is a pronounced resentment on the part of very many men against knowledge that is beyond their capacity. As a result, wherever a democratic impulse governs theology, it seeks the lowest common denominator. The ignorant and foolish piously bleat for "the simple, old-time gospel," when the reality is that their simple-minded gospel is a modern invention. While certain basic doctrines of the Bible are uncomplicated ones, the Bible as a whole is not a simple book, and it gives us no warrant for passing over its complexities to dwell on its simplicities, because both aspects are inseparably one. No one can call the prophets simple reading, nor the epistles of Paul elementary, and the two together make up a major portion of the Bible, and they do not exhaust its complexity. The demand for simplicity is usually *a demand for perversion*, and it is not surprising therefore that the gospel of a democratic era is also a perverted one.

The demand for simplicity is not only a demand for perversion, but it is also *a demand for suicide*, and the people, church, or institution which pursue it have charted a course for assured death. Bark has rightly called attention to a critical failure of the Roman mentality: "they confused simplicity with strength, as if one could not exist without the other."[1]

Socialism is an excellent example of the fallacy of simplicity. As society grows more complex, it accordingly needs more decentralization and specialization. The greater the complexity of a society, the greater its need

---

[1] William Carroll Bark, *Origins of the Medieval World* (Garden City, New York: Doubleday Anchor Books, 1960 [1958]), 144.

for free growth in terms of its increasingly refined and specialized abilities. The socialist, however, recognizes only one valid and independent form of specialization, that of the statist controllers or managers. His answer to social complexity is an imposed simplicity, an enforced regression to a household economy. In a simple, frontier household, at brief periods in history and out of necessity, one man assumed most of the major economic functions and made the family an independent world. Such a condition has been infrequent and also primitive. Specialization means the freedom to pursue one's chosen calling without the necessity of performing countless tasks for which others are best suited. Socialism, the political and economic fallacy of simplicity, is also by its nature suicidal.

The first four ecumenical councils faithfully declared the *complexity* of the Biblical faith with respect to certain doctrines. Then as now intellectually lazy persons resented any doctrine which was beyond their intelligence. The doctrines of the faith had to be reduced to the level of man's sloth. The basic work had been done by the first four councils. The fifth council, the Second Council of Constantinople, A. D. 553, had to contend with both the civil and religious hostility to and lack of comprehension of the complexities of Christian doctrine. Justinian I, an able and well-intentioned emperor, called the council in the hope that it would smooth over differences between contending theological schools and thereby unify the empire religiously. The council, by its emphasis on the details of theological complexities, only served to divide the empire. The reaction to the council was on the whole not favorable then, and it was rather grudgingly accepted, and the attitude of Christians since has been one of neglect or weariness with its details.

"The Sentence of the Council" stated the council's strong sense of responsibility to speak out against impiety:

> Our Great God and Saviour Jesus Christ, as we learn from the parable in the Gospel, distributes talents to each man according to his ability, and at the fitting time demands an account of the work done by every man. And if he to whom but one talent has been committed is condemned because he has not worked with it but only kept it without loss, to how much greater and more horrible judgment must he be subject who not only is negligent concerning himself, but even places a stumbling-block and cause of offense in the way of others? Since it is manifest to all the faithful that whenever any question arises concerning the faith, not only the impious man himself is condemned, but also he who when he has the power to correct impiety in others, neglects to do so.
>
> We therefore, to whom it has been committed to rule the church of the Lord, fearing the curse which hangs over those who negligently

perform the Lord's work, hasten to preserve the good seed of faith pure from the tares of impiety which are being sown by the enemy.[2]

The emperor might expect peace and unity, but the council was determined to stand in terms of the truth. The emperor, basically a devout man, did not try to set aside the council's work. To a measure, Justinian's edict preceding the council had pointed out its task by calling for a condemnation of the works of Theodore of Mopsuestia, master of Nestorius, Theodoret of Cyrus, and the letter of Ibas of Edessa. Justinian's hope was that a condemnation of the theology of the school of Antioch would please the Monophysites, who now commanded the school of Alexandria. The council did condemn the Antiochene theology, but without retreating from Chalcedon's stand, so that both Antioch and Alexandria were now cut off from the orthodox faith.

Theodore of Mopsuestia (c. A. D. 350-428) held to a semi-Pelagian doctrine of man. For him, sin was the consequence of mortality, not its cause, so that finitude was man's basic problem and the root of his sin and fall. Man the sinner has free-will and is self-determining, so that Christ's role as Savior is not the determinative factor in the sinner's life. Grace is not prevenient but cooperating, that is, man saves himself with God's cooperation. For Theodore of Mopsuestia, any confusion of the two natures of Christ was unthinkable, but his reasons were not orthodox. For him, there was no substantial union between God and man in the incarnation but rather a voluntary one, which began with conception. The indwelling of God in Christ was by good will, not by substance nor by operation. There were strong elements of universalism in Theodore of Mopsuestia's thought, and the fullness of salvation for him meant the fullness of ultimate union with God.[3] His thinking represented a milder version of that philosophy which governed the school of Antioch.

The Monophysites felt towards these Antiochene ideas as Stalin felt towards Trotsky. The hatred was bitter and intense, but it was nonetheless a family quarrel. The Monophysites asserted, as their name indicated, the one nature of Christ. For them, as Rainy pointed out, "Christ is *of* two natures, but not *in* two natures."[4] Ostensibly, they were protecting the doctrine of God and Christ's deity. But, as Rainy noted, "what was this 'nature' which was neither divine nature simply nor human nature simply?"[5] Christ was seen as possessing a single nature which was neither

[2] Percival, *Decrees and Canons of the Councils,* 306. As Percival points out, the concluding sentence of the first paragraph has reference to Pope Vigilius.
[3] L. Patterson, *Theodore of Mopsuestia and Modern Thought* (London: Society for Promoting Christian Knowledge, 1926), 17, 19f., 21, 35ff., 47ff., 62-65.
[4] Robert Rainy, *The Ancient Catholic Church, From the Accession of Trojan to the Fourth General Council (A. D. 98-451)* (New York: Charles Scribner's Sons, 1902), 403.
[5] *Ibid.*

the simple divine nature nor the simple humanity. This brought Christ perilously close to the position of Arius' Christology. Either the Christ of Monophysite thought was neither God nor man but an intermediate figure, or else he was a God into whose being humanity had been absorbed. In either case, the confusion of the two natures was paramount. In the one case, Jesus Christ is neither consubstantial with God or man, and, in the other, man becomes consubstantial with God. One Monophysite sect, the Aphthartodocetae, held that the body of Jesus Christ was made incorruptible, not by virtue of the resurrection but by the union with the divine nature, i.e., by the communication of the properties of the divine nature to the human nature. In the modern era, Monophysite thinking has been in evidence in Henry Ward Beecher's *Life of Christ* and in Swedenborgianism, and the humanism in both cases is clearly in evidence.

These were the problems facing the Second Council of Constantinople. Schaff referred to this council as "a mere supplement to the third and the fourth."[6] Supplements are, however, often both necessary and important. The basic faith with respect to the Trinity had been defined: errors now had to be corrected and prevented.

The Council issued fourteen anathematisms. Although the traces of the doctrine of Mary's perpetual virginity are not accepted by all orthodox Protestants, this council has been accepted by all orthodox branches of the church. The first anathema declared:

I

If anyone does not confess that the Father, the Son, and the Holy Ghost have one nature or essence, one power and might; (or does not confess) the co-essential (consubstantial) Trinity, one Godhead in three hypostases or persons worshipped, let him be anathema. For there is one God and Father of whom are all things, and one Lord Jesus Christ through whom are all things, and one Holy Spirit in whom are all things.[7]

This is simply an insistence on the orthodox doctrine of the Trinity. The Trinity is not one God if the three persons are not equal and equally of one nature, power and might. Variations from the orthodox doctrine result in tritheism and unitarianism. There is no possibility of survival for the church as a Christian body if departures from trinitarianism are not anathematized.

II

[6.] Schaff, *Creeds of Christendom*, I, 44.
[7.] These and the succeeding anathemas are taken from Bishop Charles Joseph Hefele: *A History of the Councils of the Church*, IV (Edinburgh: T. & T. Clark, 1895), 329-342. See also Percival, 321-316.

If anyone does not confess that there are two births of God the Word, the one from eternity of the Father, out of time and incorporeal, and the other in the last days, in that He came down from heaven, and was made flesh of the holy, glorious Godbearer, and ever-virgin Mary, and was born of her, let him be anathema.

Jesus Christ as very God is therefore eternally existent, "out of time and incorporeal," eternally the begotten of the Father and one God with Him. In His humanity, Jesus Christ is very man of very man, born of the virgin Mary. The reality of His humanity and deity is declared by this statement.

III.

If anyone says that the Word of God who worked miracles is one, and that Christ who suffered is another; or says that God the Word is become the same as the Christ who was born of a woman, or is in Him as one is in another, and that it is not one and the same our Lord Jesus Christ, the Word of God, who became flesh and man, and that the miracles which He wrought and the sufferings which He voluntarily endured in the flesh are not His, let him be anathema.

This statement underscores both Chalcedon and Ephesus. Because the incarnation was real, and the union of the two natures a true union, it is impossible to treat Christ as two persons, ascribing certain acts to the divine nature and others to the human nature. There are two natures but one person, and to ascribe the miracles and the suffering to any but that one person, Jesus Christ, is to deny the incarnation. The statement clearly is hostile to a Nestorian union of the two natures, whereby the person of God and the person of Jesus remain distinct, but it is clearly hostile also to a Monophysite denial of the humanity after the incarnation. The assumption is that there are two natures in the one person in perfect union. To see, as some scholars have, attempts at conciliation with the Monophysites in these anathemas is groundless: their cutting edge strikes in both directions. The confusion and absorption of the humanity into the Godhead is condemned: those who "say that God the Word is become the same as the Christ who is born of a woman, or is in Him as one is in another," are condemned.

IV.

If anyone says that the union of God the Word with man has taken place only by grace, or by operation, or by equality of honour and distinction, or by a carrying up and condition or by power, or by good pleasure, as though God the Word were pleased with man, from its seeming well and good to Him concerning him — as the raving Theodore says; or that it has taken place through the sameness of name, according to which the Nestorians call God the Word Jesus (Son) and Christ, and so name the man separately Christ and Son, and so clearly speak of two persons, and hypocritically speak of one person and of one Christ only according to designation, and honour, and dignity, and worship. But if anyone does not confess that the union of God the Word with the flesh enlivened by a reasonable and thinking soul, according to synthesis (combination), or according to hypostasis. as the holy Fathers said, and that therefore there is only one person, namely, the Lord Jesus Christ, one of the Holy Trinity, let him be anathema. As, however, the word union (*enosis*) is taken in different senses, those who follow the impiety of Apollinaris and Eutyches, assuming a disappearance of the natures which come together, teach a union by confusion; whilst the adherents of Nestorius and Theodore, rejoicing in the separation, introduce a merely relative union. The Holy Church of God, on the contrary, rejecting the impiety of both heresies, confesses the union of God the Word with the flesh by a combination, i.e., personally. For the union by combination (synthesis) not only preserves, in regard to the mysteries of Christ, that which was come together (the two natures) unconfused, but allows of no separation (of the persons).

This statement again anathematizes both Nestorians and Monophysites. The incarnation is a true union, without confusion or change, of the two natures in one person, Jesus Christ. To speak of the union as merely a moral identification, or a union of activity or operation, is to deny the incarnation. Eutyches, specifically named, was a forerunner of Monophysite thought. His teaching, and all teachings, declaring a disappearance of one nature after the union, or their confusion, are condemned. Both Nestorianism and Monophysitism are "heresies." This anathema denounces those who "hypocritically speak of one person and of Christ" but in actuality "clearly speak of two persons."

V.

If anyone so understands the expression, one Hypostasis of our Lord Jesus Christ, that thereby is meant the designation of the union of many hypostases, and hereby undertakes to introduce into the mystery of Christ two hypostases or two persons, and often having introduced two persons, speaks of one person according to dignity, honour, and worship, as Theodore and Nestorius in their madness maintained: and if any one slanders the holy Synod in Chalcedon, as though it had used the expression, one hypostasis, in this impious sense, and does not confess that the Word of God was personally united with flesh, and that therefore there is only one hypostasis or one person, as also the holy Synod in Chalcedon confessed one hypostasis of our Lord Jesus Christ, — let him be anathema! For the holy Trinity, when God the Word, one of the holy Trinity was incarnate, did not suffer the addition of a person or hypostasis.

Again the condemnation cuts both ways, and Chalcedon's definition is made the test of orthodoxy. The way to unity of Monophysite and orthodox is through the submission of all to Chalcedon. This was an anathema hardly likely to conciliate Monophysites, but conciliation was not sought at the price of truth.

VI.

If anyone says that the holy, glorious, ever-virgin Mary is called Godbearer by abuse and not truly, or by analogy, as though a mere man were born of her, and not as though God the Word were incarnate of her, but that the birth of a man were connected with God the Word, because He was united with the man born; and if anyone slanders the holy Synod of Chalcedon, as though, in accordance with this impious opinion held by Theodore, it called the virgin Godbearer; or, if anyone calls her manbearer or Christbearer, as though Christ were not God, and does not confess her as Godbearer, in the proper sense and in truth, because God the Word, who was begotten of the Father before all worlds, was incarnate of her in the last days; and (does not confess) that in this pious sense the holy Synod of Chalcedon confessed her to be Godbearer — let him be anathema.

Again the reality of the incarnation is insisted upon, as against Nestorianism and Theodore of Mopsuestia. Nestorianism having been condemned, the humanists had withdrawn to the as yet uncondemned position of Theodore for a safe haven. The council now condemned the root and the branch alike. Attempts to read Chalcedon in terms of Theodore were also condemned: when Chalcedon and the earlier councils spoke of Mary as *thetokos*, they meant it in terms of orthodox Christology, not in terms of a voluntary union.

VII.

If anyone, speaking of the two natures does not confess that he acknowledges in the Godhead and manhood the one Lord Jesus Christ, so that by this lie signifies the difference of natures, of which the unspeakable union takes place without confusion, without the nature of the Word being changed into that of the flesh, nor that of the flesh into the nature of the Word — for each remains what it was in nature after the personal union has taken place — or who takes that expression in reference to the mystery of Christ in the sense of a separation into parts, or, confessing the two natures in relation to the one Lord Jesus, the incarnate Word of God, takes the differences of these of which HE was composed, but which is not destroyed by the union — for HE is one of both, through one both — takes this difference not as an abstraction, but uses the duality in order to separate the natures, and to make them separate persons (hypostases), — let him be anathema.

The sixth anathema spoke of those who twist the orthodox doctrine and speak of the incarnate one "as though Christ were not God." In the seventh anathema, some more of these stratagems are cited, and they are answered in terms of Chalcedon. The basic result of the heresies was the denial of the incarnation. Either the two natures were so divided that no true union took place but rather only a voluntary association, or else the two natures were confused and the humanity absorbed into the divinity. The practical and philosophical result of both Nestorianism and Monophysitism was the apotheosis of man; both represented the triumph of pagan humanism and of imperial theology. Western liberty is the product of Chalcedonian Christology and of the trinitarianism of the Athanasian Creed. Explicit or implicit humanism will attempt either to separate the man Jesus from the person of God except by a voluntary association open to all, or to give him a divinity which is open to all men. Upon all such, the anathema of the council stands.

VIII.

> If anyone does not take the expressions, "of two natures," the Godhead and the manhood, the union took place, or, the one incarnate nature of the Word, as the holy Fathers taught, that from the divine nature and the human, personal union having taken place, one Christ was constituted, but endeavours, by such expressions, to bring in one nature or essence of the Godhead and manhood of Christ, let him be anathema. For when we say that the only-begotten Word was personally united, we do not say that a confusion of the natures with each other has taken place; but rather we think that, whilst each nature remains what it is, the Word has been united with the flesh. Therefore, also, there is one Christ, God and man, the same who is of one substance with the Father as to His Godhead, and of one substance with us as to His manhood. For the Church of God equally condemns and anathematises those who separate and cut asunder the mystery of the divine economy of Christ, and those who confess it.[8]

Again, Chalcedon is stressed and the Monophysite confusion of natures is condemned. The sophisticated doctrines of the Monophysites could not conceal their basically Hellenistic and humanistic thrust. For Athanasian and Chalcedonian creedalism, the true universal is the triune God. By introducing a confusion of natures into the person of Christ, humanity is made one with the universals, with the ultimate realities of the universe. Humanity thereby becomes its own god. Sovereignty is transferred from God to man, and salvation also becomes more and more man's work, in that man is now the new universal. The Monophysite Coptic liturgy had already come to a position of celebrating man as well as God. Thus, an earlier hymn, while still paying its respects to "the Holy equal Trinity," finds the congregation singing:

> In the name of the Father and
> the Son and the Holy Ghost,
> the Holy equal Trinity.
> Worthy, worthy, worthy, the
> Holy Virgin Mary.
> Worthy, worthy, worthy, Thy
> servants the Christians.[9]

---

[8] For the last clause, Percival translates "who introduce confusion into that Mystery."

The Reformation doctrines of justification, predestination, and sovereign grace are simply the logical and necessary concommitant of Chalcedon and of the Athanasian Creed, and all these together simply the Biblical faith. Humanism makes man the new universal, and the state becomes the unified god on earth. As a result, while the form of Christian doctrine can be retained, the heart of that doctrine can be negated by introducing man into the Godhead and by making man the new universal. When Scholasticism reintroduced Aristotle's humanism into Western history, the consequence was the decline of orthodox Christianity and its trinitarian answer to the problem of the one and the many and universals. The universals of Scholasticism became the Hellenic ideas or forms, and the Trinity itself was reevaluated in terms of these forms to become substance (the Father), structure (the Son), and process (the Spirit), so that the Trinity became simply the common being of the universe analyzed into its aspects. The universals thus had no small immanence, and the struggle of medieval Europe came increasingly to be a contest between claimants to the title of concrete universal, i.e., the immanent expression of ultimate order. Church, state, and university alike claimed supremacy and sovereignty, as did the anarchic and ultimate individual of such groups as the Adamites and other movements of the day. The mystics also claimed the same realization of the universal in their experience.

Any and every departure from Ephesus and Chalcedon, and from the Athanasian Creed, was a venture into humanism and the supplanting of God by man.

IX.

> If anyone says that Christ is to be worshipped in two natures, by which two kinds of worship are introduced, the one for God the Word, the other for the man; or if anyone, by taking away the flesh, or by confusion of the Godhead and manhood, or preserving only one nature or essence of those which are united, thus worships Christ, and does not worship God made flesh together with His flesh with one worship, as the Church of God received from the beginning, — let him be anathema.

In the ninth anathema, several forms of perversion of the faith of Chalcedon are cited and condemned. *First,* some worshipped both natures of Christ, His humanity as well as His deity, thereby introducing man-worship into Christianity in the name of obedience to the faith. *Second,* others confused the two natures and therefore worshipped man in this manner and introduced humanity into the nature of the Godhead. *Third,* still others reduced the two natures to one by absorption and thus again destroyed the Biblical distinction between God and man and their

---

9. Aziz S. Atiya, "Historical Introduction," *Coptic Music* (Folkways Records, Album FR 8960, New York, 1960).

differing beings. The bridge between the uncreated being of God and the created being of man was uniquely bridged without confusion in Jesus Christ; attempts to make the bridge a natural one by confusion or absorption have as their goal and meaning the obliteration of the distinction between God and man. This obliteration serves to make man his own god.

X.

If anyone does not confess that our Lord Jesus Christ crucified in the flesh is true God, and Lord of glory, and one of the Holy Trinity, let him be anathema.

God can be eliminated from a philosophy or religion not only by a confusion with humanity, so that God and man become either basically or potentially one, but also by a radical and total isolation and separation from one another. If God is made "the wholly other," a hidden god who does not reveal himself (as for Arianism and neo-orthodoxy), he ceases to be god over man. A hidden god who has not spoken nor can speak, who has no revelation nor an infallible word, must surrender the universe by default to man. Man at least speaks; man at least has some kind of word, so that speaking man replaced the silent god as the lord of being. Denials of the reality of the incarnation, and the reality of Christ's crucifixion, while ostensibly protecting God from the world of mutability and passion, were in actuality protecting man from interference by God. If the crucified and risen Christ is simply a remarkable man, then he portends a new world of potentiality for man as the lord of creation. If this crucified and risen Christ be very God of very God, as well as very man of very man, then man is under God's government and decree as a creature.

XI.

If anyone does not anathematise Arius, Eunomius, Macedonius, Apollinaris, Nestorius, Eutyches, and Origen, together with their impious writings, and all other heretics condemned and anathematized by the Catholic and Apostolic Church and by the four holy Synods already mentioned, together with those who have been or are of the same mind with the heretics mentioned, and who remain till the end in their impiety, let him be anathema.

It is not sufficient to be against heresy; one must also be against heretics. The notion that one can hate sin and love the sinner is a contradiction. Can one hate theft and love the thief who robbed him, or hate murder but love the murderer of his family, or hate rape but love the rapist who raped his loved ones? True, this idea that it can be done is commonplace, but it is an evidence of moral degeneracy. The council named various heretics and condemned them and required all orthodox believers to unite in their condemnation. Those who refuse to condemn the heretics are themselves guilty of impiety and are anathema. Either men separate from heresy and heretics in terms of the faith, or they are separated from the faith and from the faithful.

XII.

If anyone defends the impious Theodore of Mopsuestia, who says (a) God the Word is one, and another is Christ who was troubled with sufferings of the soul and desires of the flesh, and who by degrees raised himself from that which was more imperfect, and by progress in good works and by his way of life became blameless; and further, that as mere man he was baptized into the name of the Father, and of the Son, and of the Holy Ghost, and through baptism received the grace of the Holy Spirit, and was deemed worthy of sonship, and was worshipped with reference to the person of God the Word, like the image of an emperor, and that (only) after the resurrection he became unchangeable in his thoughts and completely sinless; and (b) again, as the same impious Theodore says, the union of God the Word with Christ was of such a nature as the apostle says there is between man and wife: "the two shall be one flesh"; and (c) among other blasphemies, dared to say that, when the Lord, after the resurrection, breathed upon His disciples, saying, "Receive the Holy Ghost," He did not give them the Holy Ghost, but only breathed upon them as a sign; (d) and again, that the confession of Thomas, on touching the hands and the side of the Lord after the resurrection, "My Lord and my God," was not spoken concerning Christ by Thomas, but that, astonished at the miracle of the resurrection, Thomas praised God who raised Christ; (e) and what is still worse, in his exposition of the Acts of the Apostles, Theodore compares Christ with Plato, Manichaeus, Epicurus, and Marcion, and says that, as each of these devised his own doctrine and gave to his disciples the name of Platonists, Manichaeans, Epicureans, and Marcionists, in the same manner, when Christ also devised a doctrine, after Him they were called Christians. — If anyone, then, defends the forenamed most impious Theodore and his impious writings, in which he poured out the above-mentioned and other countless blasphemies against the great God, our Saviour Jesus Christ, and does not anathematise him and his impious. writings, and all who adhere to him, or defend him or say that he has given an orthodox interpretation, or who have written in defense of him and his impious writings; and who think or have ever thought the same, and remained to the end in this heresy — let him be anathema.

In analyzing Theodore of Mopsuestia's teachings, the council placed its finger clearly on its basic humanism. Jesus Christ was reduced to the ranks of one teacher among many, and he was at best a great man who by moral excellence became an image or icon of God even as the images of an emperor represent the emperor and are worshipped. This reference, "like the image of an emperor," is significant, in that the images of the emperors again became central with the iconoclastic controversy. It is also significant in that an image or icon is not the substance; the emperor or the god depicted is. Christ as the icon of the Father in this sense is one possible icon or image among many, and one possible teacher among many. Thus, in the name of worshipping Christ as the image of the Father, those who were using Theodore of Mopsuestia's terminology to shield their Nestorianism were actually demoting Christ even as they worshipped Him. When the door is opened to many images and many teachers, ostensibly all are exalted, but in actuality all are demoted, in that truth becomes the property of none. An unrevealed god means an unrevealed truth, and an unrevealed god is also a possibly non-existent god and a nonexistent truth. Man then becomes his own way, truth, and life, and objective truth is replaced by subjective truth.

XIII.

If anyone defends the impious writings of Theodoret which are directed against the true faith, and against the first and holy Synod of Ephesus, and against the holy Cyril and his twelve chapters, and (defends) all that he wrote in defence of Theodore and Nestorius, the impious ones, and others who think the like with those named, with Theodore and Nestorius, and receive them and their impiety, and for their sakes call the teachers of the Church impious, who maintain and confess the hypostatic union of God the Word; and if he does not anathematise the impious writings named, and those who thought and think the like, and all who have written against the true faith or the holy Cyril and his twelve chapters, and have persevered in such impiety — let him be anathema.

The writings of the bishop and church historian, Theodoret, a friend of Nestorius, were also subjected to scrutiny and condemnation. Theodoret has many modern defenders. The fact remains, however, that his defense of Nestorianism was clear-cut and his position not orthodox. The condemnation of men long since dead became necessary at the council, because contemporary heretics were taking refuge behind the opinions of Theodore, Theodoret, Ibas, and others to escape the reproach of Nestorianism.

XIV.

If anyone defends the letter which Ibas is said to have written to Maris the Persian, in which it is denied that God the Word became flesh and man of the holy Godbearer and ever-virgin Mary, and in which it is maintained that he was born of her a mere man, called the temple; and that God the Word is one and the man is another; and in which the holy Cyril who proclaimed the true faith of Christ is accused as a heretic, and as if he had written the same as the impious Apollinaris; and in which the first holy Synod of Ephesus is censured, as though it had condemned Nestorius without examination and trial; and the twelve chapters of the holy Cyril called impious and opposed to the true faith, and Theodore and Nestorius and their impious doctrines and writings defended; if anyone defends the letter in question, and does not anathematise it, together with those who defend it, and say that it is right, or a part of it, and who have written or do write in defence of it or of the impieties contained in it, and venture to defend it or the impieties contained in it by the name of holy Fathers of the holy Synod of Chalcedon, and persevere therein to the end — let him be anathema.

The Ibas referred to was Bishop of Edessa in Syria from 435 to 457; Ibas translated the works of Theodore of Mopsuestia into the Syriac and distributed them extensively throughout Persia and Syria. He was accused of Nestorianism and twice acquitted, but the Robber Council of Ephesus, 449, deposed him. Chalcedon reestablished Ibas after examination, as it did Theodoret also, after Theodoret finally consented to the anathemas against Nestorius. The Second Council of Constantinople avoided condemning Theodoret and Ibas but condemned simply their writings which taught specified errors. In Ibas' case, the letter in question is cited as one "which Ibas is said to have written," implying doubt. The letter contained such statements as this: "Those who maintain that the Word was incarnate, and made man, are heretics and Apollinarians."[10] Ibas' position apart from this letter, was suspect.

The Second Council of Constantinople thus ably defended the work of Ephesus and Chalcedon. It represented no further development, but it did represent an able defense of the faith and its work was needed. It is not enough, in dealing with a present danger, to avoid it by citing the fact that someone dealt with the matter in the past. If an enemy attacks today the enemy must be fought today, but without a surrender of past victories. A church cannot say, if men arise within its ranks denying the infallibility of Scripture, that it cannot deal with these men today, because the confession dealt with the matter a few centuries ago. Rather, it must affirm the old confession by a new condemnation of heretics. This the Second Council of Constantinople did.

The council, moreover, was unafraid of complexity and refinement of doctrine. It drew the line sharply, because the alternative was to erase or at the least to blur the line between Christianity and humanism. A retreat towards simplicity of faith is a retreat into death. The scorn men reserve for those whose teachings are difficult is no evidence of character but is in their throats the death-rattle of a church and culture. The churches today which draw the line sharply are small and lonely congregations, growing only with difficulty, whereas the modernists and Arminians who erase the line of offense and introduce humanism into the church seem to flourish. But their growth is simply the growth of corruption, and their only light the phosphorescence of decay.

---

10. Landon, *Manual of Councils*, I, 200.

Chapter Ten

The Doctrine of Grace

In Pelagianism, humanism came to the fore with its doctrine of man. Pelagius frankly and plainly asserted the plenary ability of man to live without sin: "I say that man is able to be without sin, and that he is able to keep the commandments of God."[1] Pelagius held, *first*, that all might be sinless if they chose, and many had been so. *Second*, each man is born without any impediment or entailment of sin or moral weakness from Adam or his ancestors. *Third*, man therefore has no need for divine grace in overcoming sin.[2] As Matheson noted, "Paganism knows nothing of sin, it knows only of sins: it has no conception of the principle of evil; it comprehends only a collection of evil acts." Warfield added, "This is Pelagianism too."[3]

The British monk, Pelagius, who was the exponent of this form of humanism, is said to have been originally named Morgan. The times of his birth and death are not known, but he appeared in Rome c. 400 and began to teach his doctrines. The great champion of orthodoxy against Pelagianism was St. Augustine. Since it is outside our purpose to analyze the controversies as such, and the men and writings involved, but rather the creedal and conciliar movements, the great work of St. Augustine cannot be discussed here.

[1.] Benjamin Breckinridge Warfield, *Studies in Tertullian and Augustine* (New York: Oxford, 1930), 293.

[2.] *Ibid.*

[3.] *Ibid.*, 296n.

The Council which confronted Pelagianism was the Second Synod at Orange (Arausio) in Southern Gaul, July 3, 529. This council has been called a victory of Semi-Augustinianism by Schaff,[4] and this is largely true, but, because it was a victory of Semi-Augustinianism, it was also a victory for Semi-Pelagianism.

The text of the 25 canons appears in Leith, and summaries of the canons, with the full Latin text, are to be found in Hefele.[5] Landon's summary gives the essential point of these 25 canons more briefly, by summarizing the key ones:

1. Condemns those who maintain that the sin of Adam has affected only the body of man by rendering it mortal, but has not affected the soul also.

2. Condemns those who maintain that the sin of Adam hath injured himself only, or that the death of the body is the only effect of his transgression which has descended to his posterity.

3. Condemns those who teach that grace is given in answer to the prayer of man, and who deny that it is *through grace* that he is brought to pray at all.

4. Condemns those who teach that God waits for our wish before purifying us from sin, and that He does not by His Spirit give, us the wish to be purified.

5. Condemns those who maintain that the act of faith, by which we believe in Him who justifieth, is not the work of grace, but that we are capable of doing so of ourselves.

6. Condemns those who maintain that man can think or do any thing good, as far as his salvation is concerned, without grace.

7. Condemns those who maintain that some come to the grace of baptism by their own free will, and others by the supernatural help of divine mercy.[6]

The eighteen other canons are essentially sentences taken from the works of St. Augustine and Prosper. Three propositions were appended to the 25 canons, holding

1. That all baptised persons can, if they will, work out their salvation.

2. That God hath predestined no one to damnation.

3. That God, by His grace, gives to us the first beginning of faith and charity, and that He is the Author of our conversion.[7]

[4.] Schaff, *History of the Christian Church,* III, 866-870.
[5.] Leith, *Creeds of the Church,* pp. 37-45; Hefele, *History of the Councils,* IV, 152-169.
[6.] Landon, *Manual of Councils,* 11, 4f.
[7.] *Ibid.,* II, 5.

The council thus was in some respects a retreat. The victories won by Augustine and his followers were weakened. Fisher's comment is pertinent:

> The Council asserted the necessity of prevenient grace, and the necessity of grace at every stage of the soul's renewal, and affirmed that unmerited grace precedes meritorious works, that all good, including love to God, is God's gift, that even unfallen man is in need of grace. But not only is predestination to sin denied, but there is no affirmation of unconditional election or irresistible grace. Moreover, free-will is said to be "weakened" in Adam, and restored through the grace of baptism. The creed is anti-Pelagian, but the tenets of Semi-Pelagianism are only in part explicitly condemned. It was sanctioned by the Roman Bishop, Boniface II.[8]

Even more, since Augustine had clearly asserted double election, to damnation and to salvation, Augustine himself was in effect condemned by the Council of Orange.

Strict Augustinianism had its adherents in the later centuries, men such as Bede, Alcuin, and Isidore of Seville, but the church steadily moved away from Augustinianism until the Reformation. The consequences were far-reaching.

Pelagianism is essentially the assertion of man's ability to save himself; it is a belief that man does not need God to attain the perfect life. The implications of this doctrine for both church and state, as well as for every other sphere, are very great. If man is able, then the state, the church, and the university are able to save man.

In political theory, Pelagianism has meant that the state is not restricted to the role of a ministry of justice. The state becomes man's mediator and savior. The Pelagian state offers cradle to grave security. It faces every problem in the confidence that, given sufficient time and power, it will provide the answer. The Pelagian state is confident that it can abolish sickness and disease, poverty and hunger, crime and lawlessness, and, through nationalized science, possibly even death itself. Pelagianism asserts the plenary ability of man to save himself, and the Pelagian state believes in the plenary power of the state to save man and to create a paradise on earth. Because the Pelagian state believes in its *plenary ability,* it works to seize that *plenary power* which it holds is necessary for the exercise of its abilities and plans. As a result, Pelagianism in politics is inescapably totalitarian. It cannot place any brakes on the state, nor can it be justifiably suspicious of the state, since it has no real doctrine of sin, only a catalogue of sinful acts. The decline of the doctrine of sovereign grace is marked by the rise of the sovereign state.

---

8. Fisher, *History of Christian Doctrine,* 197.

Pelagianism in ecclesiology, with respect to the doctrine of the church, again has far-reaching consequences. The church *of* the mediator makes itself *the* mediator progressively, as Pelagianism develops. The authority and sovereignty which properly belong to Christ begin to accrue to the Pelagian church, and the infallibility of Christ and His enscriptured word are progressively transferred to the church. The Pelagian church weakens the dependence of men on God and His grace and increases their dependence on the institution of the church. Grace and power are transferred from Christ's work to the church's work, and the church progressively becomes the saving power and the saving society. Interest in orthodox Christology wanes, and interest in Pelagian ecclesiology increases. Because the power recognized by the Pelagian church is essentially human power, it seeks to aggrandize human power. This is done in two ways: *first,* the Pelagian church seeks numerical strength by union with other Pelagian churches and by laxer standards, in order to present a strong front in terms of human reckoning. *Second,* the Pelagian church seeks power by an alliance with the state. Its goal is essentially the same, a paradise on earth by human effort, and accordingly the Pelagian state and the Pelagian church form a common front to destroy every trace of the Christian state and the Christian church. The common goal is a one world order in which the dream of Pelagius, man's perfectibility by man, is realized. Because the Pelagian church believes more and more openly in man as his own god, it moves from a slighting of God to the attempt to abolish God and to proclaim the death of God. The Pelagian church, like its state, is essentially totalitarian: it is its own god and law.

Pelagianism is no less apparent in the academy than it is in church and state. Education today is largely applied Pelagianism.[9] Education in this perspective becomes a program of salvation. Through education, all man's problems will be solved. Knowledge is power, and the educator is thus the key to the social regeneration of man. The Pelagian school sees ignorance, not sin, as man's basic handicap and problem, and, accordingly, it seeks to remove this impediment. Man must be awakened out of his ignorance to the vast world of his potentialities. The school is the institution whereby man can enter into his godlike powers and master himself and the world. The Pelagian school is thus hostile to the Christian state and the Christian church no less than to the Christian school, and it seeks their destruction. By alliance with the Pelagian state and church, it works to create paradise on earth.

But Pelagianism infects every sphere. The artist believes in the regenerating power of the esthetic experience. The Pelagian women come

---

[9.] See R. J. Rushdoony, *Intellectual Schizophrenia* (Presbyterian and Reformed. Philadelphia, 1961) and *The Messianic Character of American Education* (Craig Press, Nutley, New Jersey, 1963).

to believe in the power of their sex to save mankind, and feminism is the result. The economists have plans whereby monetary trickery will create perpetual prosperity, and so on. Plenary ability means plenary planning, plenary controls, and plenary tyrants and tyranny. The social and historical consequences of Pelagianism have always been disastrous. In the name of exalting man, man is debased by these planners.

The doctrine of sovereign grace alone provides a bulwark for liberty, for sovereign grace, faithfully believed and applied, means also a sovereign restraint upon man's pretensions. To God alone belongs dominion. Either God predestines, or man and the state do. If God is not sovereign, the state will be. The foundations of liberty are laid with Augustinian materials. It is either Christ or the state; a man cannot have two masters or two saviors. The triumph of Pelagianism is always the enslavement of man.

Even as subordinationism was a compromise which surrendered orthodox trinitarianism, even when closest to it, so the Council of Orange surrendered the doctrine of grace by compromising it, even as it defended Augustinianism to a large degree. Truth is exact and precise, and the slightest departure from the truth is the substitution of falsity for truth. The long canons of Orange are on the whole excellent, but they are compromised by the element of error.

Chapter Eleven

The Procession
of the Holy Ghost

Subordinationism, in its broader significance, had a double implication: *first*, it treated the Father as true God but gave a lesser status to the Son and to the Holy Ghost, so that, while nominally trinitarian, it was actually uncongenial to trinitarianism. *Second,* as a result of this subordinationism, the revealed order, i.e., the revelation of God the Word and of His enscriptured word, the Bible, took a lesser place to the natural word of God, creation, and its order of power, the state. In subordinationism, the world became the domain of the state, and the element of revelation was seen as an addition to rather than a necessary part of man's life. In and through subordinationism, the messianic state was reintroducing its claims.

The Augustinian development culminating in the Athanasian Creed was hostile to this subordinationism. It was a logical conclusion of this development to add to the Nicene Creed the *Filioque*, the clause concerning the procession of the Holy Ghost from the Son as well as the Father: "who proceedeth from the Father and the Son." The phrase was lacking in earlier forms of the creed, because the issue had not yet arisen, but the concept was thoroughly Nicene and Athanasian.

The first known inclusion of the *Filioque* is at the Council of Toledo in Spain of A. D. 589, which sealed the triumph of orthodoxy over Arianism in Spain.[1] The clause had not appeared in the earlier creeds because the question had not come up. There was more general assent earlier to the procession of the Holy Ghost than later, when Monophysite and Arian thinking had developed their implications more fully. In John 14:16-18, 26, 27, the Holy Ghost, the Comforter, is seen as coming from both the Father and the Son, and v. 18 is taken by commentators in this sense. This was also true in the early church. The sophistication of doubt came later.

The Second Council of Toledo of 447 adopted the canon: "The Father is unbegotten, the Son is begotten, the Paraclete not begotten but proceeding from the Father and the Son."[2] But at this time, while asserted against the Arian beliefs, the words were not added to the creed. The Council of 589 met when King Reccared became orthodox and brought the Goths of Spain into orthodoxy. He asked the council or synod to cite and anathematize the Arian heresies and to instruct the people. A general confession with twenty-three anathematisms was formulated, and the *Filioque* added to the creed. The confession declared:

1. If anyone still holds the doctrine and communion of the Arians, let him be anathema.

2. If anyone does not confess that the Son of God, our Lord Jesus Christ, is begotten of the substance of the Father without beginning, is like to and of one substance with the Father, let him be anathema.

3. If anyone does not believe that the Holy Ghost proceedeth from the Father and the Son, and is coeternal with and like unto the Father and the Son, let him be anathema.

4. If anyone does not distinguish the persons in the Trinity, let him be anathema.

5. If anyone declares the Son and Spirit inferior to the Father, let him be anathema.

6. If anyone does not believe that Father, Son, and Spirit are of one substance, one omnipotence, and eternity, let him be anathema.

7. If anyone maintains that the Son is ignorant of anything, let him be anathema.

8. If anyone ascribes a beginning to the Son or Spirit, let him be anathema.

9. If anyone maintains that the Son, in His Godhead, was visible or capable of suffering, let him be anathema.

---

[1] This Council of Toledo of May 8, 589, is called the Fourth Council by John M'Clintock and James Strong, *Cyclopaedia of Biblical, Theological, and Ecclesiastical Literature*, vol. X, "Toledo, Councils of" (New York: Harper, 1894), 453, and is called the Third Council of Toledo by Schaff, *Creeds of Christendom*, I, 26, and is the Fourth Council according to Landon, *Manual of Councils*, II, 153. But Landon lists a synod of c. 405 as the second, whereas this is not listed by M'Clintock and Strong, who give the title to that of c. 447, held during the time of Leo I, but not listed by Landon.

[2] Badcock, *History of the Creeds*, 216.

10. If anyone does not hold the Holy Ghost as the true Almighty God, as the Father and the Son, let him be anathema.

11. If anyone declares any other faith than that of Nicaea, Constantinople, Ephesus, and Chalcedon to be the Catholic faith, let him be anathema.

12. If anyone separates the Father, Son, and Spirit in regard to glory and Godhead, let him be anathema.

13. If anyone believes that the Son and Spirit are not to be honoured along with the Father, let him be anathema.

14. If anyone does not say: "*Gloria et honor Patri, et Filio, et Spiritui Sancto,*" let him be anathema.

15. If anyone defends or practices rebaptism, let him be anathema.

16. If anyone regards as good the abominable treatise which we composed, in the twelfth year of Leovigild, in order to mislead the Romans to the Arian heresy, let him be anathema.

17. If anyone does not condemn the Council of Ariminum with all his heart, let him be anathema.

18. We confess that we have been, with all our heart, etc., converted from the Arian heresy to the Catholic Church. The faith which our King has confessed before the Synod we also confess and teach to our congregations. If anyone does not hold this faith, let him be anathema maranatha (1 Cor. xvi. 22).

19 to 22. If anyone rejects the faith of the Synods of Nicaea, Contantinople, Ephesus, and Chaldaea, let him be anathema.

23. This condemnation of the Arian heresy we have subscribed with our own hands. The definition of those Synods of Nicaea, etc., we have subscribed. They contain clearly the true doctrine of the Trinity and Incarnation. If anyone falsifies this holy doctrine, and separates himself again from the Catholic communion which we have now obtained, he is guilty before God and the world.[3]

The reference in no. 16 is to the heretical synod, an Arian Synod, at Toledo in 581 or 582, summoned by Leovigild, King of the West Goths, an Arian who persecuted orthodoxy severely. This synod published a *Libellus* to pervert the orthodox, and the bishops now anathematised their previous work. The same factor, condemnation of compulsion at a Synod, is apparent in the condemnation in no. 17. The Council of Ariminum, A. D. 359, met at Ariminum in Roumania. As long as the council was free, it was anti-Arian and orthodox. When its orthodoxy became apparent, force was applied to bring about an Arian conclusion. Trickery was used also, Valens inserting a declaration that the Son was not a creature like other creatures. The simple bishops read this as a denunciation of Arianism, when it

---

[3.] Hefele: *History* of *the Church Councils,* IV, 417f.

actually was an assertion of the Son's creatureliness, although unlike other creatures. Ariminum was quickly and universally condemned. Those who call attention to the fact that the early councils were often called by a king or emperor fail to note this significant fact: the councils were free of dictation from the state, and a dictated council was a false council. The state could suggest or advise, but it could not command the council.

As Schaff has pointed out, the *Filioque* was not an accidental addition but a necessary development of the orthodox faith, the inevitable implication of orthodox Christology:

> The *double* procession follows inevitably from the consubstantiality of the Father and the Son, and from the identity of the Spirit of God and the Spirit of Christ. It also forms a connecting link between the Trinity and Christology, and between Christology and Anthropology, by bringing the Holy Spirit and His work into more immediate connection with Christ, and, through Him, with the church and the believer. It was therefore not accidental that the same Augustine, who first taught clearly the double procession, developed also those profound views of sin and grace, which took permanent root in the West, but had no influence in the East.[4]

The Arian and generally heretical depreciation and subordination of Jesus Christ was the depreciation of revelation. To the degree that revelation was slighted, to that degree nature was asserted as the primary and basically self-sufficient order. God then became at best the first cause of nature, and Greek humanism was again triumphant. If nature is the basic and ultimate order, and Jesus is at best a product of nature, then the state is the true order of the world, and the saving order. The determination of history, moreover, passes from the Trinity to the state, from eternity to time, from the supernatural to the natural. Subordinationist Christology was imperial Christology, and the imperial, and later caesaropapal doctrines of God saw God essentially as the author of a primary nature and a governing agency, the state. The sure voice of God was therefore the natural voice, the state. The work of grace and of revelation then became a kind of addition to nature. The Scholastic concept of the *donum superadditum* was basically humanistic as well as non-Biblical. The implications of Scholasticism were thus subordinationist.

The Augustinian doctrines of sin and grace rested in the Biblical perspective and in an anti-subordinationist Christology and trinitarianism. Yeomans pointed out that

> The *filioque* is vitally connected with the advance of the Western church towards a strong anthropology (in connection with the doctrine of sin and grace), while the Eastern stopped in a weak Pelagian and synergistic view, crude and undeveloped. The procession

---

4. Schaff, *History of the Christian Church,* III, 688f.

only *de Patre per Filium* would put the *church* at arm's length, so to speak, from God; that is, beyond Christ, off at an extreme, or at one side of the kingdom of divine life, rather than in the centre and bosom of that kingdom, where all things are hers. The *filioque* puts the church, which is the temple and organ of the Holy Ghost in the work of redemption, rather *between* the Father and the Son, partaking of their own fellowship, according to the great intercessory prayer of Christ Himself. It places the church in the meeting-point, or the living circuit of the interplay, of grace and nature, of the divine and the human; thus giving scope for a strong doctrine of both nature and grace, and to a strong doctrine also of the church itself.[5]

Because of subordinationism, the development of the state was furthered in the East; because of this anti-subordination, the development of the church became possible in the West, and both the high doctrine of the church of medieval Europe and the Reformation are products of this orthodox, antisubordinationist trinitarianism. The revealed order and the natural order are both directly and fully placed under the Trinity; church and state are ministries of God, alike responsible to Him whose decree governs all things. The state is the ministry of justice, and the church is the ministry of the word and the sacraments; both are alike ordained by the Trinity and are under the triune God. God and Christ are not maintaining competing orders, as subordinationism at best implied, with the order of God ostensibly the superior one. Rather, the triune God alone has universal jurisdiction; to church and state, in their respective areas of justice and of the word and sacraments, God has given limited and subordinate authority. In all things they are subject to Him. As Gelasius I (492-496), pope and saint of the Church of Rome, declared to the emperor:

> There are two powers who have sovereign rule over the world: the spiritual and the temporal authority: the sacred authority of the bishops is so much greater, as on the day of judgment they must render an account of the actions of kings. You know, magnaminous emperor, that your dignity surpasses that of other princes of the earth: nevertheless, you are obliged to submit to the power of the ministers in sacred things, for it is to them you address yourself to know what are the sources of your safety, and the rules which you ought to follow in receiving the sacraments, and in disposing of religious things. The bishops persuade the people that God has given you a sovereign power over temporal things, and they cause them to submit to your laws. In return, you should obey, with entire submission, those who are destined to distribute to you the holy sacraments. If the faithful ought blindly to follow the orders of bishops who acquit themselves worthily in their functions, so much the more ought they to receive the decree of the pontiff of Rome, whom God has established as the first of his bishops, and whom the Church has always recognised as its supreme chief. [6]

---

5. *Ibid.*, III, 689n.

Here, in an early and faulty form, is the first major formulation of the concept of sphere sovereignty, or sphere law, which came into its own with Calvinism, and, in particular, with Abraham Kuyper. According to this concept, whose origins are in the Old Testament, God has established laws for the various spheres of creation, and these law-spheres are coordinate. Universal jurisdiction belongs to none of the many spheres but to the triune God alone. Neither church, state, school, or any other sphere can claim universal jurisdiction validly, although the claims have been asserted, because sovereignty and dominion belong to God alone.

Anti-subordinationism also made the Reformation doctrine of justification inevitable. Subordinationism gave primacy to nature, and hence to the natural ability of man. As a result, man becomes in effect his own savior, and grace is cooperating grace, not prevenient. If the Holy Ghost proceeds only from the Father, then the Holy Ghost, in a system which accords primacy to nature, becomes absorbed into nature. It becomes the act of nature, a charismatic act, but essentially a natural act, because the charism is either naturalized or made an appendage to nature. An example of this is the Russian saint, St. Seraphim, "ascetic, contemplative and Pneumatophore." St. Seraphim "considered that the chief aim of a Christian is to 'acquire' the Holy Ghost."[7] The Holy Ghost in such thinking is an asset which can be acquired by human activity in its natural evolvement upward. As S. Bulgakov said, "Man is the logos of the world, and through him the world thinks and learns to know itself." The world works upward; nature's upward reach is this religious faith. "Man is a microcosm; he unites within himself the world; humanity contains the image of the world; it is the *eikon of eikons,* for it is the image of God."[8] The world of nature and God are virtually identified here. "The image of the world" and "the image of God" are correlative terms for Bulgakov. The work of the Holy Ghost is to further the work of man's ascent into deification. "The Orthodox Faith sees in the Church, that is, the concrete historical Church, the concentration of the theanthropic process."[9] The state is man's true order, and the church is the concentrated area in which the social process of deification, the theanthropic process, occurs, where humanity and the state ascend upwards. The kenotic Christ of Eastern thought abandons His deity in the world in order to lead man, by His union and example, into the path of deification. The Russian liturgy declares of Christ, "Thou hast become poor like us, and has deified the earthly by thy union with it."[10] These are natural conclusions from the

[6] M'Clintock and Strong, III, 765.

[7] Nadejda Gorodetzky, *The Humiliated Christ in Modern Russian Thought* (London: SPCK, 1938), 99n.

[8] S. Bulgakov, "Religion and Art," in E. L. Mascall, editor, *The Church of God, An Anglo-Russian Symposium* (London: SPCK, 1934), 180f.

[9] G. P. Fedotov, "Orthodoxy and Historical Criticism," in Mascall, 97.

naturalization of the Holy Ghost. Whereas the opposition of the Eastern Church to the *Filioque* was originally primarily technical, i.e., the addition was made without a general council, and secondarily theological, it is now essentially theological. One Greek Orthodox theologian, Rhosse, states, "It is not only technically illegal and illegitimate, but essentially wrong .... Even as a theological opinion it is vicious and inadmissible."[11] This is strong language, to call the *Filioque* "vicious." And why "inadmissible"? Mesalora has told us: "One thing is evident — there is but one principle or source in the Godhead .... To this the Western addition of the *Filioque is* diametrically opposed .... The belief in one single principle in the Godhead is demanded by a logical conception of the Triune God."[12]

What is explicit and implicit in Mesalora's statement? *First,* Mesalora, and the Greek Orthodox Church, is formally trinitarian; "the Triune God" is affirmed formally. *Second,* it is held that "there is but one principle or source in the Godhead," and also that "one single principle in the Godhead is demanded by a logical conception of the Triune God." *Third,* this "one principle," "this single principle," is identified with God the Father. Any "logical conception of the Triune God" requires the inclusion of the entire Trinity in the activities of the Trinity; the economy of the Trinity may variously involve the three persons, but the great work of St. Augustine was to call attention to the equal work of the entire Trinity in creation, redemption, and providence. "Functions and acts, like the theophanies in the Old Testament, which had been ascribed to the Son were attributed by Augustine to the whole Trinity. (De Trinitate, L. 11, 9-18) By him the numerical unity of the persons in respect of substance was unequivocally taught."[13] To eliminate the Son from the procession of the Holy Ghost was not only Biblically unsound but philosophically unitarian in implication. The Kenosis of the Son was transferred from time, where it was wrongly asserted, to eternity as well. God the Son was emptied of His Godhead, and God the Father made the "single principle in the Godhead" to the exclusion of the Son. *Fourth,* the position subordinated also the Holy Ghost, since God was seen as the principle figure. In the Augustinian view, the act of procession involves without subordination all three persons of the Trinity; the Holy Ghost is economically given a different role than the Father and the Son, but the authority, sovereignty, power, and glory remain the same, in essence and in act.

This anti-subordinationism of the West led to the Reformation. Augustine's trinitarianism meant, as has been noted, his Biblical view of

---

[10] Nicholas Arseniev, *We Beheld His Glory* (London: SPCK, 1937), 124.

[11] Frank Gavin, *Some Aspects of Contemporary Greek Orthodox Thought* (Milwaukee: Morehouse, 1923), 126f.

[12] *Ibid.,* 126.

[13] Fisher, *History of Christian Doctrine*, 146f.

grace and sin. Subordinationism made nature sovereign, but grace cannot be sovereign if nature is sovereign. The continual eruption of the doctrine of grace, and of predestination, in the Western Church was due to its orthodox trinitarianism. The faith having not been compromised at this crucial point in the liturgical confessions, the resistance to false doctrine would not die, and revolt erupted repeatedly in assertion of sovereign grace.

In 1875, in Bonn, Germany, a synod or "Union Conference" of Old Catholic, Eastern, and Anglican Churches met for five days, beginning on August 12. The meeting adopted certain resolutions whose basic purpose was to bring closer union between the various churches, so that the element of peace-making was a major factor in the deliberations, rather than a forthright defense of the faith. The resolutions declared:

Preliminary Resolutions

1. We agree together in receiving the ecumenical symbols and the doctrinal decisions of the ancient undivided Church.

2. We agree together in acknowledging that the addition of the *Filioque* to the Creed did not take place in an ecclesiastically regular manner.

3. We acknowledged on all sides the representation of the doctrine of the Holy Ghost, as it is set forth by the Fathers of the undivided Church.

4. We reject every proposition and every method of expression in which in any way the acknowledgment of two principles of *arche* and *aitai* in the Trinity may be contained.

On The Procession of the Holy Ghost

We accept the teaching of St. John of Damascus respecting the Holy Ghost, as the same is expressed in the following paragraphs, in the sense of the teaching of the ancient undivided Church.

1. The Holy Ghost goes forth out of the Father as the Beginning, the Cause, the Source of the Godhead.

2. The Holy Ghost goes not forth out of the Son, because there is in the Godhead but one Beginning, one Cause, through which all that is in the Godhead is produced.

3. The Holy Ghost goes forth out of the Father through the Son.

4. The Holy Ghost is the Image of the Son, who is the Image of the Father, going forth out of the Father and resting in the Son as the force beaming forth from Him.

5. The Holy Ghost is the personal Production out of the Father, belonging to the Son, but not out of the Son, because He is the Spirit of the Mouth of the Godhead, which speaks forth the Word.

6. The Holy Ghost forms the mediation between the Father and the Son, and is bound together to the Father through the Son.[14]

Apart from its plain intent at compromise, this statement carries the amazing premise that only those symbols and doctrines are binding on the churches which were a product "of the ancient undivided church," i.e., of the first six, or, some would say, seven councils. This premise has been often asserted, but no branch of the church has ever regarded such a limitation as valid for itself. Moreover, the premise by passes the authority of the Scriptures in favor of the authority of the councils. This is implicit humanism, in that it asserts that, if an undivided council meets again, it can legitimately and without error define the faith. It is simply the substitution of conciliar infallibility for papal infallibility. In either case, it is human authority, not the word of God which is determinative. Moreover, the third of the "Preliminary Resolutions" is nonsense. The Nicene fathers did not give assent to any Arian subordinationism such as the "Union Conference" did, and Augustine certainly gave a strong testimony for the Procession from the Son. What the Conference marked, rather than any significant contribution to doctrinal development, was doctrinal compromise and reviving Arianism. The subsequent history of the churches involved gives further evidence of their departure from orthodoxy.

The reason for the cavalier compromise of the Conference was due to its theological apostasy. In 1861, Stanley could write of the doctrine of double procession, "It is an excellent specimen of the race of 'extinct controversies.'" After a thousand years of controversy, Stanley said, "now the whole question is laid completely to rest. In the West it is never seriously discussed. In the East it is remembered, and will never, perhaps, be forgotten; but it is more as a point of honor than of faith."[15]

When a controversy is based on real and fundamental issues, the principles involved never become extinct, but the men who neglect those principles do.

And this extinction faces many Western Churches. In 1967, the Episcopal Church of the United States, in its trial liturgy for communion, turned its back on the West. The Nicene Creed was altered to conform to Eastern usage: "We believe," and the procession of the Holy Spirit was limited to the Father, the *Filioque* clause being dropped.[16] From a personal, individual confession, the new liturgy went to a collective confession. The believer was no longer tied to the faith confessed: it was a collective

---

[14.] M'Clintock and Strong, *op. cit.*, VIII, 611.

[15.] Arthur Penrhyn Stanley, *Lectures on the History of the Eastern Church* (New York: Scribner, 1865), 142f.

[16.] *The Liturgy of the Lord's Supper* (The Church Pension Fund, New York, 1967), 7f.

affirmation rather than a personal witness made basic to the life of the person and the person's community of faith.

Chapter Twelve

Canon Law

The term "canon law" has an unpleasant sound in modern ears: it connotes the "tyranny" of the church, the middle ages, oppression, and much else of the same ilk. In truth, however, the concept of canon law means liberty.

It is often assumed that Calvin was a strong enemy of canon law. In the *Institutes IV,* x, Calvin dealt with "The Power of Legislation, in Which the Pope and His Adherents Have Most Cruelly Tyrannized Over the Minds, and Tortured the Bodies of Men." But Calvin did not have true canon law in mind but the perversions of it: "Whatever edicts have been issued by men respecting the worship of God, independently of his word, it has been customary to call human *tradition.*"[1] Of "human laws" i.e., laws having no warrant in the word of God, Calvin said, "If they are designed to introduce any scruple into our minds, as though the observance of them were essentially necessary, we assert, that they are unreasonable impositions on the conscience. For our consciences have to do, not with men, but with God alone."[2] Man has no need to add to God's law, because "Every thing pertaining to the perfect rule of a holy life, the Lord has comprehended in his law, so that there remains nothing for men to add to that summary."[3] The "sole legislator" is God, and men cannot lawfully assume this honor to themselves.[4]

[1.] *Institutes,* Bk. IV, ch. x, i.
[2.] *Ibid.,* IV, x, v.
[3.] *Ibid.,* IV, x, vii.
[4.] *Ibid.,* IV, x, viii, cf. William Cunningham: *Historical Theology,* vol. I, (London: Banner of Truth Trust, 1960 [1862]), 438.

Calvin's hostility was not to canon law as such but to the abuses of it. Calvin himself was simply trying to restore the rule of true canon law. Canon law in its true sense means not only the liberty of the church but the liberty of man and society.

To understand the implications of canon law, it is necessary to realize that ancient society was unitary, and it had a single, visible, human sovereignty. It was totalitarian in practice and in faith. A visible 'divine' authority governed the whole of life and admitted the existence of no independent order. For the ancient state, the uncontrolled was the enemy, and the controlled was the subject. Neither man nor any of his activities and institutions possessed any free, uncontrolled, or independent domain wherein the state had no jurisdiction. The sovereignty of the state meant that man was the creature of the state and entirely its subject.

But Biblical faith asserted instead the sovereignty of God and the ultimacy of His decree and law, so that man, the state, and every institution were under God and His law. Instead of the sovereign state providing the overall shelter for all things, the sovereign God is that over-lord, and all of man's institutions are directly under God and His word. Instead of a mediatorial state, Christ is man's mediator. The Bible provides a legal mandate for the institutions, and the state is made the ministry of justice, and the church the ministry of the word and the sacraments. The family is under God's law, as is agriculture, commerce, science, education, and all things else. Neither the church, nor the state, nor any other institution has a legitimate overall power of control. But the state in antiquity, and again today, has played the overall role of god, the sovereign over every realm and with basic and ultimate power over every realm. The state can permit or grant to its children or creatures certain privileges, but it cannot tolerate their denial of its sovereign authority. For the church therefore to issue canons placing Christians under the canons of Christ, under the laws of God was a denial of the sovereignty of the state and of its canons. It was a shattering of the concept of the totalitarian unitary state.

Calvin had no desire to destroy canon law, therefore, but rather to restore the true canon or rule, the word of God, to Geneva. The independence of the church required it. Political absolutism, however, then as now, has been hostile to canon law. Instead of the multiple law orders, and multiple variety of courts, which characterized the era of Christian feudalism, absolutism in the state has worked steadily to reduce all human society to one law-order, the state. Every other realm must be subjected to the state rather than to God: the church, economics, science, education, agriculture, the arts, all things are made aspects of the life of the state (rather than of man under God) and therefore under the government of the state. The supposition of the state in its absolutism is twofold. *First*, by asserting overall sovereignty and jurisdiction, the state is usurping the power and prerogative of God. The state makes itself the ultimate creator and lawgiver rather than God. *Second,* the state declares itself to be the true man as well as the true god. Every God-given aspect of the life of man, the state declares both to be its creation and also an aspect of its life. When the states makes religion, economics, science, education, agriculture, the arts, and all other law spheres aspects of its life, it is denying that it is one among many law spheres in which man operates and claims instead to be the overall governor of the law spheres, and also the state claims to be the true man for whom these law spheres exist, to serve the state and to further its dominion. The state by this says in effect, the true man is the state, so that man is not truly man outside the state. This faith was common to antiquity.

The destruction of the concept of canon law is necessary for the success of totalitarianism. The state cannot rule absolutely unless it can reduce man to a single law sphere, the state, and deny valid jurisdiction to every other law sphere. This destruction has largely been accomplished, and, in every branch of the church, canon law is not only over-laid with human tradition but is also regarded as a relic of the past. Man's true law sphere is seen as the state. In the political sphere man must realize the good life and true brotherhood, and the world's hope is in politics.

When Pope Paul VI, on Monday, October 4, 1965, appeared before the United Nations to make his plea for a peaceful world order, he in effect abandoned canon law, in that he saw, as the saving order, and man's true order, not the transcendental Kingdom of God, but an immanent and united world order. Speaking as "the Pontiff of Rome" and "the bearer of a message for all mankind," he said that this was his message: "We might call our message a ratification, a solemn moral ratification of this lofty institution," i.e., the United Nations.[5] Since the United Nations claims world-wide jurisdiction, and since the U.N. reduces all religions to a level of equality by prohibiting any discrimination with respect to creed, the pope's speech in effect declared that the true kingdom is the U.N.'s kingdom of man, and rather than defending Christ's declaration of the supremacy of His kingdom over all realms and institutions (John 19:11, Matt. 26:64), the pope reduced the kingdom Christ may possess to an adjunct of man's kingdom.

The social gospel is likewise a denial of canon law. It sees a one undivided realm, the state, as the true order of God and man. The state is given the overall jurisdiction and sovereignty over church, school, family, business, farming, and all things else which belongs only to God. The essential function of the social gospel is to render all things unto Caesar and nothing to God.

[5.] *The Tidings,* Los Angeles, October 8, 1965, 7.

True canon law is the application of the canon or rule of Scripture to the problems of life. Pelliccia said, of the word "canon," that "writers of Roman history used" the term "to describe a muster-roll of soldiers and their commissariat."[6] Truly Biblical canons are the muster-roll of defenders of the faith, protectors of the faithful, and applications of Scripture to the problems of the day. When canons are restricted to the formal polity of the church and say nothing concerning the application of doctrine to the problems of the world, the real function of the canon law is lost, and nothing but an ecclesiastical *Roberts' Rules of Order* remains.

When, for example, churches pass resolutions supporting civil violence, equalitarianism, community organization for picketing and demonstrations, they are clearly violating the Biblical law and are moving in terms of human traditions. A false canon or rule has then been applied to life, a canon other than the infallible word of God.[7]

The application of a valid canon is apparent in a measure taken in 1966 by a church in Wisconsin, unfortunately, however, destined to be neglected. The measure in question specified the problem and applied God's law to it:

> The Council of the Racine Christian Reformed Church overtures Classis Wisconsin to overture Synod:
>
> I. To reaffirm its decision as articulated in the Acts of Synod 1912 regarding Socialism, namely, that it is an error and a departure from our principles. (See Acts of Synod 1912, Art. 47, p. 38 which reads as follows: "The consistories shall take the same attitude toward such persons which they take over against all departures from our principles.")
>
> A. Formal ground: This decision has been buried in oblivion and most of our leaders are totally unfamiliar with it.
>
> B. Material grounds:
>
> 1. Socialism is in conflict with man being the image bearer of God, who as such is a responsible creature who is individually accountable to God. The Christian may not shun any facet of his personal and covenantal God-ordained responsibilities by shifting them to the state.
>
> 2. Socialism is in conflict with the First Commandment of the Moral Law in that it gives priority to the State above God as the supreme authority over man. God is the great benefactor and not the State. Socialism is the direct opposite of this making the State the distributor of wealth and regulator of life. Men are then forced by circumstance to look to the State rather than to

---

6. Alexius Aurelius Pelliccia, *The Polity of the Christian Church* (London: Masters, 1882 [1829]), 51.
7. See the Editorial "Re: Church Strikes and Boycotts," in *The Presbyterian Journal*, March 6, 1967, 14.

Divine Providence for the source of their daily material sustenance.

3. Socialism is in conflict with the Eighth Commandment of the Moral Law which insists upon the legitimacy of private property, forbids any form of stealing said property and demands of the individual faithful stewardship of such property.

4. Socialism is in conflict with the Tenth Commandment of the Moral Law which forbids all coveting of the neighbor's possessions and all notions of statist redistribution of wealth which is the trumpeting position of Socialism.

5. Socialism advances the idea of centralization of power which is the very purpose of Satan and of both the beasts out of the sea and the earth as set forth in Revelation 13. Further, it advocates "one world" which will certainly be under the anti-christ which we may not advocate or support in any degree or form.

II. To do its utmost to disseminate the knowledge of this Biblical position with grounds throughout the denomination in the way that Synod believes to be most effective.

Grounds:

1. Many Christian Reformed people are unaware of our ecclesiastical stand which as stated above has been largely ignored and buried with the passage of time.

2. The gradual drift toward Socialism and state welfarism in the United States and Canada has rendered us unconsciously vulnerable to the departure from these Biblical principles.

3. The current accelerated adoption of socialist and state welfarist measures in the United States and Canada makes it a matter of paramount importance that our people be aware of our denominational position and see Socialism for what it is, a diabolical evil.

III. To require of all our ministers, professors, teachers and denominational employees and all in positions of leadership that they be sincerely committed to our position, that they strictly adhere to this position in their church life and private conduct and that they faithfully champion this position and warn our constituency against all departures therefrom.

Grounds:

1. They have a great influence upon the membership of the Christian Reformed denomination.

2. They play a strategic role in shaping and molding the future thinking of the membership of our denomination by virtue of the great influence which they exert upon our covenant youth.

3. They function as an important segment of the total Christian witness which God requires our denomination to bear in this vale of darkness.

In such a statement, it is the word of God which provides the canon, not humanism, Greek philosophy, or some other principle. Dooyeweerd has shown how Roman legal concepts essentially altered the medieval church's concept of canon law.[8] From a Biblically informed perspective, all things are subject to the laws of God. Every area of law is a sphere which is separate from others, so that a state has no right to interfere in the sphere of the church, or, for example, in the arithmetical sphere. The laws of mathematics, as well as the laws of the church and of the state, are alike of God's creating, and no one sphere can arrogate to itself God's creative power and overall sovereignty. For the state to claim that it can rule over mathematics, the church, or economics, is to violate its mandate and to ensure social disaster. While the spheres have an interdependence, in that not one is in any sense complete in itself, or a living world by itself, this interdependence rests on their common creation by God to provide a world of possible liberty for man. Life is not numerics, nor is it the state, school, church, economics, science, or any one of the other spheres, and for one law sphere to attempt to provide the sovereignty and unity over all is to reduce man into slavery to a limited aspect of life.

For man to be free, therefore, the canon law had to be applied as a regulative principle to limit man in his every sphere and relation. Canon law ceases to be truly canonical when it fails to place these limitations on man in his total activity. The law then has a canon other than Scripture.

[8.] Herman Dooyeweerd, *A New Critique of Theoretical Thought*, III, (Philadelphia: Presbyterian and Reformed Publishing Company, 1957), 233ff.

Chapter Thirteen

Constantinople III:
The Abolition of God

The Sixth Ecumenical Council, the Third Council of Constantinople, met in 680-681. It is the last of the councils acknowledged by the Eastern and Western churches alike, and orthodox Protestantism as well. The seventh Ecumenical Council, the second Council of Nicea, 787, is not recognized by Protestants, because of its defence of images.

The problem again was humanistic heresy. For some, this statement is guilty of reductionism, of over-simplification; they are insistent on seeing good faith on all sides, but with intellectual misunderstandings governing some or all of the participating theologians and bishops. The problem, we are told, was a complex one; it was compounded by the differences of meaning created by Greek and Latin terms; it was further compounded by rather dubious psychologies, derived from the ancient world, which governed the conciliar definitions of Christ. We cannot therefore too readily agree with the conciliar definitions of orthodoxy and heresy, it is suggested.

The answer to this is that in terms of Biblical faith man's basic problem is not inadequate knowledge but sin. Man sinned deliberately and wilfully against God: he sought to make himself rather than God the ultimate source of truth and law, the basic point and frame of reference. As Van Til has written, "as a sinner man seeks to make himself, instead of God, the ultimate aim as well as the ultimate standard in life." Moreover, Van Til has added, "Here then is the heart of the matter: in Adam man has set aside the law of his Creator and therewith has become a law to himself. He will be subject to none but himself. He seeks to be autonomous. He knows that he is a creature and ought to be subject to the law of his Creator." But man revolts against this. "He makes himself the final reference point in all predication."[1] Sinful man is not neutral; his knowledge is geared to one end, to establish his own autonomy. The only relationship he will tolerate with God is a democratic one: on that Arminian basis, with man casting the deciding vote against God and Satan by voting for himself, man finds God tolerable. It is ridiculous to assume that there is anything neutral about man as he approaches Christ. Every non-neutral fiber of sinful man's being is aquiver as he approaches Christ and seeks either to eliminate Christ or to integrate him into his system.

The Third Council of Constantinople met to deal with monothelism, an attempt to integrate Jesus Christ into an implicitly non-Christian perspective. Monothelism conceded the victory to Chalcedon; it accepted as necessary to religious respectability the doctrine of the two natures, but it insisted that Christ was subject to one will only, the human will being either merged into the divine or absorbed by it. This doctrine represented an attempt by the emperor Heraclius to unite the Eutychians and Monophysites with the orthodox and bring religious unity to the empire. In the course of its history, Monothelism gained many prominent advocates. Sergius, patriarch of Constantinople, did the theological work for Heraclius and his successors, Pyrrhus, Paul, and Peter continued it. Honorius, pope of Rome, also advocated it. Other prominent Monothelite churchmen were Theodorus of Pharan, Cyrus of Alexandria, Macarius of Antioch, and Stephen, his disciple; all were condemned by name at the sixth council. Sophronius, a Palestinian monk, was early a leader in the struggle against Monothelism. Martin I, pope of Rome, also led in the battle against the heresy and was banished to the Crimea by the emperor. When Pope Martin stood before the civil authorities in Constantinople on trial, he was denied the right to call attention to the heresies of the Monothelites: "Don't mix here anything about the faith, you are on trial for high-treason. We, too, are Christians and orthodox." Martin replied, "Would to God you were! But even on this point I shall testify against you, on the day of that dreadful judgment." A Greek abbot, Maximus, was also prominent in the battle against Monothelism, and for this lie was scourged and had his right hand and his tongue cut off by the emperor, dying soon thereafter on August 13, 662. St. Maximus had earlier been private secretary to Heraclius before entering the church. Maximus had been responsible for the Lateran synod of 649 called by Martin I and had written its condemnation of Monothelism. Emperor Constans II had his right hand and tongue publicly cut off to prevent further writing and speaking for the faith by Maximus, who rejected every flattering and threatening effort to silence him.

[1.] Cornelius Van Til, *A Christian Theory of Knowledge* (Philadelphia: Westminster Theological Seminary, 1954), 27, 26.

The men who defended the faith were aware of the perils. They were not immune from the fear of man, but they were even more subject to the fear of God. In the midst of each council was placed the Holy Gospels, to indicate not only the authority of Scripture but the presence of Jesus Christ as the sovereign head of every true council and Christian gathering. The intense earnestness of the delegates, and their hostility to the slightest deviation from the faith rested on the belief that heresy represented not a lack of understanding but a deliberate attempt to subvert and destroy the faith, to attack and abolish God. The Enlightenment has so warped man's perspective that men believe salvation is knowledge, and sin is therefore ignorance; the will of man is therefore governed by his mind and the information available to the mind. But this psychology is alien to Biblical faith: man's sinful nature governs his mind and will and bends them to its purposes. Man's problem is not ignorance but sin, not a lack of knowledge but a will to abolish God from the world. The unregenerate man is governed by the desire to be his own god and to will the death of God.

God can be abolished from philosophical consideration by variations of three ways. *First,* there can be an outright denial of God; it can be held that God does not exist, and that the concept is unnecessary.

Second, instead of a denial of God, the denial of man can be used to abolish God. If man be reduced to mere sensations, or an animal whose mental processes are worthless, man cannot know God because by definition he can know nothing. To deny God means also to deny man, and hence these two approaches go hand in hand.[2] Charles Darwin relied on this denial of man. He did not deny that God seemed to be an inescapable concept and reality, that it was not possible to explain the world apart from Him, but, rather than acknowledge God, Darwin denied man and any validity to man's thinking and mind. His own admission of this fact is quite revelatory of his unwillingness to accept any thinking which led to God. In a letter to W. Graham, of July 3, 1881, Darwin told him:

> Nevertheless you have expressed my inward conviction, though far more vividly and clearly than I could have done, that the Universe is not the result of chance. But then with me the horrid doubt always arises whether the conviction of man's mind, which has been developed from the mind of the lower animals, are of any value or at all trustworthy. Would any one trust in the convictions of a monkey's mind, if there are any convictions in such a mind?[3]

Darwin did *not* conclude, from this untrustworthiness of man's mind, that his own scientific hypotheses were untrustworthy. It did not occur to him

---

[2.] See R. J. Rushdoony, *By What Standard?* (Philadelphia: Presbyterian and Reformed Publishing Company, 1958, 1965).

[3.] Francis Darwin, editor, *The Life and Letters of Charles Darwin,* vol. I (New York: Basic Books, 1959), 285.

to invalidate science and evolution by this view of man: it was only used against God. This is, of course, childish thinking but it is even more clearly sinful thinking.

Third, God can be denied by an affirmation of God which leaves Him as an adjunct of man, or the captive of man. God can be then praised fulsomely, but the glory and the power are quietly transferred to man.

The Monothelites were in effect abolishing God by an affirmation which introduced humanity into the Godhead and made man one with God, so that Christianity was in effect nullified. They did this in the name of Christianity, but the consequences were humanistic atrophy.

At the Sixth Council, the letter of Pope Agatho was an important statement of the case against Monothelism. Agatho strongly affirmed the position of Chalcedon:

> But when we make a confession concerning one of the same three Persons of that Holy Trinity, of the Son of God, or God the Word, and of the mystery of his adorable dispensation according to the flesh, we assert that all things are double in the one and the same our Lord and Saviour Jesus Christ according to the Evangelical tradition, that is to say, we confess his two Natures, to wit the divine and the human, of which and in which he, even after the wonderful and inseparable union, subsists. And we confess that each of his natures has its own natural propriety, and that the divine has all things that are divine, without any sin. And we recognize that each one (of the two natures) of the one and the same incarnated, that is, humanated (*humanati*) Word of God is in him unconfusedly, inseparably and unchangeably, intelligence alone discerning a unity, to avoid the error of confusion. For we equally detest the blasphemy of division and of co-mixture. For when we confess two natures and two natural wills, and two natural operations in our one Lord Jesus Christ, we do not assert that they are contrary or opposed one to the other (as those who err from the path of truth and accuse the apostolic tradition of doing ...).[4]

For Hellenism, the confusion and co-mixture were natural and necessary; hence its humanism. Matter represented the world of inchoate being, whereas form represented divine being, and the universe is the product of the co-mixture of the two. The Biblical perspective of created being and the uncreated and creating being of God was totally alien to Hellenism. Greek philosophy could understand a total co-mixture and confusion, it could not understand incarnation. As a result, as it approached the doctrine of the incarnation, it tried to force it into the mold of co-mixture and confusion as the logically necessary step. Christ as the supreme form must of necessity be co-mingled with matter to provide the logical structure or logos for all men and all philosophy. The Monophysites were thus insistent on a single nature: here in this one nature a co-mingling and confusion took place. But

---

4. Percival, *Decrees and Canons*, 330f.

Chalcedon and Constantinople II blocked this from consideration by declaring it to be heresy. Logically, the Hellenic, and especially the neoplatonic tradition, required the confusion and co-mixture, and so it reappeared as Monothelism, the doctrine of two natures but one will. Had this doctrine triumphed, the church would either have stagnated or become a new channel for the redevelopment of Hellenism. Both things happened, but the condemnation of Monothelism made possible the survival of orthodoxy.

From the Hellenic perspective, man's salvation involves ascent on the scale of being into deification. Man progressively must forsake the world of matter for the world of form, i.e., spirit. Wherever Hellenism prevailed, there asceticism and monasticism prevailed. In the Western Church, asceticism and monasticism, after an early triumph, declined, and they are increasingly becoming relics rather than the central force. In the Monophysite churches, the monastic orders control all higher offices because they represented by definition the higher truth and power of the church.

The Definition of Faith of the council spoke of the flesh and will of Christ's humanity as "deified," but by this it meant that, under the doctrine of economic appropriations the human flesh and will were totally governed by the divine nature and will and were thus one without confusion with the deity.[5] It was, the Definition said, an "economic conversation." After reviewing the conclusions of the five previous councils, the Definition declared:

> Defining all this we likewise declare that in him are two natural wills and two natural operations indivisibly, inconvertibly, inseparably, inconfusedly, according to the teaching of the holy Fathers.
>
> And these two natural wills are not contrary the one to the other (God forbid!) as the impious heretics assert, but his human will follows and that not as resisting and reluctant, but rather as subject to his divine and omnipotent will....
>
> We glorify two natural operations indivisibly, immutably, inconfusedly, inseparably in the same our Lord Jesus Christ our true God, that is to say a divine operation and a human operation, according to the divine preacher Leo, who most distinctly asserts as follows: "For each form does in communion with the other what pertains properly to it, the Word, namely, doing that which pertains to the Word, and the flesh that which pertains to the flesh."
>
> For we will not admit one natural operation in God and in the creature, as we will not exalt into the divine essence what is created,

---

5. On this point see John of Damascus, *Exposition of the Orthodox Faith,* Chapter XVII.

nor will we bring down the glory of the divine nature to the place suited to the creature.

> We recognize the miracles and the sufferings as of one and the same (Person), but of one or of the other nature of which he is and in which he exists, as Cyril admirably says. Preserving therefore the inconfusedness and indivisibility, we make briefly this whole confession, believing our Lord Jesus Christ to be one of the Trinity and after the incarnation our true God, we say that his two natures shone forth in his one subsistence in which he both performed the miracles and endured the sufferings through the whole of his economic conversation, and that not in appearance only but in very deed, and this by reason of the difference of nature which must be recognized in the same Person, for although joined together yet each nature wills and does the things proper to it and that indivisibly and inconfusedly. Wherefore we confess two wills and two operations, concurring most fitly in him for the salvation of the human race.[6]

Monothelism, the council said plainly, did two things: *first*, it exalted "into the divine essence what is created," and, *second*, it brought "down the glory of the divine nature to the place suited to the creature." Against this humanistic confusion the council was adamant.

In explaining their Definition to the emperor, the council, declaring that Satan "has raised up the very ministers of Christ against him," explained its decision in the Prosphoneticus:

> And as we recognize two natures, also we recognize two natural wills and two natural operations. For we dare not say that either of the natures which are in Christ in his incarnation is without a will and operation: lest in taking away the properties of those natures, we likewise take away the natures of which they are the properties. For we neither deny the natural will of his humanity, or its natural operation: lest we also deny what is the chief thing of the dispensation for our salvation, and lest we attribute passions to the Godhead ....

> Therefore we declare that in him there are two natural wills and two natural operations, proceeding commonly and without division ....[7]

The Monothelites, by absorbing the human will into the divine will, opened the door for the similar absorption of the wills of all redeemed men into the divine will, so that sanctification became progressive deification. Neander observed, concerning this:

> The question concerning the relations of the human and the divine will to each other in Christ was connected also in a way that deserves notice, with the question respecting the relation of the human to the divine will in the redeemed in their state of perfection. At least, many among the Monothelites supposed the final result of the perfect development of the divine life in believers would be in them, as in the

---

6. Percival, 345f.
7. *Ibid.*, 347.

case of Christ, a total absorption of the human will in God's will; so that in all, there would be a subjective, as well as objective identity of will which, consistently carried out, would lead to the pantheistic notion of an entire absorption of all individuality of existence in the one original spirit. Maximus well understood this, and contended earnestly against the notion.[8]

In 711, a Monothelite, Philippicus or Bardanes became emperor, and the persecution of orthodoxy was resumed for two years, until Anastasius II dethroned him and ended the persecution.

John of Damascus (680-764) was the last Eastern theologian to give the issue significant attention. In his "Exposition of the Orthodox Faith," John made it clear that any other than the orthodox position was a denial of the incarnation:

> But if those who declare that Christ has only one nature should say also that that nature is a simple one, they must admit either that He is God pure and simple, and thus reduce the incarnation to a mere pretence, or that He is only man, according to Nestorius. And how then about His being "perfect in divinity and perfect in humanity?" And when can Christ be said to be of two natures, if they hold that He is of one composite nature after the union? For it is surely clear to every one that before the union Christ's nature was one.[9]

The Third Council of Constantinople made it clear that the incarnation was not a pretence: it was real. The council made it equally clear that the ostensible Christianity of the Monothelites was a pretence: it was a humanism which in effect abolished God, and no theologian could miss its implications. They, for their part, declared: "we will not exalt into the divine essence what is created, nor will we bring down the glory of the divine nature to the place suited to the creature." The position of the Monothelites was a deadly one, and, despite the earnestness of some of its humble believers at some points in the history of Monothelites as well as the Monophysites, the position was one of sterility and decay. It was not orthodox Christianity, and it had none of the vigor of Biblical faith. It was not an honest and open humanism, and thus it could not develop in terms of its real meaning. Its basic vigor was in hostility, and its destiny has been decay and death.

[8.] Augustus Neander, *General History of the Christian Religion and Church,* vol. III (Boston: Crocker & Brewster, 1855), 183.
[9.] John of Damascus, "Exposition of the Orthodox Faith" chapt. III, in *Nicene and Post-Nicene Fathers,* Series Two, vol. IX, 47.

Chapter Fourteen

Iconodulism

The Sixth Ecumenical Council, the Third Council of Constantinople, was held in 680-681. A little more than a century later, the Seventh Ecumenical Council, the Second Council of Nicea, was held in 787. Although, apart from two papal legates sent from Rome, this seventh council was limited to the Eastern Church, Rome recognized it as ecumenical, and only the Gallican Church in the West withheld recognition for a time. In the century between the sixth and seventh councils, the theological climate had changed; the change had long been in process, but now it commanded the church.

Neoplatonisim was now dominant as the philosophy undergirding theology, monasticism, ecclesiology, and political science. For neoplatonism, the universe is a vast scale of being, from brute matter to pure and divine spirit. Man can *look* upward or downward, and he can *move* upward or downward on the scale of being. He can develop the divinity of his soul or spirit by ascending upwards towards pure spirit, or he can debase that spark of divinity by turning to the world of sensations and matter. Rational knowledge has as its goal the realities or Ideas of being, and the realm of Ideas is Mind or the Divine. The goal of knowledge is mystical union with the One, the World-Soul. The influence of neoplatonism, especially through Plotinus, was extensive on Arab thought as well as on Jewish and Christian thinkers.

Monasticism was applied neoplatonism. It called for an ascent in the scale of being by a forsaking of the material for the spiritual world. The idea that spiritual living was somehow superior to material living had no ground in

123

Biblical thought. For the Bible, both body and soul were created wholly good by God, and both are alike totally depraved by virtue of the fall of man; body and soul, the whole man, are involved in man's attempt to be as God. Both body and soul are alike redeemed in Jesus Christ and have a glorious destiny in Him. Monasticism veered from monism to a semi-Manichaeanism. In monism, all being is one being, the difference being that some forms, such as matter, represent a thinness of being, and spirit represents a higher, purer more concentrated being. In semi-Manichaean-ism, spirit is good, matter evil, and true being is spirit, and false being is matter.

Neoplatonism infected both church and state. For ecclesiastical neoplatonism, the church, as the realm of spirit, represented the higher order, whereas the state, as the agency of the material world, represented a lower order. For political neoplatonism, the state represents the logos or structure of being. The state therefore is the highest manifestation of being in the material world, and its ruler is the representative of the Idea of being.

Set in a Christian context, with neoplatonism, both church and state saw themselves as continuations of the incarnation. Chalcedonian theology saw the gap between created being and God's uncreated being as bridged only in Jesus Christ, without confusion and without change. For neoplatonism, all being was seen as one being, and Jesus Christ was the leader in the process of ascent. In Jesus Christ the process of ascent came to open, institutional focus in history; the Idea had become flesh and was leading men into the same realization of the Idea, the open and full manifestation of the Idea in history as the means of overcoming history. The image or icon of the Idea manifested itself in the institution of the church or state. Man, according to the Bible, was created in the image of God; man was thus an icon of God. The image or icon of Christ could also be manifested in several ways, basically in carved and painted images, and in an institution.

The image was one aspect of the continuing incarnation. The saints were represented in icons as aspects of the incarnate Idea; even as they incarnated the Idea, so their icons incarnated them. The icons of saints were seen as sufficiently real to be introduced as sponsors at baptisms. It was held that some images had been made without human hands, that some, indeed, had been miraculously produced by Christ Himself.[1]

The emperor's image had been the subject too of extensive religious veneration. This veneration antedated the fall of Rome. The emperor's image was carried in religious processions and hailed with the cry, "Blessed is he that cometh in the name of the Lord." Churchmen were increasingly agreeable to this, and in 602 Pope Gregory I placed the images of the sinful

---

[1.] Augustus Neander, *General History of the Christian Religion and Church*, III, (Fifth American Edition, 1855), 201.

Emperor Phocas I in the Lateran. Statues of Constantine were adored and received sacrifices, candles, incense, and prostration.[2]

There were thus two institutional incarnations in the world, church and state, and in both East and West there was a struggle on the part of both to limit the extent of the incarnation in the other. The iconoclastic controversy was the form the struggle took in the East. Both sides were iconodules, venerators of icons; the imperial party simply became iconoclastic with reference to the church. As Ladner pointed out, the imperial party, with reference to the church, saw that narrowing the extension of Christ's government in the world widened the extension of the emperor's worship."[3] The iconoclastic controversy was a phase of a larger imperial program. As Finlay noted, "It embraces a long and violent struggle between the government and the people, the emperors seeking the central power by annihilating every local franchise, and even the right of private opinion, among their subjects .... The emperors wished to constitute themselves the fountains of ecclesiastical as completely as of civil legislation."[4] The undergirding philosophy of the struggle was Hellenism.[5] The first appearance of images in any relation to the church was among the Gnostic followers of Carpocrates, who called themselves Gnostics primarily. These Gnostics made religious use of "images of the philosophers of the world," i.e., of Pythagorus, Plato, Aristotle, and Christ and others.[6]

The image represented the continuity of being between heaven and earth. The true saint was a man who had transcended the limitations of matter to become a spiritual being. Neoplatonism made asceticism an intellectual and spiritual virtue, an ascent in being and hence an ascent in knowledge and virtue. Asceticism thus was assumed to be indicative of superiority. As Pickman observed, "It was the chosen weapon of the humanitarian. That is why before long a physician who did not become a monk lost his practice."[7]

[2.] Ernst H. Kantorowicz, "The 'King's Advent' and the Enigmatic Panels in the Doors of Santa Sabina," *The Art Bulletin*, December, 1944, vol. XXVI, no. 4, 207-231; E. Kantorowicz, "Ivories and Litanies," *Journal of the Warburg and Courtauld Institutes*, vol. 5, 1942, 56-81; E. Kantorowicz: *Laudes Regiae, A Study in Liturgical Acclamations and Mediaeval Ruler Worship* (Berkeley: University of California Press, 1946), 17n.7, 102, 110.
[3.] Gerhart B. Ladner, "Origin and Significance of the Byzantine Iconoclastic Controversy," in *Mediaeval Studies*, II, 1940 (New York: Sheed and Ward, 1940), 135.
[4.] George Finlay, *History of the Byzantine Empire From DCCXVI to MLVII* (London: J. M. Dent, 1906), 10.
[5.] See George Florovsky, "Origen, Eusebius, and the Iconoclastic Controversy," in *Church History*, June, 1950, vol. XIX, no. 2, 77-96.
[6.] Irenaeus, *Against Heresies*, Bk. I, ch. XXV, 6, in *Ante-Nicene Christian Library*, vol. V, Irenaeus vol. I, 96.
[7.] Edward Motley Pickman, *The Mind of Latin Christendom*, (London: Oxford, 1937), 457.

Both church and state claimed to be the true extension of the incarnation and therefore the only legitimate image bearers. For the church, the imperial icons represented idolatry. For the imperial party, the church's icons were idolatrous.

For the imperial party, the emperor was the true vicar of Christ. The gold coins of Byzantium most often bore the head of Christ crowned with the imperial diadem and robed in the emperor's garments. Laws were promulgated in the name of "The Lord Jesus Christ, Our Master." By the side of the imperial throne was another, empty save for the Gospel, before which men bowed: "It is the throne of Christ, our true Sovereign." The emperor was Christ present as Lord. The emperor's palace was thus a church in a real sense, with even the porter ordained as a priest. The throne was installed in an apse. "His receptions were not audiences, but revelations. He did not merely make an appearance, he manifested himself." His meals "were full of subtle allusions to the Last Supper." Since the entire meal was a religious ritual, no mistakes were permitted. Anyone who dropped a plate was decapitated, and "the guests who witnessed such a sacrilege must have their eyes put out." Any attempt to assassinate the emperor was a crime against God, although a successful attempt was then God's will. The emperor was absolute in his sovereignty, and "His power, theoretically universal, did not stop at the frontiers of the Empire. Like the Church and for the same reason, his sway was oecumenical."[8] Liudprand, in his *Antapodosis,* gives us a vivid picture of the pageantry and pomp of the emperor's audiences.[9] Gold was heavily used in Byzantium, with golden domes on the churches, and golden crosses. The emperor lived in a surrounding of gold, with his clothing interwoven with gold, because the Book of Revelation spoke of the heavenly Jerusalem as a city of gold.[10] The coronation of the emperor, as of Nicephorus, was the coronation of Christ, and "he emerged as the image of Christ himself."[11] The imperial party thus was wedded to the concept of the empire as the continuation of the incarnation, and the church simply an arm of the empire, and the emperor as the true vicar and representative of Christ.

The churchmen who opposed this position saw its implications. Theodore of Studium wrote, "Unless the Emperor be subject to the law, there are but two possible hypotheses: either he is God, for divinity alone transcends law; or nothing remains but anarchy and revolution."[12]

[8.] Rene Guerdan, *Byzantium, Its Triumphs and Tragedy* (New York: C. P. Putnam's Sons, 1957), 17-26.

[9.] F. A. Wright, translator, *The Works of Liudprand of Cremona* (London: Routledge, 1930), 207-212.

[10.] Guerdan, 45f.

[11.] *Ibid.,* 50f.

[12.] Charles Diehl, *Byzantium: Greatness and Decline* (New Brunswick, New Jersey: Rutgers University Press, 1957), 168.

Theodore championed the church's icons and held that there was divinity not only in the image but also in the artist. The artist poured forth his divinity in creating the image, even as God ostensibly poured forth His divinity into His creation. The defense by the church was thus equally neoplatonistic.

The iconoclastic emperors were heretical, and their background was largely Monophysite. The emperors who ended the iconoclastic controversy, and Constantine VI and Irene who called the Seventh Ecumenical Council, the Second Council of Nicea, 787, were ostensibly orthodox, but their decision left the state essentially unchanged; the church had merely retained the use of icons. It had not altered the position of the emperor or empire. Although the struggle did not end until February 19, 842, a day which came to be celebrated as the Feast of Orthodoxy, the decision of 787 largely prevailed. The comment of Percival is indicative of the essentials of the Council's action in 787:

> The council decreed that similar veneration and honour should be paid to the representations of the Lord and of the Saints as was accustomed to be paid to the "laurata" and tablets representing the Christian emperors, to wit, that they should be bowed to, and saluted with kisses, and attended with lights and the offering of incense. But the Council was most explicit in declaring that this was merely a veneration of honour and affection, such as can be given to the creature, and that under no circumstances could the adoration of divine worship be given to them but to God alone.[13]

Theodosius, one of the bishops at the Council, declared,

> For if the people go forth with lights and incense to meet the "laurata" and images of the Emperors when they are sent to cities or rural districts, they honour surely not the tablet covered over with wax, but the Emperor himself. How much more is it necessary that in the churches of Christ our God, the image of God our Saviour and of his spotless Mother and of all the holy and blessed fathers and ascetics should be painted?[14]

This statement indicates the nature of the final settlement. The conflict had been over the religious use of imperial icons versus the religious use of ecclesiastical icons, both institutions claiming to be the true extension of the incarnation. Now the designation of worship was withdrawn from the icons, and their use mutually permitted without disturbing the state's power or sovereignty. Near the end of Session I, "John, the most reverend bishop and legate of the Eastern high priests said: This heresy is the worst of all heresies. Woe to the iconoclasts! It is the worst of heresies, as it subverts the incarnation of our Saviour."[15] The incarnation, in this

---

[13.] Percival, *Decrees and Canons of the Seven Ecumenical Councils*, 526.
[14.] *Ibid.*, 535.
[15.] *Ibid.*

perspective, *required* continuation, and the icons were thus the continuation of the incarnation, and denial of the icons was thus subversion of the incarnation. This meant that two continuing incarnations were implicitly allowed, one in the state, the other in the church.

The iconoclastic "conciliabulum" held in Constantinople in 754 had condemned icons as a violation of Chalcedon and of all the six councils. This council called itself the Seventh Ecumenical Council, but it was later condemned as a mock council. No patriarch was present, nor any deputies from Rome, Alexandria, Antioch, or Jerusalem, but 338 Eastern bishops attended. This Council was called by Emperor Constantine Copronymus (Constantine V, 741-773), who had himself styled the Thirteenth Apostle by a subservient church synod. This council of 754 abolished all images and pictures from churches. The theological acumen of this council was in nearer conformity with the earlier councils and represented clearer thinking than did the later recognized council of 787. The council of 754 declared:

> After we had carefully examined their decrees under the guidance of the Holy Spirit, we found that the unlawful act of painting living creatures blasphemed the fundamental doctrine of our salvation — namely, the Incarnation of Christ, and contradicted the six holy Synods. These condemned Nestorius because he divided the one Son and Word of God into two sons, and on the other side, Arius, Dioscurus, Eutyches, and Severus, because they maintained a mingling of the two natures of the one Christ.

> Wherefore we thought it right, to shew forth with all accuracy, in our present definition the error of such as make and venerate these, for it is the unanimous doctrine of all the holy Fathers and of the six Ecumenical Synods, that no one may imagine any kind of separation or mingling in opposition to the unsearchable, unspeakable, and incomprehensible union of the two natures in the one hypostasis or person. What avails, then, the folly of the painter, who from sinful love of gain depicts that which should not be depicted — that is, with his polluted hands he tries to fashion that which should only be believed in the heart and confessed with the mouth? He makes an image and calls it Christ. The name Christ signifies *God and man.* Consequently it is an image of God and man, and consequently he has in his foolish mind, in his representation of the created flesh, depicted the Godhead which cannot be represented, and thus mingled what should not be mingled. Thus he is guilty of a double blasphemy — the one in making an image of the Godhead, and the other by mingling the Godhead and manhood. Those fall into the same blasphemy who venerate the image ....

> ...Whoever, then, makes an image of Christ, either depicts the Godhead which cannot be depicted, and mingles it with the manhood (like the Monophysites), or he represents the body of Christ as not made divine and separate and as a person apart, like the Nestorians.

The only admissible figure of the humanity of Christ, however, is bread and wine in the holy Supper. This and no other form, this and no other type, has he chosen to represent his incarnation. Bread he ordered to be brought, but not as a representation of the human form, so that idolatry might not arise. And as the body of Christ is made divine, so also this figure of the body of Christ, the bread, is made divine by the descent of the Holy Spirit; it becomes the divine body of Christ by the mediation of the priest who, separating the oblation from that which is common, sanctifies it.

...Christianity has rejected the whole of heathenism, and so not merely heathen sacrifices, but also the heathen worship of images.[16]

This statement indicates the awareness of the issues: the definition of Chalcedon undergirds all the councils, and it is heresy to confuse the two natures, as the iconodules did implicitly. But the point was still missed: the illustration that painting an image of Christ mingled the two natures confused the issue. How could the two natures be confused in a portrait of Christ, when the two natures were present in Him? Then the council of 754 introduced confusion into the sacrament, "the only admissible figure of the humanity of Christ." This bread is then made "the divine body of Christ by the mediation of the priest." Here again neoplatonism entered in, and the way was clearly prepared for the medieval doctrine of the Host. The extended incarnation was transferred from the images to the elements of the sacrament. Instead of being a subservient council, the council of 754 was implicitly closer to medieval Rome in its doctrine of the church than was the council of 787 in its ecclesiology. The council of 754 also declared that "no prince or secular official shall rob the churches, as some have done in former times, under the pretext of destroying images."[17] The integrity of the church as a separate domain was clearly implied.

The Decree of the Second Council of Nicea, 787, said in part:

To make our confession short, we keep unchanged all the ecclesiastical traditions handed down to us, whether in writing or verbally, one of which is the making of pictorial representations, agreeable to the history of the preaching of the Gospel, a tradition useful in many respects, but especially in this, that so the incarnation of the Word of God is shown forth as real and not merely phantastic, for these have mutual indications and without doubt have also mutual significations.

We, therefore, following the royal pathway and the divinely inspired authority of our Holy Fathers and the traditions of the Catholic Church (for, as we all know, the Holy Spirit indwells her), define with all certitude and accuracy that just as the figure of the precious and life-giving Cross, so also the venerable and holy images, as well in painting and mosaic as of other fit materials, should be set forth in the

---

[16.] *Ibid.*, 543f.
[17.] *Ibid.*, 545.

holy churches of God, and on the sacred vessels and on the vestments and on hangings and in pictures both in houses and by the wayside, to wit, the figure of our Lord God and Saviour Jesus Christ, of our Spotless Lady, the Mother of God, of the honourable Angels, of all Saints and of all pious people. For by so much more frequently as they are seen in artistic representation, by so much more readily are men lifted up to the memory of their prototypes, and to a longing after them; and to these should be given due salutation and honourable reverence, not indeed that true worship of faith which pertains alone to the divine nature; but to these, as to the figure of the precious and life-giving Cross and to the Book of the Gospels and to the other holy objects, incense and lights may be offered according to ancient pious custom. For the honour which is paid to the image passes on to that which the image represents, and he who reveres the image reveres in it the subject represented.[18]

The first point in this Decree is well taken. If the incarnation is real, it can be portrayed; an unreal incarnation, one which is "merely phantastic," cannot be depicted. Put in modern terms, a true and real Christ can be photographed; a mythical one cannot. The second point is equally valid. Honor paid to the portrait is honor to the one portrayed. To despise a symbol is to despise the one symbolized. Thus, the monk Stephanos brought on his arrest by deliberately insulting the imperial image. He took out a coin, in an imperial audience, and, calling attention to the image of the emperor, trod it under foot, saying, "What punishment must I suffer, should I trample his coin, which bears the emperor's image, under my feet? judge from it, what punishment he deserves who insults Christ and his mother, in their images."[19] As the Council knew, the tabernacle had its carved images, i.e., of the cherubim on the ark, pomegranates, etc., and the Bible forbade the worship, not the decorative use of these figures. But the carvings of the tabernacle were *never* the object of religious bowing, of incense, lights, or anything else. The Council justified the veneration of images by citing the Biblical instances of veneration of men in its letter to the emperor and empress:

And finally, those looking to obtain some gift, venerate those who are above them, as Jacob venerated Pharaoh. Therefore because this term has these many significations, the Divine Scriptures teaching us, "Thou shalt venerate the Lord thy God, and him only shalt thou serve," says simply that veneration is to be given to God, but does not add the word "only"; for veneration being a word of wide meaning is an ambiguous term; but it goes on to say "thou shall serve him *only*," for to God alone do we render latria.[20]

18. *Ibid.*, 550.
19. Neander, III, 220.
20. *Ibid.*, 573.

This argument concedes that veneration and worship are identical. God is venerated or worshipped, and images are also; the commandment is said to allow wider latitude to veneration, but service is restricted to God alone. The ostensible Biblical justification is a poor one, in that the word "only" as well as "serve" modify and explain the act of veneration or worship. And the veneration of superiors, monarchs, and parents was a requirement of the law, a respect for God-ordained authorities rather than for the persons involved as men.

The images were needed because the church thereby presented itself as the continuing incarnation. Asceticism was a form of this same continuing incarnation, in that the monks ascended upward on the ladder of being and became little Christs virtually; the monks of Athos in the 14th century, claimed in moments of ecstasy to have realized the light of the divine glory, the uncreated essence of God. This experience was not even Christian in form, let alone content, in that it was a product of fasting plus concentration on one's navel. When Barlaam condemned this practice of navel-watching as ungodly and anti-Christian, a Synod was called, and Barlaam and his party were cited as heretics and condemned. Today, on the Sunday of Orthodoxy, in the Greek Church, Barlaam's name is mentioned first in the list of those anathematized for heresy. Those whom Barlaam called the "navel-souled ones" had triumphed.[21]

The liturgy of the Eastern Church is dramatic and enthusiastic, designed to further God-possession, to extend the incarnation more deeply into the life of the church, and the monastic clergy, with its dedication to this liturgy, represents a permanently enthusiastic element.

The importance of the continuing incarnation to Nicea II appeared clearly in Canon VII:

> *That to churches consecrated without any deposit of the reliques of the Saints, the defect should be made good.*
>
> Paul the divine Apostle says: "The sins of some are open beforehand, and some they follow after." These are their primary sins, and other sins follow these. Accordingly upon the heels of the heresy of the traducers of the Christians, there followed close other ungodliness. For as they took out of the churches the presence of the venerable images, so likewise they cast aside other customs which we must now revive and maintain in accordance with the written and unwritten law. We decree therefore that relics shall be placed with the accustomed service in as many of the sacred temples as have been consecrated without the relics of the Martyrs. And if any bishop from this time forward is found consecrating a temple without holy relics, he shall be deposed, as a transgressor of the ecclesiastical traditions.[22]

[21.] Michael Choukas, *Black Angels of Athos* (Brattleboro, Vermont: Stephen Daye Press, 1935), 31.

[22.] Percival, 560.

The relics and images are here equated, and both are seen as necessary to the church; indeed, a church is defective, it is stated, without relics, and a bishop consecrating a church without relics is to be "deposed, as a transgressor." The relics of the saints, even more than their images, represented their holy estate. The relics were venerated, and, by the 9th century, were believed to have healing powers. Pelliccia discussed the subject in his chapter, "Of the Canonization (Apotheosis) of Saints." Apotheosis, of course, means deification. Pelliccia spoke of the custom in antiquity of deifying heroes and deceased rulers. This was, he said, an excellent plan "for infusing into men stimulating incentives of virtue." This custom, in a new form, "was at length, with most excellent judgment, carried out in the Christian religion."[23] "Some persons in the middle ages irreverently put the relics of Saints in the same vessel with the Eucharist itself, but this was forbidden by councils in the sixteenth century."[24] This practice was not at all surprising; it was a logical development. Since the relics were an extension of the incarnation, and the Eucharist was itself an incarnation, to bring the two together was simply a conclusion of pious logic.

The church thus was not truly a church, not fit to be consecrated, if all it had was the Bible; it needed relics, the visible presence of an invisible power. The church had changed. Hellenism had triumphed in the church, and neoplatonistic humanism had become its orthodoxy. Those who contemplated their navels were to find more support in the church than those who believed in and studied the word of God.

[23.] A. A. Pelliccia: *Polity of the Christian Church*, 382ff.
[24.] *Ibid.*, 162.

Chapter Fifteen

The Ascension
and the Session

The Apostles' Creed declares that Jesus Christ not only rose again from the dead, but that "He ascended into heaven, And sitteth on the right hand of God the Father Almighty." Two very closely related doctrines are here cited, the Ascension, and the Session.

The Ascension is the visible passing of Christ from earth to heaven in the presence of His disciples. It occurred on the Mount of Olives, forty days after the resurrection (Mark 16:19; Luke 24:50, 51; Acts 1:1-11). The Ascension was predicted by the Old Testament (Psalms 24, 68, 103, 110), and by Christ (John 6:62; 20:17). It was prefigured by the translation of Enoch (Gen. 5:24; Heb. 11:5), and of Elijah (2 Kings 2:11). The New Testament deals doctrinally with the Ascension in 2 Corinthians 13:4, Ephesians 2:6, 4:10, 1 Peter 3:22, 1 Timothy 3:16, and Hebrews 6:20. Neither the doctrine nor the predictive prophecies, nor the event, will be accepted by those who as a matter of humanist faith deny the infallible word.

The 4th article of the Articles of Religion of the Church of England and the Protestant Episcopal Church reads: "Christ did truly rise again from death, and took again his body, with flesh, bones, and all things appertaining to the perfection of Man's nature; wherewith he ascended into Heaven, and there sitteth, until he return to judge all Men at the last day."

The Westminster Larger Catechism deals with the matter in several questions. In two of these, it is declared:

Q. 51. What was the estate of Christ's exaltation?

A. The estate of Christ's exaltation comprehendeth his resurrection, ascension, sitting at the right hand of the Father, and his coming again to judge the world.

Q. 53. How was Christ exalted in his ascension?
A. Christ was exalted in his ascension in that, having after his resurrection often appeared unto and conversed with his apostles, speaking to them of the things pertaining to the kingdom of God, and giving them commission to preach the gospel to all nations; forty days after his resurrection, he, in our nature and as our head, triumphing over enemies, visibly went up into the highest heavens, there to receive gifts for men, to raise up our affections thither, and to prepare a place for us, where himself is and shall continue till his second coming at the end of the world.

Bishop Pearson, in his commentary on the creed, spoke of the ascension as transient, as the way, and the session as permanent, as the end. Pearson added:

As therefore when we say *Christ* ascended, we understand a literal and local ascent, not of his Divinity (which possesseth all places, and therefore being every where is not subject to the imperfection of removing any whither), but of his humanity, which was so in one place that it was not in another: so when we say the place into which he ascended was heaven, and from the exposition of the apostles must understand thereby the heaven of heavens, or the highest heaven, it followeth that we believe the body with the soul of *Christ* to have passed far above all those celestial bodies which we see, and to look upon that opinion as a low conceit which left his body in the sun.[1]

Pearson's last reference, to Christ leaving His body in the sun, was to a doctrine taught by the Hermians, a heretical sect of the 2nd century who denied that water baptism was taught by Christ. The Hermians held that man's soul was made of fire and spirit, and the true baptism was by "fire." The Seleucians, followers of Seleucus, a philosopher of Galatia, who adopted Valentinian Gnosticism around 380, taught that Jesus adopted a body for appearance only, not an actual flesh and blood body. The world was not created by God but was held to be eternal. The soul was animated fire, created by the angels. Christ, said the Seleucians, was not in session with the Father but had left His body in the sun. They also denied water Baptism. For them, all the pleasures of happiness are physical, corporeal delights. The position of both groups was basically Manichaean, a point made by Gregory Nazianzen and Augustine. (Gregory Nazianzen: *Epist. I ad Cledonium*, p. 739. Augustine, *Tract 34* in Ioan 2). The Manichaean attack was on the ascension as the way to the session, i.e., to prevent the God-centered exaltation of Christ's redeemed saints, in order to make possible man's autonomous exaltation.

[1.] John Pearson: *An Exposition of the Creed* (London: Scott, Webster and Geary, 1836. Revised by W. S. Dobson), 410.

The doctrine of the Session is the perpetual presence of our Lord's human nature in the highest glory of heaven, at the right hand of God the Father. The body of Jesus Christ is thus locally and physically present in heaven, and hence it is the Holy Spirit whom He sends to men. The result of this exaltation of the Session is that it brings the redeemed to God, into the divine presence, in closest communion. It made possible the exaltation of all the saints into the communion of heaven, "that where I am, there ye may be also" (John 14:2, 3). The Session is repeatedly cited in the Gospels and Epistles, but Mark's story of the ascension is unique in citing the Session in that context (Mark 16: 19).[2]

In the Scriptures, the Ascension, Session, and Second Coming are all closely linked together to the Resurrection and the Last Judgment. They are part of the exaltation and victory of Jesus Christ. Davies, in commenting on the fact that to St. Paul Christ is Lord by virtue of His resurrection and ascension, stated:

> So closely allied with this conception of the Ascension that it is all but indistinguishable from it is the further belief that the Ascension issues in the enthronement of Christ in Messianic majesty as King at the right hand of God; "for he must reign, till he hath put all his enemies under his feet" (1 Cor. 15:25). Thus through the Ascension Christ has become God's vicegerent over the universe, yet His reign is not one of peace but of glorious warfare as He continues "to subject all things unto himself" (Phil. 3:21).[3]

By the ascension, God exalted Jesus Christ to the status of Lord: "Wherefore God also hath highly exalted him, and given him a name which is above every name: That at the name of Jesus every knee should bow, of things in heaven, and things in earth, and things under the earth; And that every tongue should confess that Jesus Christ is Lord, to the glory of God the Father" (Phil. 2:9-11).

Prior to the incarnation, men of faith saw God's hand in history and accepted it, but their sense of desolation and loneliness was expressed by David in Psalm 22; that isolation was experienced to the uttermost by Christ on the cross, and it was ended by His ascension and session. Man now is restored to communion with God in Christ, and the communion is closer than that of Eden. Man in the person of Jesus Christ sits in session with the triune God, in warfare against evil and in judgment over it. The subject of Revelation is the "wrath of the Lamb" (Rev. 6:16) against the oppressors of His people.

[2.] See Edward F. Hills, editor, John W. Burgon, *The Last Twelve Verses* of *the Gospel According to S. Mark*, (The Sovereign Grace Book Club, 1959), 256.

[3.] J. G. Davies, *He Ascended Into Heaven, A Study in the History of Doctrine* (London: Lutterworth Press, 1958), 61.

The ascension of Christ is declared to be the presentation of the "first-fruits" of the new humanity to God the Father (1 Cor. 15:23). The first of everything belonged to God, according to the Law, to indicate that all things, men, animals, crops, were His in their totality. The first-fruits therefore represented the symbolic dedication of the entire fruit. Moreover, "If the first-fruits were holy, the lump was also holy" (Rom. 11:16), i.e., the entirety partakes of the character of the representative. Christ is the first-fruit of the new creation, of the new humanity created by God; He is the second and last Adam (1 Cor. 15:47-49). Therefore, "Ourselves also, which have the first-fruits of the Spirit, even we ourselves groan within ourselves, waiting for the adoption, to wit, the redemption of our body" (Rom. 8:23). In the ascension, the whole body of the elect is presented to the Father, holy in the first-fruit, Jesus Christ. In the session, the whole body of the elect is present at the right hand of God the Father, declaring war on the ungodly and seeking redress for the evils they have suffered. That victory which the elect seek is assured by the Ascension, "which marks the reversal of man's verdict upon Jesus of Nazareth by the verdict of God."[4]

This teaching was strongly emphasized by the early church. Justin Martyr emphasized the doctrine of election together with the ascension, declaring:

> And that God the Father of all would bring Christ to heaven after He had raised Him from the dead, and would keep Him there until He has subdued His enemies the devils, and until the number of those who are foreknown by Him as good and virtuous is complete, on whose account He has still delayed the consummation — hear what was said by the prophet David. These are his words: "The Lord said unto my Lord, Sit Thou on my right hand, until I make Thine enemies Thy footstool. The Lord shall send to Thee the rod of power out of Jerusalem; and rule Thou in the midst of Thine enemies. With Thee is the government in the day of Thy power, in the beauties of Thy saints; from the womb of the morning have I begotten Thee." (Ps. XC. I etc.) That which he says, "He shall send to Thee the rod of power out of Jerusalem," is predictive of the mighty word, which His apostles, going forth from Jerusalem, preached everywhere; and though death is decreed against those who teach or at all confess the name of Christ, we everywhere both embrace and teach it. And if you also read these words in a hostile spirit, ye can do no more, as I said before, than kill us; which indeed does no harm to us, but to you and all who unjustly hate us, and do not repent, brings eternal punishment by fire.[5]

---

4. Davies, *op. cit.*, 63.

5. Justin Martyr, First Apology, ch. XLV, in *Ante-Nicene Christian Library*, II, *The Writings of Justin Martyr and Athenegeras*, 45f.

The confidence of the early church is here clearly apparent: Christ has ascended to triumph; although the enemies of Christ may kill the Christians, it is the enemies who have cause to fear if they do not repent, because Christ is the great Lord and judge over all men. The ascension of Christ is the exaltation of all the elect. Athanasius declared: "And the term in question, 'highly exalted,' does not signify that the essence of the Word was exalted, for He was ever and is 'equal to God,' but the exaltation is of the manhood."[6] Chrysostom said of this exaltation, "we who appeared unworthy of earth have been led up today into the heavens: we who were not worthy of the preeminence below have ascended to the Kingdom above: we have scaled the heavens: we have attained the royal throne, and that nature, on whose account the Cherubim guarded paradise, today sits above the Cherubim."[7]

"Thus the Ascension is the necessary prelude to the intercession," Davies noted.[8] By means of the ascension, the believers intercede with God against the evil ones, and their victory is assured in Christ. Of the Feast of the Ascension, one anonymous preacher declared, "Every Christian festival condemns the devil, but this one especially."[9]

Concerning the Session and intercession the Larger Catechism of the Westminster Divines declared:

> Q. 54. How is Christ exalted in his sitting at the right hand of God?
> A. Christ is exalted in his sitting at the right hand of God, in that as God-man he is advanced to the highest favor with God the Father, with all fullness of joy, glory, and power over all things in heaven and earth; and doth gather and defend his Church, and subdue their enemies; furnisheth his ministers and people with gifts and graces, and maketh intercession for them.
>
> Q. 55. How doth Christ make intercession?
> A. Christ maketh intercession, by his appearing in our nature continually before the Father in heaven, in the merit of his obedience and sacrifice on earth, declaring his will to have it applied to all believers; answering all accusations against them; and procuring for them quiet of conscience notwithstanding daily failings, access with boldness to the throne of grace, and acceptance of their persons and services.

To be seated at the right hand is to be seated in the position of trust and power; Pearson wrote that "the *right hand* of God signifies the glorious majesty of God ... the exceeding great and infinite power of God." It is "the right hand of power" (Matt. 26:64; Mark 14:62; Luke 22:69). Among its

---

6. Athanasius, "Four Discourses Against the Arians," Discourse I, 41, in *Nicene and Post-Nicene Fathers*, Series Two, vol. IV, 330.
7. Cited by Davies, *op. cit.*, 116.
8. *Ibid.*, 122.
9. *Ibid.*, 123.

many meanings, it means "the right hand of judicature," so that Christ is thereby "manifested and declared to be the great judge of the quick and the dead." It is Christ's inheritance, in its full promised meaning, of the throne of David (Acts 2:36). Both temporal and spiritual enemies shall be made His "footstool" (Heb. 10:12; 13). According to Pearson, "For the destruction of these powers was Christ *exalted* to the right hand of God, and by his regal office doth he subdue and destroy them all." Christ destroys the power of sin in His saints, and he subjugates the reprobate to His absolute power eternally. Death also is destroyed by Christ (1 Cor. 15:20). "Enemies we all have been; under his feet we shall be, either adopted or subdued." There is not limitation to Christ's power. The session "signifieth an *omnipotent* power, able to do all things without any limitation."[10]

The apostate activities of man are imitative, because man is not God; his thinking therefore is not creative but analogical. Man's wisdom is to think God's thoughts after Him, to understand the universe and himself in terms of God's creative purpose and prior interpretation. Apostate man plans a world order in terms of God's kingdom, but without God.

First, man's dream of the kingdom is immanent; the kingdom, a paradise on earth, is entirely of this world; it originates in man and is to be man's private world and possession, an area held without benefit of God and with God held at bay. Instead of a transcendental unity, man seeks therefore a temporal unity. Since the true order is of man, the unity and authority for that order must be located and held within history by man.

Second, this one-world order is to be the exaltation of man by man, and this humanistic dream calls for man's exaltation in contempt of God and as an offensive action against Him. The very exaltation of man in this perspective involves war against God as the very ground of man's exaltation.

Third, the humanistic doctrine of the Session sees man as the lord of history. The elite scientific planners, as the epitome of free man, are to sit in the position of omnipotence and power and govern man and nature.

History involves therefore inescapable warfare. God, having created man in His image, offered man the position of viceregent under God over creation. Man sought this same position in autonomy from God and in rebellion against God. God in Christ reestablished man, restored him to grace, and opened afresh by the re-creation of man in Christ man's glorious destiny.

The divine Session is the sole and total omnipotence and government of the Trinity over all creation. Man is given a favored position in the divine session, a position made possible by grace and received by the total submission and obedience of Jesus Christ. Man's own exaltation in the

---

10. Pearson, *op. cit.*, 405-438.

eternal kingdom involves his own perfect sanctification after death. The government is God's, not man's, and man's position in perfect obedience is that of a viceregent, not that of God.

The purpose of humanism, of every non-Christian movement and of all heresy and apostasy, is to seize the throne for man, to place man in the place of God and to create a man-centered Session over all creation and history.

The Unitarian poet, William C. Gannett, saw man's fulfilment in this ascension of man to become a god. Writing in 1871, he declared that everyone's last name is God:

> It's Mary, Maud, and Katy,
> John-God, and Willie-God.[11]

For Frederick L. Hosmer, writing in 1904, the city of man, "The Commonwealth of man" is "The City of our God!"[12] In 1918, Gannett saw the coming peace conference as a new Sinai:

> Humbly, forgivingly, then shall the nations
> Seek them together a Sinai untrod,
> Hear the New Law in a Tryst of the Peace-makers,
> Frame a New World for the peoples of God![13]

In 1904, Gannett saw the "coming glory" as the "Glory of the Man Complete!" This new man-god would go

> Onward, upward, through the ages
> Shaping Nature to its plan.[14]

This was a romantic expression of the apostate dream. The practical demonstration of the same hope is less poetic. During the French Revolution, plans were made to depopulate France by killing twelve to fifteen millions of the French people in order to effect a "revolutionary transfiguration." The scheme was actually explained in print. It was held that "depopulation was essential." "Guffroy in his journal expressed the opinion that only five million people should be allowed to survive, whilst Robespierre was reported to have said that a population of two millions would be more than enough." Others asserted that "eight millions was the figure generally agreed on by the leaders."[15]

The humanistic order claims for itself the absolute right of judgment which properly belongs only to God. Thus, Joshua Lederberg, Ph.D., professor of genetics at Stanford, has said, in defending abortion, "We cannot insist on absolute rights to life of a piece of tissue just because it

---

11. "Jesus Who?" in Frederick L. Hosmer and William C. Gannett, *The Thought of God in Hymns and Poems,* First Series (Boston: Beacon Press, 1918 [1885]), 61.
12. *Ibid.,* Third Series, 7.
13. *Ibid.,* Third Series, 87.
14. *Ibid.,* Third Series, 89.
15. Nesta Webster, *The French Revolution, A Study in Democracy,* 424-429.

bears a resemblance to humanity."[16] The plain implication is that the state should have this absolute right.

Unless the ascension and session of Jesus Christ be confessed, men will seek their own ascension into omnipotence and their own session of absolute power over man. For a man to confess Christ and to espouse statism or socialism is to involve himself in serious contradiction and the practical denial of Christ. The divine Session and the statist, socialist session are mutually exclusive and incompatible. Calvin said of the ascension and session, that it meant that Christ was "inaugurated in the government of heaven and earth."[17] The essence of the humanistic and socialist state is that it is the enthronement of man into the government of heaven and earth. The consequence is warfare against God and Christ. There is no victory possible for men who wage war against God. But neither is there any hope for men, who, in the direct line of fire, fail to see that a war is on.

16. Jim Hazelwood, "The Shattering Impact of Science," Oakland, California, *Tribune*, Thursday, April 13, 1967, 1.
17. *Institutes*, Bk. II, xvi, xv.

Chapter Sixteen

The Last Judgment

The Apostles' Creed, after declaring the divine Session, reads, concerning Christ, that "From thence he shall come to judge the quick and the dead." The Nicene Creed affirms, "And he shall come again, with glory, to judge both the quick and the dead; Whose kingdom shall have no end." The verdict on history will come from beyond history, even as the determination of history is from eternity, from the triune God, for, in Stauffer's words, "Nothing can happen without God willing it, willing it to happen so, and willing it beforehand."[1] As Stauffer, who is by no means orthodox, has written,

> That is not fatalism. The fatalist sees everything that happens in the world and its history subjected to the oppressive coercion of an impersonal fate, while the biblical writers know of the guiding will of a personal God who hears and answers our prayers. That is not determinism. The determinist conceives of human decision as being effected by sub-personal casual factors that are alien to the will. This reduces the will to an appearance (as among the Essenes, according to Jos. Ant. 13. 172). By contrast the Scriptures conceived of our will as conditioned by a will of a supra-personal kind, by the will of God, who wills man's will, and by his willing first quickens man to his specific reality.[2]

Moreover, as Stauffer has noted, "Christ once came to the earth as the *rex triumphaus* the *deus salvator revelatus.*"[3] History is a succession of

---

[1] Ethelbert Stauffer: *New Testament Theology* (New York: Macmillan, 1956), 52.
[2] *Ibid.*, 266, n. 100, n. 101.
[3] *Ibid*, 216.

judgments, wherein God comes in clouds of judgment, and all these crises and judgments are for the shaking of the nations, to destroy the reprobate realms of man and to establish by sifting Christ's faithful in His realm. As God declared through Ezekiel, "I will overturn, overturn, overturn it; and it shall be no more, until he come whose right it is; and I will give it to him" (Ezek. 31:27). The purpose of this overturning, according to St. Paul, is "the removing of the things that are shaken, as of things that are made, that those things which cannot be shaken may remain" (Heb. 12:27). The successive judgments have as their purpose the removal by destruction "of things that are made," i.e., of the humanistic and apostate orders of history, so that Christ's kingdom, "which cannot be shaken may remain." These are all partial judgments, forerunners of the final judgment.

Humanism, however, has not left this doctrine of judgment untouched. The parable of Matthew 25:31ff. has been used by the humanists to convert the last judgment into a triumph of humanism! Joachim Jeremias provides a notable example of this. For Jeremias, the parable of the separation of the sheep and the goats gives the criterion by which the heathen will be judged. The parable is actually concerning the judgment of the professing church. Jeremias instead sees it as a judgment, not of the Shepherd's own flock, but of another flock! But Jeremias then contradicts himself when he states that "separate" is "a shepherd's technical term" for dividing the goats from the sheep in Palestine at the end of the day. In other words, it is the shepherd's flock, Christ's church, which is being judged. But Jeremias still sees it as a judgment of the heathen:

> Perhaps, in view of such a saying as that in Matt. 10:32f., where Jesus says that he will intercede at the last judgment for those of his disciples who have confessed him before men, he might have been asked, But then, by what criterion will the heathen who have never known you be judged? Are they lost? (for such was the contemporary opinion). Jesus replies, in effect: The heathen have met me in my brethren, for the needy are my brethren; he who has shown love to them has shown it to me, the Saviour of the poor. So, at the last judgment, the heathen will be asked about the acts of love that they have shown to me in the form of the afflicted, and they will be granted the grace of a share in the kingdom, if they have fulfilled the Messiah's law (James 2:8), the commandment of love. Thus for them justification is available on the ground of love, since for them too the ransom has been paid (Mark 10:45).[4]

First of all, the idea that unbelievers had any right to salvation never occurred to anyone in the New Testament era, and it is never a concern of either Christ or the apostles. *Second,* Jeremias makes a totally humanistic concern the ground of salvation. Not Christ but man is the test. Faith is

---

[4.] Joachim Jeremias, *Rediscovering the Parables* (New York: Charles Scribner's Sons, 1966), 163.

manward, not Godward. *Third*, justification is given a non-Christian ground, humanistic love, rather than God's grace. Thus, not only is man the *object* of faith and religious concern, he is also the *source* of grace and salvation. *Fourth*, as has been noted, Jeremias chooses to disregard the fact that the shepherd is judging and dividing his own flock, the church, not the heathen outside. It is the separation of the unbelievers in the church from the church, and the ground of it is the shepherd himself.

Fifth, this parable is part of a discourse on the judgment of the church, of true Christians as against nominal ones. Matthew 24:42-51 concludes the declaration concerning the fall of Jerusalem, and then the end times, both instances of judgment, by warning the church to be prepared for judgment by means of true faith and obedience. *Three parables* then illustrate the distinction between true believers and nominal church members, *first*, the parable of the wise and foolish virgins; *second*, the parable of the talents, i.e., profitable vs. unprofitable servants; *third*, the separation of the sheep and the goats (Matt. 25).

In this last parable (Matt. 25:31ff.), a profession of faith by both sheep and goats is *presupposed;* both are followers of the Shepherd, both alike profess to be of His flock. The question is one of division in terms of the reality of their professed faith. True faith is saving faith: even a cup of cold water in His name then has its reward (Mark 9:41). The witness to faith required by the Shepherd is confessional, confessional in that it manifests faith and confesses it under stress. This confession has a double aspect: *First*, the fruits manifest the tree, and works confess the faith; *second*, the church had been warned that persecution would be its portion (Matthew 5:10-12; Luke, 6:22-23; 1 Peter 4:13, 14; 2 Cor. 4:17; 2 Tim. 2: 12, etc.), but that the Lord would be with them in their trials (Matt. 10:19, 20). To visit imprisoned Christians often took courage, because it meant identification as a believer, and, in the persecutions of the early church, such attention from official sources was serious. St. Paul spoke with feeling of Onesiphorus, who "was not ashamed of my chains" (2 Tim. 1: 16), and this word comes from a period before the general persecution of Christians.

St. Paul spoke of "discerning the Lord's body" in two ways: *first*, in knowing the meaning of the communion elements, understanding and believing in His atonement and His resurrection, and, *second*, in avoiding the "divisions" whereby Christian brethren were not recognized nor shared with at the "Lord's supper" (1 Cor. 11:17-34). They were thus not recognized as fellow members in Jesus Christ, and the Lord's body was not discerned.

In this parable of judgment, the "goats" have failed to discern the Lord's body because they were not truly members of Him; they refused to know him in the persons of His oppressed and suffering saints, because they are the "cursed," who know him not. Not knowing Christ, how could they have communion with His members? Refusing to recognize Christ in His glorious person, how could they recognize Him in His suffering and oppressed saints? (Matt. 25:41-46) The audacity of these sinners is notable: they dare to contradict Christ on judgment day; the saints in humility fail to recognize the full scope of their faith; the sinners deny the meaning of their sin.

The interpretation of Jeremias is not only an alien and humanistic one forced onto the Scripture, but Jeremias' own comments give it the lie.

It should be added that such interpreters do not believe in the reality of the Biblical judgment. For them, the creeds and Scriptures are simply myths and symbols. Thus George Hedley "defends" the creeds as "venerable tradition" which deal with "Not events, but values," and these values "constitute the essence of the creeds." "Childish literalism" is condemned for believing the creeds literally, and "adolescent Literalism" for denying the creeds, for "It is only in myth and symbol that man can come close to expressing the inexpressible. It is in the poetry of the ancient creeds that the everlasting faith of the church yet rings out to the world."[5]

But it would be a serious mistake to say that these humanists do not believe in the judgment, nor in a heaven and hell; they do believe, and very literally, but not in the Biblical judgment, heaven and hell. Because they are established by God as inescapable aspects of man's history, judgment, heaven, and hell are inescapable categories of thought. If a man denies the Biblical version, it is only to create a humanistic version.

In a very important passage, Karl Marx said in part:

> For a *popular revolution* and the *emancipation of a particular class of civil society* to coincide, for *one* class to represent the whole of society, another class must concentrate in itself all the evils of society, a particular class must embody and represent a general obstacle and limitation. A particular social sphere must be regarded as the *notorious crime* of the whole society, so that emancipation from this sphere appears as a general emancipation. For one class to be the liberating class *par excellence*, it is necessary that another class should be openly the oppressing class.[6]

For Marx, it was necessary, *first*, for one class to identify itself as "the liberating class," as man's savior. *Second*, to do this, "it is necessary" to identify another class as "the oppressing class," as the devil. *Third*, Marx felt it necessary, as his many writings reveal, that revolution, culminating in judgment, be demanded against this demonic oppressing class. The world revolution would culminate in the last judgment. *Fourth*, there would be a

---

[5.] George Hedley, "Reflections: on Criticizing the Creeds." Oakland, California, *Tribune*, Saturday, April 22, 1967, 24-B.

[6.] Karl Marx, "Contribution to the Critque of Hegel's Philosophy of Right," in *Early Writings*, T. B. Bottomore, translator, editor (New York: McGraw-Hill, 1963), 56.

hell for the oppressors, and the Soviet Union has its slave labor camps, and a heaven, the communist utopia or paradise on earth, for the faithful.

The details differ, but every world-view and every faith has its versions of judgment, heaven, and hell. For some, hell is existence, and heaven is nirvana and nothingness. But the basic categories remain. The relativists, nihilists, and existentialists who deny all absolute values and laws demand judgment on God, law, and morality; hell for them is a world of absolute values, which they wage war against, and heaven is a world beyond good and evil.

But to transfer final judgment, heaven, and hell from the eternal order to time is to absolutize history and to enthrone man as god. It means the destruction of liberty, because history ceases to be the realm of liberty and testing but becomes the place of final trial. Having made the final judgment temporal, the humanist cannot permit liberty, because liberty is hostile to finality; liberty presupposes trial and error and the possibility of serious waywardness when and where man is sinful and imperfect. History cannot tolerate both trial and error and insist on finality and the end of trial and error. The humanistic utopias are all prisons, because they insist on a finality which man does not possess. Accordingly, the socialist utopias demand the "reeducation" of man in the post-revolutionary world, in the era beyond the judgment. The "new era" is the new heaven on earth: how can perverse man dwell therein without being broken by "revolutionary justice," i.e., a continuation or extension of the last judgment? The result is perpetual tyranny, as immoral man and dissenting godly man are forced into the strait jacket of the socialist heaven.

Development is thus denied to both man and history. Epistemological self-consciousness brings the parallel development of the wheat and the tares, of saints and sinners, and God does not permit finality to invade history until the end of history (Matt. 13:30).

The humanist, however, believes so passionately in a final judgment that he insists on bringing it into history before history can develop its implications. Dewey demanded the "Great Community," the Fabians their "Great Society," and every other version and sect of humanists has its apocalypse and last judgment. The humanists fail to introduce heaven, but they successfully establish hell on earth.

But history refuses to terminate on man's orders, because it runs on God's time, and not in terms of man's myths. As a result, the final orders which men build have an inevitable habit of decay, and the order which claims to be final ensures its own destruction as the movement of history crushes it underfoot in its unrelenting march to epistemological self-consciousness. Man's "final" orders come in with pride and go out in shame and destruction, but Jesus Christ "shall come again, with glory, to judge both the quick and the dead; Whose kingdom shall have no end."

Chapter Seventeen

The Church

An article of the faith according to the Apostles' Creed is "The holy Catholic Church," or, in the words of the Nicene Creed, "I believe one Catholic and Apostolic Church."

This is now for many faithful Christians the only difficult article of the creed; in view of the apostasy of the institutional church and its obscene waywardness, it sometimes takes a strong stomach to confess the creed at this point. This same revulsion is felt by Jesus Christ, who declared to the Laodicean Church, "I will spew thee out of my mouth" (Rev. 3:16). But such churches are not churches but synagogues of Satan (Rev. 2:9), not an article of faith but a necessary enemy as the church separates in terms of Christ.

The Westminster Confession of Faith, chapter XXV, "Of the Church," defines the church clearly:

> I. The catholic or universal Church, which is invisible, consists of the whole number of the elect, that have been, are, or shall be gathered into one order, under Christ the head thereof; and is the spouse, the body, the fullness of him that filleth all in all.
>
> II. The visible Church, which is also catholic or universal under the gospel (not confined to one nation, as before under the law), consists of all those throughout the world, that profess the true religion, together with their children; and is the kingdom of the Lord Jesus Christ, the house and family of God, out of which there is no ordinary possibility of salvation.

147

III. Unto this catholic visible Church, Christ hath given the ministry, oracles, and ordinances of God, for the gathering and perfecting of the saints, in this life, to the end of the world: and doth by his own presence and Spirit, according to his promise, make them effectual thereunto.

IV. This catholic Church hath been sometimes more, sometimes less, visible. And particular churches, which are members thereof, are more or less pure, according as the doctrine of the gospel is taught and embraced, ordinances administered, and public worship performed more or less purely in them.

V. The purest churches under heaven are subject both to mixture and error; And some have so degenerated, as to become not churches of Christ, but synagogues of Satan. Nevertheless, there shall be always a Church on earth, to worship God according to his will.

VI. The Lord Jesus Christ is the only head of the Church, and the claim of any man to be the vicar of Christ and the head of the Church, is unscriptural, without warrant in fact, and is a usurpation dishonoring to the Lord Jesus Christ.[1]

The marks of the true church are thus, *first,* the true preaching of the Word of God, the infallible Scriptures; *second,* the right administration of the Sacraments, i.e., in faithfulness to Scripture; and, *third,* the faithful exercise of discipline in terms of Scripture.

The *means of grace* are the word and the sacraments. Of the relationship of the Church to the means of grace, Berkhof has written:

> The Church is not a means of grace alongside of the Word and the sacraments, because her power in promoting the work of the grace of God consists only in the administration of these. She is not instrumental in communicating grace, except by means of the Word and of the sacraments. Moreover, faith, conversion, and prayer, are first of all fruits of the grace of God, though they may in turn become instrumental in strengthening the spiritual life. They are not objective ordinances, but subjective conditions for the possession and enjoyment of the blessings of the covenant.[2]

Moreover, as Berkhof also pointed out, the means of grace cannot "of themselves confer grace, as if they were endued with a magical power to produce holiness." This does not signify that the means of grace can be regarded "as purely accidental and indifferent."[3] Although they are simply the *means,* not the source, they are the God-appointed means of grace.

[1.] Section VI was substituted for the original reading by later revisers. The original reading was: "There is no other head of the Church but the Lord Jesus Christ: nor can the Pope of Rome, in any sense, be head thereof; but is that Antichrist, that man of sin and son of perdition, that exalteth himself in the Church against Christ, and all that is called God."

[2.] Louis Berkhof: *Systematic Theology* (Grand Rapids: Eerdmans, 1946), 604.

[3.] *Ibid.,* 608.

The doctrine of *visibility* is an important and central aspect of the definition of the Church. As the Confession declares, "This catholic Church hath been sometimes more, sometimes less, visible." The catholic or invisible Church is defined in Section I as "the whole number of the elect, that have been, are, or shall be gathered into one, under Christ the head thereof." This means that the invisible Church is more inclusive a term than the Church Triumphant, in that it embraces far more than the church in heaven.

The visible Church, however, is on earth; it is not a perfect Church, and "The purest churches under heaven are subject both to mixture and error." The pure churches are those in whom "the doctrine of the gospel is taught and embraced, ordinances administered, and public worship performed more or less purely in them." Because Jesus Christ declared that "the gates of hell shall not prevail against" His Church (Matt. 16:18), "there shall be always a Church on earth, to worship God according to his will." "The gates of hell" means the powers, council, or authority of hell, the city council in ancient times convening publicly before the gates; "prevail" here has the force of "withstand," and the Berkeley Version translates it, "the gates of hell shall not hold out against her." This connotes clearly *aggressive* action against hell by the Church, and *defensive* action by hell. It is heretical thinking to assume that the action of the Church is defensive; it is dangerous and creates a mood receptive to the enthronement of Satan for the Church to assume that its position is a defensive retreat towards the rapture or towards the second coming. The Church, however small, and however much a Gideon's band, is the aggressor against the powers of darkness, who, in constant frenzy, try to barricade themselves, in their towers of Babel, against the sovereign and omnipotent God.

The more faithful the Church, the greater its visibility, i.e., the more clearly it witnesses to the word and power of Christ in this world. But the true Church is not alone in claiming visibility, in claiming to be the visible representative of Christ's invisible order. The state claims its own kind of visibility; the state sees itself as the visible expression of the true order of man, and, sometimes also, of whatever gods may be. It then becomes a contest, *first*, as to who represents God's true order, and, *second*, what is the order which is to be represented?

The humanistic order strives for visibility, *first*, as the dominant force in man's society, as the omnipresent fact on the human scene, and, *second*, as the new order of salvation. Accordingly, man's dominant concern in the era of humanism is political, since politics is the area where the hidden deity becomes visible. The 19th century was thus the era of political visibility; the religion of most men tended increasingly to become political. "Democracy" as the hope of the world found its culminating messianic expression in Woodrow Wilson's dream of making the world safe for democracy by war and diplomacy.

Especially after the mid-20th century, man's hope became more and more politico-economic. U Thant, Secretary General of the United Nations, declared in 1967, "In this century political ideology has taken the place formerly occupied by religion as a main source of strife in the world." To have peace, we must therefore transcend political ideology by syncretism and move in terms of economics instead. After all, as U Thant pointed out, "The simplest citizen can grasp the fact that a fraction of the money that will be spent throughout the world on armaments in 1967 could finance economic and social programmes, both national and global, on a scale hitherto undreamed of." In other words, if people will overlook their political differences, and will unite in terms of socialistic economics, they will see the visible "breakthroughs" of human development which would make the world "rival all the utopias of the philosophers."[4]

Since the visibility which the false churches strive for is the appearance of the world socialist order, i.e., total statism, part of the false church's mission is the dismantling and the disappearance of the church. Various plans are regularly suggested for eliminating segments of the church as a first step. Thus, Dr. John Dillenberger, Dean of San Francisco's graduate theological union, has declared, "If we sold five out of every six church buildings in the country and put all that money to better use in serving the needs of the people," the mission of the church would not suffer but would probably be enhanced.[5] Such a plan has already been in operation in Communist countries. Dillenberger's concern is a humanist one, with human need, not the Biblical commission. The purpose of the synagogues of Satan is thus to make the church invisible in the sense of being non-existent as a church, and the state visible as the true order of man.

As against this, the Christian must affirm, "I believe one Catholic and Apostolic Church," one universal church established in the apostolic faith, and "the gates of hell shall not hold out against her," for "this is the victory that overcometh the world, even our faith" (1 John 5:4).

Since visibility means power, the false churches strive for a visibility which will give them world power. The pseudo-visibility is a claim to represent in a plenary ability the infallibility and authority of God. Whether Protestant, Roman Catholic, or Eastern, the church then identifies itself with the incarnation, speaks under its own terms with plenary authority, and declares that its sacraments accomplish what Christ alone is empowered to do. Instead of God being the Rock on which the

4. U Thant, "What Could We Build If We Worked Together?" in Alcan advertisement, *U. S. News & World Report,* vol. LXII, no. 18, May 1, 1967, 59f.
5. "If the Churches Sold 5 Out of 6 Buildings —" in Oakland, California, *Tribune,* Wed., May 3, 1967, 7.

church is founded, the church becomes the rock. The term "rock" is in Scripture always a symbol of the triune God, and its use by Jesus Christ in reference to Peter confirmed this. This was known to the early church, and subsequently, and was well stated by Aelfric in a homily:

> Jesus then said, "What say ye that I am?" Peter answered him. "Thou art Christ, the living God's Son." The Lord to him said for answer, "Blessed art thou, Simon, dove's child." (Bede the expounder unveils to us the deepness of this lesson.)

> The Lord said to Peter, "Thou art rockon." (Literally stonen, having the same relation to stone as rocken to rock, golden to gold, earthen to earth, &c.) — For the strength of his faith, and for the firmness of his confession, he received that name; because he joined himself with steadfast mind to Christ, who is called a Rock by the apostle Paul.

> "And I will build my church upon this rock"; that is, upon the faith which thou confessest. All God's convocation is built upon the rock; that is, upon Christ; because he is the ground-wall of all the structures of his own church.

> All God's churches are accounted one convocation; and this is built with chosen men, not with dead stones; and all the building of those lively stones is laid upon Christ; because we are, through faith, accounted his members and he is our "aller" head. Who(soever) builds off the ground-wall, his work shall fall, to (his) great loss. Jesus said, "The gates of hell shall not have power against my church." Sins and erroneous doctrine are hell's gates, because they lead the sinful (man) as it were through a gate into hell's torment. Many are these gates; but none of them shall have power against the holy convocation, which is built upon the firm rock, Christ; because the believer, through Christ's protection, escapes the perils of the devilish temptations.[6]

Very early too a pseudo-visibility was claimed by means of the doctrine of transubstantiation. Within the ranks of the ostensibly orthodox this was advocated by Paschasius Rhadbertus, Abbot of Corbie but answered about A. D. 840, at the request of the Emperor Charles the Bold, by Bertram, monk of Corbie, who defended the doctrine of the real presence as against transubstantiation.[7] The Catechism of the Council of Trent taught that in the consecrated wafer there are the nerves and bones as well as the body and blood of Christ.

The true church, "This catholic Church, hath been sometimes more, sometimes less, visible." How is this greater visibility apparent? The visibility of the Church is not in its institutional presence, but in its fulfilment of its calling. When the Church truly fulfills her calling, the consequences are apparent in the diffusion and enforcement of God's law

---

[6.] E. Thomson, editor, *Select Monuments of the Doctrine and Worship of the Catholic Church in England Before the Norman Conquest*, 95-99.

[7.] W. F. Taylor, editor, translator, *The Book of Bertram, "De Corpore et Sanguine Domini."* London: Simpkin Marshall, 1880.

order, so that every area of life is brought under the dominion of the triune God. A living tree manifests itself by green leaves and fruit; a living Church is visible in that it bears fruit unto God. If the visibility which the church seeks is the visibility of man, it will bear fruit unto humanism and will make human welfare the test of faith.

After St. Augustine, we can therefore say that two cities, empires, or orders are seeking realization in history, are attempting to become the visible order of history. These two are the City of God and the City of Man. The strategy of the City of Man is to deny the antithesis between the two orders in order to neutralize and destroy the City of God.

Humanism seeks to destroy Christianity and the Church in a number of ways. One common means is to redefine God into a humanistic concept. Thus, one humanist has written:

> Theists and atheists will come to agreement and mutual understanding when they admit their inability to understand the Supreme Cause of the universe, and agree to give it a name — to call IT GOD.
>
> The time has come for us to rescue the word God from the sordid meanings now sometimes given to it: such as being a vengeful being in human form, temperamental and jealous of other similar gods and merciful only to those who grovel before him. Let us respond to our beliefs by setting God up on a pinnacle of immutable justice and fair dealings for men of all races, colors and creeds. But let us recognize that anything finite is beyond identification by the infinite mind.[8]

The next step is to separate God from religion and the church. Thus, one clergyman has written, in a book dedicated to this cause, "I am on the staff of an Anglican parish in Toronto. I claim to be a Christian and an Anglican; yet I can say, in all seriousness, that there is no God." This same clergyman writes, "Jesus, like Yahweh, is the great Atheist .... He took advantage of people's hospitality, fed upon their food ... rode the best vehicles he could achieve, lived it up among drunkards and maybe got drunk." Moreover, "It is one of the discoveries of the present age that you can be a Christian and an atheist." Church worship gets no respect: "It is obvious that our present services are useless."[9]

At the same time, it is held that churches must withdraw from any attempt to influence social life, because the place of religion is in private life. The area of Christianity is held to be the private life of the believer. In other words, all social life must be humanistic, and only the inner life Christian. But true religion is a total concern; any area vacated by a religion

---

8. Hugh Auchincloss Brown, "A Definition of God," in *The American Rationalist*, vol. 9, no. 3, September, 1964, 12.
9. "The Attack Upon Christianity," in The *Canadian Intelligence Service*, vol. 17, no. 4., April, 1967, 4.

is only occupied by another religion, because all life is inescapably religious. Thus, to ask Christianity to confine itself to personal piety is to demand that it commit suicide, and pietism is a step in the direction of suicide. The concern of the Church is the word of God, but the word speaks to all of life. If the proclamation of the gospel be not catholic, then it has ceased to be the gospel; it is no longer the good news for every area of life and the claim of God to total sovereignty.

The false gods go, and so do the false churches, but, God being sovereign, His word endures forever, and His elect are unshakeable in Him, and His Church is destined to conquer.

Chapter Eighteen

The Communion of Saints

"The Communion of Saints" is an often neglected article of the Apostles' Creed. A late addition to the creed, the article does not appear in the Nicene Creed, in that it was not a contested doctrine. However, as Badcock has noted, its presence in the Creed was not merely to state a truth; more than that, "it must state an objective ground or necessary condition of salvation; and this ground or condition must not be alterable; in the sense of 'the things to be believed' the 'faith' had been the same ever since Pentecost." Moreover, the communion of saints cannot be some frame of mind among men; "it must express some divine act or gift."[1]

According to the Roman Catholic definition, the communion of saints is the union between the Church Triumphant (in heaven), the Church Militant (on earth), and the Church Suffering (in purgatory). The three form one church, whose invisible head is Jesus Christ, and whose visible head is the pope.

The major attention to the doctrine came with the Westminster Assembly. The Westminster Confession of Faith chapter XXVI is titled "Of the Communion of Saints":

> 1. All saints being united to Jesus Christ their head, by his Spirit and by faith, have fellowship with him in his graces, sufferings, death, resurrection, and glory: (1 John 1:3; Eph. 3:16, 17, 18, 19; John 1:16; Phil. 3:10; Rom. 6:5, 6; Rom. 8:17) and, being united to one another in love, they have communion in each other's gifts and graces, (Eph. 4:15, 16; 1 John 1:3, 7) and are obliged to the performance of

---

[1]. F. J. Badcock, *The History of the Creeds*, 246f.

such duties, public and private, as do conduce to their mutual good, both in the inward and outward man (1 Thess. 5:11, 14; Gal. 6:10; 1 John 3:16-18).

2. Saints by their profession are bound to maintain an holy fellowship and communion in the worship of God, and in performing such spiritual services as tend to their mutual edification, (Heb. 10:24, 25; Acts 2:42, 46; 1 Cor. 11:20) as also in relieving each other in outward things, according to their several abilities and necessities. Which communion, as God offereth opportunity, is to be extended unto all those who, in every place, call upon the name of the Lord Jesus (1 John 3:17; Acts 11:29, 30; 2 Cor. 8:9).

3. This communion which the saints have with Christ, doth not make them in any wise partakers of the substance of his Godhead, or to be equal with Christ in any respect: either of which to affirm is impious and blasphemous (Col. 1:18; 1 Cor. 8:6; Ps. 15:7). Nor doth their communion one with another as saints, take away or infringe the title or property which each man hath in his goods and possessions (Acts 5:4).

Since "Communion is founded in union," this chapter cites, *first,* "The union of the saints to Jesus Christ, and their communion with him; *Secondly,* the union and communion of real saints with one another; *Thirdly,* the union of saints by profession, and the communion which they are bound to maintain." So Shaw summarized the chapter.[2] Three things are cited by the Confession as aspects of this communion of saints in section 2. *First,* there is common worship; *second,* such "spiritual services as tend to their mutual edification"; and *third,* "relieving each other in outward things, according to their several abilities and necessities." The work of pastors, teachers, widows, and deacons was the official ministry of the church in these areas; all Christians had an obligation also.

The believers are thus fellow members, fellow saints, in a communion in Christ. They are saints by virtue of Christ's objective, atoning work; the communion is not of their making, but of Christ, and they enter into the communion as they are received by Christ.

But communion is neither absorption nor obliteration; neither is it identity. The believer in communion with Christ remains himself, a creature; in communion with fellow believers, he is not merged into them but retains his integrity as a person and in his family. As Hodge pointed out, the communion of saints is not "designed to supersede the fundamental principles of human society, as the rights of property and the family tie."[3] Thus, section 3 "guards against two heretical opinions; the one relating to the saints' communion with Christ; the other, to their communion with

---

[2.] Robert Shaw, *An Exposition of the Confession of Faith of the Westminster Assembly of Divines* (Philadelphia: Presbyterian Board of Publication, 1846), 296.
[3.] Archibald Alexander Hodge, *A Commentary on the Confession of Faith* (Philadelphia: Presbyterian Board of Publication, 1869), 442..

one another."[4] The purpose of salvation is not the destruction nor the transcendence of man, but the restoration of man into his appointed God-given calling and place. It was the sin of man to seek to be as God (Gen. 3:5); it is God's grace that enables man to be truly a man, God's vicegerunt on earth in Christ. It was man's sin which led and leads him to seek a false communion with other men in communism; it is God's grace which enables man to be truly a free and self-reliant man in his appointed place.

False communion is thus in two directions. *First,* the false communion of saints is the assertion that men are or can become of one substance with God. In some forms, as with Mormonism, it is asserted that men are gods, and the ontological and transcendent Trinity is denied. In other forms, as with mysticism, man transcends humanity and the material world by his experience in order to become one with God. In all the various forms of this belief, the saints are saints by their own effort and election, and it is they who establish the communion with God or the gods. The law of their social order is therefore of themselves, of their own election, because the determination of things is in their hands. History therefore must be captured by man, conquered even as the gods and men are taken by storm. The very role of God is therefore determined by man, who is himself the bridge-builder between man and God and man and man. The society or communion with God is one of exploitation; God is another vast natural resource to be developed and mined, and "revelations" are pragmatically forthcoming from the reigning saints as the necessities of history may require them. In Mormonism, or the Latter Day Saints, the power of revelation is vested in the reigning 'apostle' and his associates, and the revelations have been pragmatic, i.e., they have served the purposes of man in history rather than the purpose of a sovereign God in eternity. The captive "God" of mystical experience ravishes the soul of the mystic by sheer beauty, but, in another sense is ravished by the mystic, who by his mystical experience and discipline can appropriate "God." The mystic "denies" history because he is superior to history and potentially its lord. Instead of finding his God-given calling in history, and seeing history as man's appointed realm, the mystic treats history as a burden, and both history and its burdens must be destroyed. Thus the mystic Angela of Foligno wrote:

> I elected to walk on the thorny path which is the path of tribulation. So I began to put aside the fine clothing and adornments which I had, and the most delicate food, and also the covering of my head. But as yet, to do all these things was hard and shamed me, because I did not feel much love for God, and was living with my husband. So that it was a bitter thing to me when anything offensive was said or done to

---

4. Shaw, *op. cit.,* 302.

me; but I bore it as patiently as I could. In that time, and by God's will, there died my mother, who was a great hindrance to me in following the way of God; my husband died likewise; and in a short time there also died all my children. And because I had begun to follow the aforesaid way, and had prayed God to rid me of them, I had a great consolation of their deaths, although I also felt some grief; wherefore, because God had shown me this grace, I imagined that my heart was in the heart of God and His will and His heart in my heart.[5]

This is the psychology of a murderess, and a murderess who identifies herself with God.

The mystic can only approach history from above, as lord and god. Evelyn Underhill so approached Christ, from above. "I come to Christ through God, whereas quite obviously lots of people come to God through Christ."[6] For Evelyn Underhill, the initiative was upward, from man to God, and God's "revelation" does not come down but rather emerges from the world; the incarnation involves "complete humanity."[7] Man ascends out of history by mysticism to become one with God and then descends with power, as a living law.

Marxism is itself an inverted mysticism, with matter made the god of the system, so that man descends to identify himself with the general will of the masses and forces of materialism in order to ascend with power as the dictatorship of the proletariat.

Mysticism is basic to tyranny; it involves the identification of an elite as gods who incarnate the will and decree of history in their persons.

The Biblical communion of saints is the work of God's grace through Christ. It is not man's doing but Christ's work, and the communion is governed by His Word and law.[8]

The *second* direction of the false communion of saints is manward. Everywhere, as against the fraternity of grace, men have sought to establish a fraternity of evil. Through the centuries, secret organizations have attempted to establish an invisible bond between members, with secret symbols and goals, in order to gain an end of man's scattering and division, to undo the confusion of Babel. These hidden ties have succeeded by offering an advantage to men, i.e., by offering something more than bare fraternity, by offering power or pleasure. To this extent, therefore, their fraternity is an enforced one, having an ulterior motive. Their approach to

---

5. This passage is cited and defended by Evelyn Underhill in Charles Williams, editor: *The Letters of Evelyn Underhill* (London: Religious Book Club, 1945), 33.

6. *Ibid.*, 205, cf. 234.

7. *Ibid.*, 142f.

8. See The Westminster Larger Catechism, Q. 65, 66, 69, 82, 83, 86, 90, and The Westminster Shorter Catechism, Q. 36, 37, 38; James Benjamin Green, editor, *A Harmony of the Westminster Presbyterian Standards* (Richmond, Virginia: John Knox Press, 1951, 1965). See also John Pearson, *An Exposition of the Creed*, W. S. Dobson revision (London: Scott, Webster, and Geary, 1836), 524-537.

the concept of a world fraternity or community rests therefore on statist means. Secret fraternities have thus through the centuries had control of the state as their goal in order to impose communion on all men. The same is true of the open advocates of world communion; their method is political and statist. They believe in a world community, ostensibly, but they deny it because they insist on an enforced communion.

Because they are themselves by nature sinners, at war with God, therefore at war with man, and at war with themselves, they can neither attain nor imagine anything but an enforced communion. These men seek to realize God's appointed goal as gods without God. But the fraternity of evil is a divisive fraternity, at war within itself, made up of numerous would-be gods who know only one law other than their own will, brute force. The false communion of self-styled saints is therefore tyranny. It may at times parade under Christian forms, but its method and goal are force and the state.[9]

The radical humanists in and out of the church, and the Death of God school of thought hold to a concept of communion which is beyond good and evil and in which communion with man is communion with god. Erich Fromm has written, "God is one of the many different poetic expressions of the highest value in humanism, not a reality in itself."[10] True communion for this faith means that good and evil are denied validity as objective moral standards, and all men must be received into communion as gods without any regard to their moral status. Thus, a "Litany" popular in these circles identifies "God" with the city, with the "spick, black nigger, bastard, Buddhahead, and kike," with "all men," and calls for communion with all men as they are. Some churches have held meetings for homosexuals and worked to further homosexual "communion" with their members. In terms of this new faith, there is no God or Christ in heaven; God and Christ must be found in all our fellow men, accepted as they are without moral judgment or censure. This concept runs deeply through the so-called "Civil Rights" Revolution. It was expressed by a degenerate criminal and murderer as he was being executed. Aaron C. Mitchell was dragged screaming to the gas chamber at San Quentin, and his last words were, "I am Jesus Christ — look what they have done to me."[11]

But this total communion without law, communion beyond good and evil, militates against everything in man. No society has ever existed

---

9. See E. Belford Box, *Rise and Fall of the Anabaptists* (New York: American Scholars Publications, [1903], 1966); Frederick Engels, *The Peasant War in Germany* (Moscow: Foreign Languages Publishing House, [1850], 1956). See also R. J. Rushdoony, "Recipe for Revolution," in *News and Views*, vol. 22, no. 10, October, 1966.
10. Cited from Erich Fromm, *You Shall Be As Gods: A Radical Interpretation Of the Old Testament and Its Tradition*, by Bernard Mandelbaum, "Justifying Man's Ways to Man," *Saturday Review*, February 25, 1967, 57.
11. Dave Lamb, "Mitchell Yells, Dies in Gas Cell," Oakland, California *Tribune*, Wednesday, April 12, 1967, 1.

without class and caste lines. The more social distinctions are denied, the more force is required in society to bring men together, and the more force prevails in a society, the less the communion. The most readily discernible aspect of Soviet society to foreign travellers is the silence of people on the streets and in public places; people walk in isolation, because public speech is not the wisest of courses.

As against this enforced collectivization, which is hostile both to true community and true individualism, is the communion of saints. The enforced community of evil has, *first*, no true community to it. It cannot see men united except by force or for gain. *Second*, it also hates the individual; it denies him his integrity of person and of property. The Biblical communion of saints rests on a God-given communion with an inner bond. By the grace of God, there is, *first*, a loyalty to Christ. The true Christian views the world in terms of God's law. He sees the world in terms of a given perspective, a revealed framework, and the more he grows in grace the more sharply is his thinking governed by this Biblical framework. He is a member of Jesus Christ; he has a citizenship in heaven, a prior citizenship which governs every human relationship. His life is not his own, but Christ's.

Second, because the governing force in his life is increasingly *grace*, it is an *inner* bond which binds him to Christ and to his fellow Christians. The Christians draw together, not in terms of advantage, and often at the price of some sacrifice, in terms of this inner bond. They have a common life in Christ and therefore a common future. They are governed by a moral unity; they move in terms of the Biblical morality. And they are governed by a doctrinal unity, professing one Lord, and one faith, and one baptism in Christ. But their unity is not alone in faith and practice, but a unity in the heart. They are one people. They are closer to one another than the members of the fraternity of evil can ever be to each other, but this unity is not at the price of their particularity, their individualism. The fraternity of evil is ultimately destructive of both unity and individuality, of *both* the one and the many, but the communion of saints establishes both on their true foundation, the triune God. In Him they are truly one, and in Him they are truly themselves, so that both the unity and diversity of life come to their realization.

The one and the many is not only a philosophical and a social problem but a personal one. Man, as a creature of God, has both a need for unity in society and individuality and freedom. The non-Christian answers to the problem veer from unity as collectivism to particularity as anarchism, and they are destructive of both unity and particularity.

But David portrayed the unity of the saints, the communion of saints, as the realization and even the christening of the individual:

Behold, how good and how pleasant it is for brethren to dwell together in unity!

It is like the precious ointment upon the head, that ran down upon the beard, even Aaron's beard; that went down to the skirts of his garments;

As the dew of Hermon, and as the dew that descended upon the mountains of Zion: for there the LORD commanded the blessing, even life for evermore (Psalm 133:1-3).

As Leupold pointed out, "The oil symbolized the rich gifts of the Spirit." This communion and unity is a blessing which "the LORD commanded"; the author "traces the blessings resulting from unity to the creative blessing of God."[12] The communion of saints is the creative blessing of the triune God and the hidden, purposive unity within history.

[12.] H. C. Leupold, *Exposition of the Psalms* (Columbus, Ohio: Wartburg Press, 1959), 919f.

Chapter Nineteen

The Forgiveness of Sins

"The Forgiveness of Sins" is an article of the Apostles' Creed, and it appears in the Nicene Creed in relation to baptism: "I acknowledge one Baptism for the remission of sins."

The proclamation of "the remission of sins" is basic to the gospel. John the Baptist alerted all Israel to the coming of the Messiah, the Savior from sin, by his declaration of this doctrine in relationship to baptism. Baptism, as the sign of the new covenant, replacing circumcision, heralded the new age even as forgiveness of sins characterized the new life (Matt. 3:2, 6; Mark 1:4; Luke 3:3-6).

Where Jesus Christ is denied, the forgiveness of sins is of course denied. As Ignatius said, "He who disbelieves the gospel disbelieves everything along with it."[1] From the beginning of Scripture to the end, one doctrine of forgiveness, justification, sanctification, and communion with God is taught. This one doctrine was set forth typically in the Old Testament ordinances and fulfilled in Jesus Christ.

Forgiveness in the world of humanism has become an emotional and personal act; in the Bible, it is a *judicial and legal act*. It means that a guilty man's legal indictment or charges have been dropped, because satisfaction has been charges deferred for the time rendered, or, for some cases, charges deferred for the time being (Luke 23:24).[2]

[1.] "The Epistle of Ignatius to the Philadelphians," *Ante-Nicene Library*, I, *The Apostolic Fathers*, 234f

[2.] K. Schilder, *Christ Crucified*. Trans. by Henry Zylstra. Third edition. (Grand Rapids: Eerdmans, 1948), 134.

Because forgiveness is a juridical term, it makes all the more emphatic the fact that forgiveness is entirely of God's grace through Jesus Christ because atonement has been made by Jesus Christ and by Him alone. The person of the believer is accepted as righteous, not because of anything he has done but because of what Christ has done. The obedience and the satisfaction of Christ are the grounds of man's forgiveness: satisfaction has been rendered by Christ as the perfect man and as the federal head of the new humanity which Christ regenerates and calls unto Himself. As Robert Shaw pointed out, "Justification is a judicial act of God, and is not a change of nature, but a change of the sinner's state in relation to the law." Justification is more than the pardon of sin. It is also the "accounting and accepting their persons as righteous," as the Westminster Confession phrases it.[3] Adoption is the change of state for the justified man and is the privilege of all that truly believe in Christ (Gal. 3:26, 28). Sanctification is the progressive destruction of the whole body of sin in those who are effectually called and regenerated and have a new heart and a new spirit created within them. This sanctification is accomplished by the word, and by the Spirit indwelling in the believer.[4]

The unregenerate sinner is concerned with forgiveness, but not of sins, but rather of the consequences of sins. What the sinner wants dropped is the indictment and the penalty, with freedom granted to continue in his sin. The religious quest of non-Christian religions is the purchase of immunity from the fact of guilt and the threatening forces of retribution.

Basic to the success of Julius Caesar was his general offer of *clementia*, mercy without grace and without regeneration. Caesar's forgiveness extended to his enemies in case after case, so that Cicero had to say, "You are the only one, Gaius Caesar, at whose victory no one lost his life, except in battle."[5] Caesar could suspend the charges against his enemies, but he could not change their nature; he could not regenerate them nor himself, and they assassinated him.

Every political attempt to forgive without grace leads only to increased lawlessness and chaos, because forgiveness without salvation is simply a subsidy to sin; it is a condonation of sin which effectually says, "Go, and sin some more."

But political saviors are more often interested in perpetuating sin than in eliminating it. Sin is an important and major instrument of political power. *First* of all, in every totalitarian regime, and in every socialist order, blackmail is a major instrument of power. People who are amenable to blackmail are amenable to control. As a result, sin is politically encouraged

---

[3.] Robert Shaw, *An Exposition of the Confession of Faith of the Westminster Assembly of Divines,* 147.
[4.] See the Westminster Confession of Faith, ch. XIII.
[5.] Ethelbert Stauffer, *Christ and the Caesars,* 42-53.

and subsidized. Foreign diplomats are morally compromised in order to control them, and domestic legislators and bureaucrats are surrounded with temptation in order to keep them in a continually compromised situation. Sin is thus a basic instrument of political power and control. *Second,* religion is necessary to political power. For men to be blackmailed, sin must be reprehensible to the public, so that a legislator's immoral acts will then endanger his career. The religion preached must not be orthodox Christianity, not an uncompromising declaration of the saving power of God and man's glorious liberty in Jesus Christ. The religion of the state must be a religion of moralism. It must make sin socially reprehensible without liberating men from it. The state becomes the major patron of this religion of moralism; its priests, preachers, and evangelists proclaim the program of the state as a part of the gospel and preach moralism, to make sin terrible and grace remote. The net effect of moralistic religion is to make sinners feel more guilty and to enhance the power of the state. *Third,* the power state has a stake in perpetuating sin because guilty men are slaves. A man with a guilty conscience is not a free man; he is in bondage, and his life will reveal his inner slavery. More than a few wives have on occasion tried quietly to push their husbands into adultery in the knowledge that a guilty man is less independent and less confident in making a stand in terms of his rightful authority and responsibility. As Shakespeare's Hamlet observed, "Conscience does make cowards of us all." The effects of a bad conscience are enslaving. The power state therefore works to *promote* immorality as though it were a necessary aspect of human liberty, and to *destroy* Christianity, in order to eliminate the remedy for sin, the relief and healing for an enslaved conscience. Without the liberating power of Christianity, the forgiveness of sins through Jesus Christ, there is no possibility of overthrowing tyranny. The gospel of the tyrant state becomes the assertion that liberty is license to sin, and slavery is the liberty of moral self-government. In every such state, the courts and schools decree and interpret liberty as freedom from morality. The people are deluded into believing they are a more free people because they now possess a license to fornicate, to commit adultery, indulge in perversions freely, and read pornography. Meanwhile, as the people wallow in this "new freedom," the state rapidly extends its powers over the people, over family life, economics, education, business, labor, and agriculture, over the churches, art, science, and all things else. The promulgation of the idea that sexual and moral irresponsibility is liberty is thus the usual and necessary prelude to the destruction of liberty and the rise of statism. The "new freedom" produces the old slavery.

Where there is no forgiveness of sins, there is also the condoning of sins. A sinful society finds itself unwilling to accept the fact of judgment, because it is vulnerable to judgment. As a result, the law is steadily subverted. The death penalty is weakened or dropped. The criminal is so greatly favored in court that the prosecution of crime is handicapped. Criminal law increasingly favors the criminal. Civil law is no better. Some years ago, a study made by the Institute for the Study of Law at John Hopkins showed that "in the Supreme Court of New York County less than 7% of the amount of judgments entered by the court was ever collected by the 'successful' parties."[6] The civil courts serve the interests of the state and provide the judges and lawyers with a good living. In the power state, there is little justice for the people in the courts, because the courts are an agency of the state rather than an agency of justice. And because the state is itself in sin, it has a vested interest in sin. Justice is anathema to the social order which has everything to fear from justice and is committed to sinning as an assertion of its independence from God.

Where there is no forgiveness of sins, there is bondage to sin. A sinning people may fret against the injustice of their overlords, but they lack the moral courage to make a stand against injustice. For a sinner to war against sin is comparable to warring against himself. As a result, a corrupt people will indulge in complaints against tyranny but will be impotent in combating it.

St. Paul connected the remission of sins with boldness in approaching God: it meant the "full assurance of faith, having our hearts sprinkled from an evil conscience, and our bodies washed with pure water" (Heb. 10:16-25). If the forgiveness of sins gives boldness in relation to God, how much more so in relation to men. The relationship of the unredeemed sinner to God is one of hatred and fear; the sinner is in flight and hiding from God. The hiding of Adam and Eve was in the Garden of Eden, behind fig-leaves and in the refuge of shadows. The hiding place of modern man is in the apostate churches, and in unbelief, but no hiding place avails man against God.

The forgiveness of sins restores man into communion with God and into his rightful place as lord of the earth in Christ. The forgiveness of sins is the liberation of man from God's judgment, and from the sentence of his own heart. It is the restoration of man into his calling as man, to be priest, prophet, and king under God. It is the restoration of man into clear and true thinking, for, as Fulke Greville wrote,

> Whence all Mans fleshly idols being built,
> As humane *Wisedome, Science, Power,* and *Arts,*
> Upon the false foundation of his Guilt;
> Confusedly doe weave within our hearts,
> Their owne advancement, state, and declination,
> As things whose beings are but transmutation.[7]

---

6. William Scagle, *Law: The Science of Inefficiency* (New York: Macmillan, 1952), 3.

When man builds on "the false foundation of his Guilt," he fails to build with reason, which measures "first our own Humanity," but seeks instead to attain to divinity and to plant our Paradise in dust."[8] Whereas the sinner builds on the false foundation of his Guilt," the believer builds on Jesus Christ, the incarnate one, and his forgiveness of sins. In Christ man is freed from the burden of sin and guilt, and from sin and death, and instead of a hunted and guilty man in headlong flight from God, from himself, and from reality, he becomes a child of God and an heir of creation. The forgiveness of sins is man's great charter of liberty.

The forgiveness of sins is primarily the act of God. The question of the scribes, "Who can forgive sins but God only?" was not denied by Jesus. Instead, He demonstrated Himself to be God incarnate. He spoke of Himself as "the Son of man," a title referring to God's Messiah, and performed a miracle in evidence of His divine power (Mark 2:6-12). Forgiveness of sins is an act of God, and therefore there can be no human forgiveness on humanistic grounds such as love, emotionalism, sentimentalism, or the craving for peace. Forgiveness by man can only be ministerial, i.e., in terms of God's requirements and laws. Acting ministerially, man can forgive, knowing that what he looses is loosed in heaven, and what he binds is bound in heaven, because God is true to Himself and to His word (Matt. 16:19; 18:18; John 20:23; 1 Cor. 5:4, 5; Isaiah 22:22). Man can then move in confidence and power, because he moves in the certainty of God's word.

Because forgiveness is the act of God, it cannot become the act of man in any originating form. Man can forgive or deny forgiveness only as God's word requires it. The initiative in forgiveness is from God. Hence the persistent attempt by heretical theologians to break down the doctrine of forgiveness by universalism, by insisting that all men's sins are forgiven and that all men are saved. Universalism means that sin is established as man's basic and permanent condition, in that all men are accepted and forgiven in their sin and without judgment and regeneration. Universalism claims to be total love, but it is, if at all, the total love of evil, in that it establishes it in moral legitimacy. Universalism is the total hatred of God's regenerating purpose and plan. Universalism is moral anarchism. The universalistic doctrine of the forgiveness of sins is the establishment of evil and the denial of the significance and reality of sin. Wherever it prevails, tyranny and stagnation take over society. The forgiveness of sins in terms of Biblical faith is the framework of both liberty and progress.

[7.] Geoffrey Bullough, editor, *Poems and Dramas of Fulke Greville, First Lord Brooke,* vol. I, from "A Treatie of Humane Learning." (New York: Oxford University Press, 1945), 167.

[8.] *Ibid.,* I, 190.

Biblical forgiveness is judicial, and it is exercised in two areas, *political* and *religious*. *First*, in the political realm, forgiveness is exercised through courts of law, and Biblical forgiveness in the social or societal relations is contingent upon the fulfilment of God's law. For some crimes, forgiveness is possible only by capital punishment, for others, by restitution. Without Biblical forgiveness, crimes accumulate, and judgment mounts, as innocent blood cries out from the ground for vengeance. The crimes then accrue not only to the criminal but to the land as well, so that God's capital punishment is executed on the entire land. A city without justice is a "bloody city" and under judgment (Ezek. 24: 6-14). The purpose of civil law is to establish justice, and there is no justice without restitution. The criminal then remains socially unforgiven in God's sight, and the land shares in the criminal's guilt and judgment.

The *second* form of Biblical forgiveness is soteriological, i.e., religious with reference to salvation. Our sins are atoned for by the blood of Jesus Christ, and we are forgiven. For a land to be Christian, both forms of forgiveness must prevail. Without both forms, antinomianism and social decay are inevitable.

Chapter Twenty

The Resurrection of the Dead

The doctrine of the resurrection of Jesus Christ, and of the general resurrection, is basic to the creeds and the apostolic witness. St. Paul stated the issue bluntly: "For if the dead rise not, then is Christ not raised; And if Christ be not raised, your faith is vain; ye are yet in your sins. Then they also which are fallen asleep in Christ are perished. If in this life only we have hope in Christ, we are of all men most miserable. But now is Christ risen from the dead, and become the firstfruits of them that slept. For since by man came death, by man came also the resurrection of the dead" (1 Cor. 15:16-21).

The attitude of many persons is that Christianity, by placing faith and religion on so material a basis as the resurrection, is guilty of a materialistic and self-serving perspective. It is held that true religion should require nobility for the sake of nobility, without any other reward than the satisfaction of being what one is. But this attitude is itself the epitome of sin, in that it enthrones moral autonomy as the essence of the true life. Man as his own god, content with his autonomy, needs no reward other than the satisfaction of being himself. Biblical religion calls for obedience to God and promises rewards for obedience and curses for disobedience. The doctrine of the resurrection is basic to the Biblical order of rewards, but it is also central to the doctrine of creation and redemption.

Since Tertullian is often accused of having a negative attitude towards the body, and of showing strongly ascetic traits, it is instructive to examine Tertullian's writings in order to assess the Christian doctrine of the resurrection and its implications.

First of all, Tertullian made it clear that there is no true Christianity without the doctrine of the resurrection. "He, therefore, will not be a Christian who shall deny this doctrine which is confessed by Christians."[1] The doctrine is alien, Tertullian held, to paganism, but "The resurrection of the dead is the Christian's trust."[2]

Second, the doctrine of the resurrection is the logical conclusion to the doctrine of creation. For paganism, mortality, and therefore the flesh, is an ugly fact. Both heretic and heathen, however much they profess to be more congenial to life than the orthodox, hate the body.

> Is not their burden from beginning and everywhere an invective against the flesh — against its origin, against its substance, against the casualties and the invariable end which await it; unclean from its first formation of the dregs of the ground, uncleaner afterwards from the mire of its own seminal transmission; worthless, weak, covered with guilt, laden with misery, full of trouble; and after all this record of its degradation, dropping into its original earth and the appelation of a corpse, and destined to dwindle away even from this loathsome name into none henceforth at all — into the very death of all designation?[3]

For the pagans, life was haunted by an eternal recurrence, by change and decay in an unending and meaningless cycle. For them, the horror of flesh was its inevitable decay. Flesh was thus a kind of trap for humanity. Very early Greek thought also turned to the transmigration of souls, as with Pythagorus. It was held, by some, "that, on account of this, they should even abstain from eating animal food? May any one have the persuasion that he should abstain, lest by chance in his beef he eats of some ancestor of his?" All these absurd opinions are given intellectual respectability, "But if a Christian promises the return of a man from a man, and the very actual Gaius from Gaius, the cry of the people will be to have him stoned; they will not even so much as grant him a hearing."[4]

This point is a significant one: the world of antiquity, committed to humanism, tolerated any absurdity concerning the future life but rejected, without a hearing often, or with demands that the preacher be killed, the doctrine of the resurrection. The answer is obvious. Every one of these other beliefs, i.e., the immortality of the soul, reincarnation or transmigration, etc., all affirmed the basic divinity of man and his self-salvation. The Biblical doctrine made man a creature and God sovereign. It placed man's total life under a total God, and this was and is the offense of the doctrine of the resurrection. The immortality of the soul,

---

[1] Tertullian, "A Treatise on the Resurrection of the Flesh," chapt. III, *Ante-Nicene Library,* vol. XV, *Writings of Tertullian,* vol. II (Edinburgh: T&T Clark, 1874), 221.
[2] *Ibid.,* ch. I, 215.
[3] *Ibid.,* ch. IV, 222.
[4] Tertullian, "Apologeticus," *Ante-Nicene Library,* Vol. XI, Writings of Tertullian, vol. I, (1872), 133.

The Resurrection of the Dead   171

in its every form, is a doctrine which makes man his own god and savior; it gives man an "open" universe, i.e., free from God, which is man's to explore in time and eternity.

God having created all things for His glory, does not allow sin and the fall to frustrate His purpose; therefore, Tertullian said, "all creation is instinct with renewal." God's purpose is the restoration and fulfillment of all things. "The whole, therefore, of this revolving order of things bears witness to the resurrection of the dead."[5]

Third, not only is man's destiny the resurrection and the glory of eternal life, but his present life in the body is not to be falsely understood. Man is the sinner, *not* the body.

> We maintain, moreover, that what has been abolished in Christ is not *carnem peccati*, "sinful flesh," but *peccatum carnis*, "sin in the flesh," — not the material thing, but its condition; not the substance, but its flaw; and this we aver on the authority of the apostle, who says, "He abolished sin in the flesh."[6]

Moreover, Tertullian pointed out. it is the "works of the flesh," not the *substance* of the flesh, which St. Paul always condemns.[7]

Man, indeed, was made of the dust or clay of the earth. It was man, clay, upon whom God breathed to make a living soul. "I wish to impress this on your attention, with a view to your knowing, that whatever God has at all purposed or promised to man, is due not to the soul simply, but to the flesh also; if not arising out of any community in their origin, yet at all events by the privilege possessed by the latter in its name."[8] God obliterated the clay in man and absorbed it into flesh; the clay became another substance, flesh.[9] To speak of the body as "dirt" and therefore contemptible is to dishonor it; the body must be viewed in terms of what God made it in creation, and makes it in the resurrection. There is no shame in earth, but things must be seen in their true perspective: The body in its first creation was destined to be a vehicle for the glory of God the Son:

> Thus, that clay which was even then putting on the image of Christ, who was to come in the flesh, was not only the work, but also the pledge and surety, of God. To what purpose is it to bandy about the name *earth*, as that of a sordid and grovelling element, with the view of tarnishing the origin of the flesh, when, even if any other material had been available for forming man, it would be requisite that the dignity of the Maker should be taken into consideration, who even by His selection of His material deemed it, and by His management made it, worthy? ... The privilege has been granted to the flesh to be nobler

---

5. Tertullian, "On the Resurrection of the Flesh," ch. XII, *Writings*, II, 235.
6. Tertullian, "On the Flesh of Christ." ch. XVI, in *Writings*, II, 198.
7. Tertullian, "On the Resurrection of the Flesh," ch. XLVI, II, 295.
8. *Ibid.*, ch V; II, 225.
9. *Ibid.*, ch. V; II, 225f.

than its origin, and to have its happiness aggrandized by the change wrought in it. Now, even gold is earth, because of the earth; but it remains earth no longer after it becomes gold, but is a far different substance, more splendid and more noble, though coming from a source which is comparatively faded and obscure. In like manner, it was quite allowable for God that He should clear the gold of our flesh, from all the taints, as you deem them, of its native clay, by purging the original substance of its dross.[10]

"The gold of our flesh!" This certainly is strong praise of the body, and it represents an important element of the teaching of the early church.

The Greco-Roman view was hostile to the body. It saw the world in terms of the dialectic of form and matter, form or ideas being the higher, truer substance, and matter being the baser substance or being. There was no delight in or respect for the body in classical culture; there was a delight rather in the pleasures of the body combined with a disrespect for the body itself. As a result, this Hellenic view lent itself readily to either total license or radical asceticism. It was this Hellenic influence which introduced asceticism into the early church. Asceticism had no roots in either the Old or New Testaments, although misinterpreted texts were used to justify it.

The pagan depreciation of the body or matter led to two consequences. *First*, it led on the one hand to asceticism, to attempts to transcend the body by a denial of it. *Second*, it led to flagrant amoralism and license. The body was a submoral concern, and therefore not within the province of ethics. The body was denied by a studied moral indifference to acts of the body, so that immorality became an ascetic way, a means of renouncing the body.

Both forms of paganism continue in the modern world, although the second is especially prominent in the twentieth century.

The pagan hatred of *change* was also a form of asceticism, and it is present in virtually all anti-Christianity. The hatred of change leads to attempts to stop change, to stop history, and to create an end-of-history civilization, a final order which will end mutability and give man an unchanging world. Part of this order involves also the scientific efforts to abolish death. This hatred of change is a hatred of creation, and of its movement in terms of God's purpose. Unlike the pagan and the humanist, the orthodox Christian is committed to a respect for creation.

This respect for creation gave roots to science in the Christian west. It is not an accident of history that science in other cultures has had a limited growth and a quick withering. Both the fact of God's eternal decree undergirding all creation with law, and the fact of the resurrection, giving dignity and importance to the physical universe, made an interest in the universe and the development of science inevitable.

---

10. *Ibid.*, ch. vi; II, 226.

The pagan perspective is one of a fundamental disrespect for creation, for the universe. The central problems for the Hellenic mind were *change* and *decay*, and, wherever neoplatonism and Aristotelianism influenced the church, this emphasis returned. For the Christian who holds to a Biblical faith, change and decay are not the problems: *sin* is, and *death* is the consequence of sin. Thus, when the hymn writer, Henry F. Lyte (1793-1847), wrote, in "Abide With Me,"

> Change and decay in all around I see.
> O thou, who changest not, abide with me,

he was showing a Hellenic influence. When men began to mourn over *mutability*, they mourned as Greeks, not as Christians, because to the Christian mutability brings on God's predestined purpose. Isaiah met the complaint over mutability, "all flesh is grass," head on, affirming it in the context of God's omnipotence and eternal decree (Isaiah 40:6-31).

The Biblical affirmation of the doctrine of the resurrection, as summed up by St. Paul in 1 Corinthians 15:16-21, makes clear several facts basic to the faith. *First*, the resurrection of Jesus Christ is inseparably linked to the resurrection of all believers. *Second*, without the resurrection, our faith is in vain, and we are miserable men. We are not autonomous, and it is the epitome of insanity to imagine that our destiny and salvation is in our hands. *Third*, Jesus Christ, as very man of very man, has opened up for His church, His members, the glorious destiny that is theirs. This means a redeemed life in time, with the curse removed from body and soul, love and labor, to the extent that we are sanctified. It means, moreover, the glory of the general resurrection, and the perfection of physical life in the resurrection body and with everlasting life. Man's destiny is to be a creature under God, not to escape creaturehood. Those who rebel against the doctrine of the resurrection are in rebellion against creaturehood. Those who are redeemed by Jesus Christ rejoice in creaturehood under God, and life in the flesh is for them a blessed one, and the prospects of the resurrection a glorious one. It is therefore basic to creedalism to affirm: "I believe in ... the Resurrection of the body, And the Life everlasting," or, as the Nicene Creed even more triumphantly declares, "And I look for the Resurrection of the dead: And the Life of the world to come. Amen."

This is the Christian faith, *the resurrection*. Pagan antiquity, as well as "primitive" cultures, hold to a belief in a supernatural, immortal soul. Whether in its Hellenic form, or as animism, this view is alien to the Biblical perspective. "Immortality" is ascribed in Scripture to God alone. St. Paul declared that God "only hath immortality" (1 Tim. 6:16 cf. 1: 17), and, when the word is applied to man, in 1 Corinthians 15:53, 54, it is not declared to be a natural condition of man but a miracle of grace: "For this corruptible must put on incorruption, and this mortal must put on immortality." Immortality is seen by Paul not as a *condition* of man but as an aspect of Christ's *grace* to the sanctified (Rom. 2:6, 7). It is Jesus Christ "who hath abolished death, and hath brought life and immortality to light through the gospel" (2 Tim. 1: 10). These are the only verses in the Bible using the words "immortal" (1 Tim. 1:17) and "immortality" (Rom. 2:7; 1 Cor. 15:53, 54; 1 Tim. 6:16; 2 Tim. 1:10). The Hellenic perspective saw the soul as immortal, basically divine, and in essence under restraint because of its mixture with the earth of the body. In neo-platonism, this body was viewed as the prison of the soul, which the soul had a positive duty to renounce and transcend. Whenever and wherever the soul is seen as of another substance than the body, then contempt of the body is inevitable. The body, as of lower substance, is a baser element, and the soul either actually or potentially divine. But, this perspective, which has extensively polluted the church, and influenced many of the church fathers, Tertullian included, is not Biblical. It is hostile to a respect for the body, although conducive to license. Greek culture was congenial to license but hostile to a true materialism.

For the Bible, body and soul are alike created by God, alike fallen, depraved, and reprobate in Adam, alike redeemed in Christ and to be regarded as God's gifts and destiny for man. Both body and soul are alike to put on immortality and enjoy the glories of the resurrection.[11] Both body and soul are therefore to be treated with respect as God's creation and blessing, wonderful now, and glorious in the world to come. The assured faith of the Nicene Creed affirms: "And I look for the Resurrection of the dead: And the Life of the world to come."

---

11. The ancient Egyptian belief in the resurrection was radically different from the Biblical faith. As *The Book of the Dead* makes clear, the Egyptian belief was in the divinization of the body, and thus more congenial to other views of divinization, the difference being that divinity became a property of the body as well as the soul.

Chapter Twenty-One

Man and the Creeds

John J. Moment, in his study of the creeds, had a chapter entitled "Man in the Creeds." In a heretical exposition Moment expounded the universal fatherhood of God, the brotherhood of all men, and the divinity in all men, declaring:

> The effort to exalt Christ by minimizing the divine in our common human nature is much of a kind with that of an earlier day when the Church went even further in degrading man in order to magnify the grace of God. This process began in the fifth century with Augustine in the course of a long and bitter debate with an Irishman named Morgan, better known to history under his latinized name of Pelagius. Pelagius contended that every man has his destiny in his own hands, that any man is capable of rising in his own strength to moral perfection. Augustine, in his protest against this over-optimistic view of the race, finally, to his own considerable embarrassment, found himself defending the proposition that apart from the power of the gospel there is and can be no good in any man. It was Pelagius' opportunity to recall the Church to its earlier faith that not only is there good in every man but that good, wherever found, is God's gift of Himself and in the most literal sense divine ....
>
> We are indulging in no figure of speech but speaking quite literally when we say that in one or another of the saints of history, in one or another of our friends, we recognize a divine Presence, and this, after all, is only another term for incarnation.[1]

[1.] John J. Moment, *We Believe* (New York: Macmillan, 1942), 102f.

As against the sovereignty of God, and predestination, Moment was anxious to preserve man's liberty, the belief "that every man has his destiny in his own hands," so that man is essentially his own savior, himself divine, and therefore a kind of "incarnation." Moment was a minister in the Presbyterian Church, U.S.A., but still essentially both a Pelagian and a humanist, although a graduate of Princeton University, prior to Wilson.

Another humanist, non-Christian, is Dr. Szasz, a psychiatrist who is anxious to preserve human liberty against the dangers of psychiatry. Dr. Szasz's able critiques of psychiatry, of the concept of mental illness, which he terms a myth, and of the relationship between psychiatry and the law, are of great value and deserve a wide hearing, but his concept of liberty, while noble in intent, is weak in practice. Dr. Szasz has written:

> The individual can never escape the moral burden of his existence. He must choose between obedience to authority and responsibility to himself. Moral decisions often are hard and painful to make. The temptation to delegate this burden to others is therefore ever-present. Yet, as all history teaches us, those who would take from man his moral burdens — be they priests or warlords, politicians or psychiatrists — must also take from him his liberty and hence his very humanity.
>
> A humanistic psychiatry must, therefore, repudiate its seemingly therapeutic mandate, the pursuit of which often results, intentionally or unwittingly, in moral tranquility gained at the expense of freedom and responsibility. Instead of trying to diminish man's moral burdens, such a psychiatry must aim at increasing his powers and so making him equal to his task. And what is this task? No one has stated it better than Albert Camus when he wrote: "The aim of life can only be to increase the sum of freedom and responsibility to be found in every man and in the world. It cannot, under any circumstances, be to reduce or suppress that freedom, even temporarily."[2]

This statement quite clearly reflects the fact that Dr. Szasz is the product of a Christian culture, and his humanistic faith and goals are conditioned by that fact. He wants liberty and moral responsibility. The choice, as he sees it, is "between obedience to authority and responsibility to himself." At this point, Dr. Szasz is playing games with language and with himself. To be responsible is to be answerable to someone or something, to a law or authority beyond one's self to which we are accountable. "Responsibility to himself" means that man has no responsibility: he is free to do everything he pleases, and his every whim is his law. Beyond pleasing himself, man has no law. But, if Dr. Szasz protests that he means by "responsibility to himself" certain standards of conduct and moral law which man must conform to, then those standards have been made into an

---

2. Thomas S. Szasz, "Mental Illness is a Myth," in *Popular Psychology*, May, 1967. vol. I, no. I, 58.

authority over man which man must obey. Dr. Szasz has then asked us to choose "obedience to authority"; he has simply chosen a humanistic authority in preference to God.

Dr. Szasz is right in declaring that "The individual can never escape the moral burden of his existence." By this statement he has asserted the moral force and authority of a law transcending man. Szasz further insists on the moral necessity of man to be free. But if man is only responsible to himself, and there is no law beyond man's will, man has no responsibility to be free. Man can, if he chooses, be a slave or a free man; either choice is valid if it is his choice.

But Dr. Szasz has equated liberty with humanity, and to take from man his liberty is to take "hence his very humanity." Apparently Dr. Szasz has a special revelation which makes liberty the definition of man, because otherwise his humanism permits no definition. Man is man, and whatever any individual man is, that which he chooses to be defines his life and the sum total of meaning. Humanism is logically total anarchism, as Marx saw; pragmatically, Marx chose total collectivism as the alternative and as a more practical way of denying God's law.

Moreover, Dr. Szasz implies that unlimited liberty, after Camus, is man's true destiny. But man's true destiny, as Biblical faith asserts, calls for limited liberty and limited power. Since man is man, it cannot be otherwise. Can man reverse the time of his birth and return to a past age? Can he choose to be a chemist when his aptitudes are only those of a clerk? Can he at will determine the time of his death, or the state of his health and finances? Man is at every point limited in his liberty, because man is a creature. Man's only true liberty is a limited liberty, and his only true power is limited power.

Man is not free to be a god, because man is a creature. Man's freedom is to be that which God made him to be, and man is at all points and in all things answerable and accountable to God. It is man's sin that makes him seek an independence from God, and this quest is not only a flight from God but also from himself, because man is God's creation, and every fiber of his being witnesses at all times to God. Dr. Cornelius Van Til has pointed out that, if man the sinner could find a single button in the universe which to press would give him an experience in independence of the triune God, man would only and always press that button. But no such button exists. Man is inescapably the creature of God, and therein is his liberty and his glory.

The creeds and councils, by their unswerving insistence on the sovereignty of God, assert thereby implicitly and firmly the creatureliness of man. In this faith is man's only hope.

David, in Psalm 8, sang with delight of man's role, by faith, under God. The destiny of the redeemed man is great: "Thou madest him to have dominion over the works of thy hands: thou hast put all things under his feet" (Ps. 8:6). Man was created to exercise dominion over the earth under God; in Jesus Christ, man is regenerated to fulfil his calling.

But man, apart from God, is nothing. For man to seek an escape from God is to seek the impossible. Man cannot escape from God, Who is omnipresent, nor from himself, who is God's creation. As David said, "If I ascend up into heaven, thou art there: if I make my bed in hell, behold, thou art there" (Ps. 139:8). There is no possibility of escape, because there is no other universe, not a single fact or atom not created by God. There is no hiding place nor covering from God, so that the existentialist dream of escape from God into a freedom from God is a myth.

Man does appear, however, in the creeds and very directly and simply: "I believe," and even this appearance is by grace, the prevenient grace of God. Man was called into being, together with the whole of creation, by the creative word and power of God, and man is recalled into the presence of the triune God, and into communion with Him, by that self-same regenerating and creative word.

The nature and destiny of man is to be a man under God, to exercise dominion over the earth under God, and to triumph over sin, death, and the enemy in Christ. Every attempt to put man in the creed is an attempt to abolish God but which in effect abolishes man. Thomas J. Altizer, in defending his death of God theology in a debate with John Montgomery, said, "The Christian can rejoice in the death of God ... because he is free from any kind of ultimate norm and therefore is released to live fully in the present. He is liberated."[3] Altizer here reveals clearly the motive force of his school of thought. It is, *first,* the old Satanic temptation, man's original sin, to be as God, to be the knower or determiner of good and evil, of ultimate norms (Gen. 3:5). Therefore man wills the death of God in order to make possible man's own birth as god. *Second,* man identifies liberty and liberation as the freedom "from any kind of ultimate norm." Man lives then in a moral vacuum, a world rendered totally void of God's ultimate norms and antiseptically sealed from God. *Third,* man is then free to create his own norms, to be his own ultimate norm. This can be gained either through *anarchism,* in which each individual man is his own ultimate norm, or through *total statism,* in which the collective man's will as embodied in the dictatorship is the ultimate norm.

The result is not the death of God but the death of man. Anarchism, as Marx recognized, can only destroy man and society, but totalitarianism of this variety in particular is also destructive of man. *First,* man then has no

---

3. *Inter-Varsity News,* May, 1967, "Dialog on the Death of God," 2.

appeal against injustice, or against his own failure and sin. Since man is the ultimate norm, what appeal has man against himself, or what source of help? If the ultimate norm is the state, then he has no appeal against the state, since the state is then god. The result is absolute tyranny. The tyranny of psychoanalysis is that it gives man no escape from the infallibility of the unconscious, because man is then governed by the unconscious. Wherever humanism locates the ultimate norm, the result is the same, total tyranny. *Second,* a burden of infallibility is then placed on sinful man and his sinful state. The ultimate norm is the individual or collective man, and an ultimate norm is an infallible norm, because there is no norm over it by which it can be judged fallible. As a result, no progress is possible, since no concept of higher or lower, better or worse, can be applied to an infallible norm. *Third,* the only way in which progress can be visualized is by creating a trans-human or macro-human norm, one which makes it possible to surpass man. In terms of evolution, this means the abolition of man. Man, it is held, is to be a single cell in the new life-form of the future, "macro-life," so that the individual man will be of no more value than a cell of skin, hair, or fingernail, and as readily subject to squeezing as part of a pimple, shaving as unwanted hair, or trimming as an unwanted length of fingernail. Yet this concept of man as a single cell of the "macro-life" is seriously considered and planned for.[4]

When man becomes the object of the creed, when man is "in the creed," the result is the abolition of man. The salvation of man is to declare the Biblical creeds, to confess the triune God and to find in Him salvation, liberty, and life. When man declares, "I believe ..." he becomes the confessor of God's glory and God's truth, and the recipient of God's grace and prosperity.

[4.] Henry Still, *Will the Human Race Survive?* (New York: Hawthorne Books, 1966), 246-248.

Chapter Twenty-Two

The Foundations of Social Order

Every social order rests on a creed, on a concept of life and law, and represents a religion in action. Culture is religion externalized, and, as Henry Van Til observed, "a people's religion comes to expression in its culture, and Christians can be satisfied with nothing less than a Christian organization of society."[1] Wherever there is an attack on the organization of society, there is an attack on its religion. The basic faith of a society means growth in terms of that faith, but any tampering with its basic structure is revolutionary activity. The Marxists are in this respect more astute than their adversaries: they recognize hostility to their structure as counter-revolutionary activity, as hostility to their establishment. The life of a society is its creed; a dying creed faces desertion or subversion readily. Every creed, however healthy, is also under continual attack; the culture which neglects to defend and further its creedal base is exposing its heart to the enemy's knife. Because of its indifference to its creedal basis in Biblical Christianity, western civilization is today facing death and is in a life and death struggle with humanism.

The foundations of social order need to be examined, therefore, in order to be understood and defended. *First*, there is the creedal basis: every law order rests on and is the legal codification of a system of morality, and every morality presupposes a religion, some form of "ultimate concern." Most religions are non-theistic, but all religions are basic to one or another system of morality. Moral order is an aspect of religious order. Most

---

[1.] Henry Van Til, *The Calvinistic Concept of Culture* (Philadelphia: The Presbyterian and Reformed Publishing Company, 1959), 245.

religions are not theistic but basically humanistic. From the structural perspective, religions can be divided into two great and central classes: *theistic* and *political*. In a theistic religion, God is the source of morality and law. The order of the universe is God-given and absolute, and man's order must be patterned in terms of God's infallible word, the Bible. In political religion, politics is the source of morality and law. Aristotle wrote on politics and therefore concerned himself with ethics, and his ethics is the morality of a political order. Ethics for Aristotle basically has an immanent principle of ultimacy rather than a transcendental one. Instead of an absolute order in the universe, political religion sees a developing order which can guide and control, so that God's eternal decree is replaced by man's total planning. Man's predestination replaces predestination by God. Political morality has always been productive of political religions.

The *second* foundation of social order is the state. The state is the social organization of the creed, the legal structuring of the moral system of a society. The state cannot be amoral, because its every law is the codification of its basic morality. The state cannot be religiously neutral, because it is the religious organization of society in terms of law. When the state claims religious neutrality, it is either self-deception or a deception of the people, and it merely means a neutrality towards its old faith in order to prepare the way for the establishment of the new faith. The state is no less a religious organization than the church, and in some societies more so. In Christian society, church and state are both religious orders, the church as a ministry of grace and the state as a ministry of justice. In pagan society, the state takes priority as the religious order: the temple or the shrine then become aspects of the state's life and function. Religion can no more be abstracted from the state than from the church. Churches and states may forsake a religion and abandon their creed, but only in order to adopt a new one.

The purpose of the state varies in terms of its religion. Basically, the state can be either messianic or ministerial, either a savior or a ministry of justice. For Biblical religion, the state is the ministry of justice; for non-Christian religions, for political religions, the state is man's savior. The two concepts are mutually exclusive, and there can be no compromise between them.

The *third* foundation of social order is sovereignty. Sovereignty can be either transcendental or immanent, resting either in God or being an attribute of man and his order. Basically, the two conflicting concepts are between God's sovereignty and the claimed sovereignty of the state. If God is sovereign, then He is the creator and governor of all things, and His law over-arches, controls, judges, and assesses all things; nothing can exist or have being apart from Him. If the state is sovereign, then the state must exercise total control and judgment over all things in its world, or its

sovereignty is limited and negated. The state seeks, in terms of its claim to
sovereignty, to become the determining and over-arching power over every
domain: no sphere is allowed to function except by permission of the state.
The earth, air, water, sky all belong to the state, are used only under the law
and tax of the state, and are potentially or actually subject to repossession
by the state. The state has assumed that ultimacy over man's life which
properly belongs only to God. The creed of the state therefore requires
holy warfare against the Christian creed and faith.

Two absolute sovereignties and sovereigns cannot coexist at the same
point in time and space, claiming the same jurisdiction. Because the claims
of God and the sovereign state are mutually exclusive, their conflict is
inevitable. The warfare between Christ and Caesar is inescapable war, and
it is a war unto death.

For every sovereign order, sin and evil are a problem. Biblical
Christianity deals with sin and evil in two ways. *First,* the state as the
ministry of justice establishes restitution as the fundamental principle of
the law. The justice of God must be maintained; there must therefore be
restitution by man whenever God's order is in any way abated or breached,
or else God will exact retribution through His judgment. *Second,* the
church as the ministry of grace must proclaim the saving grace of Jesus
Christ. Jesus Christ makes atonement for man's sin against God, and He
establishes the order of God in relation to man; this order is communion
in Him. Christ's atoning work affects restitution in relationship to God,
even as civil law under God must effect restitution in relationship to man
as its duty towards God. Thus, in a higher sense, both church and state have
a calling to effect godly restitution, the state as a ministry of justice, the
church as a ministry of grace. The goal is "the restitution of all things" in
the new creation (Acts 3:21). *Restitution is thus the basic aspect of the
Christian social order.*

The *fourth* foundation of social order is thus grace. Man's problem under
any creed is the presence of personal and impersonal evil in the world. Man
assesses the nature of that evil and his answer to it is in terms of his creed.
For political religions, for humanism, evil is in the environment, and the
state's power to change that environment is its saving grace. The state must
remake man's physical and spiritual environment in order to change and
save man. Social change in terms of the state's plan is statist grace in
operation. The bad environment must be destroyed in order to free man.
This evil environment sometimes involves persons and institutions, such as
the bourgeoisie, capitalists, the clergy, Christians, churches, private
organizations, private enterprise, and so on. All these may have to be, and
frequently are, "liquidated" or destroyed as part of the process of salvation.
Those persons remaining must be "re-educated" in terms of the new creed
and out of Christianity.

For Biblical Christianity, the answer to the problem of evil is God's grace, the grace of God through Jesus Christ and the restitution of all things. Man's problem is not his environment but *sin,* man's desire to be his own god, his own law and principle of ultimacy. Man cannot save himself, either by politics, works of law or morality, or by any other means. Jesus Christ is man's only savior. Man must live under God's law order in order to live freely and happily, but the law order cannot save man, nor will that law order long survive, if there be not a sizable body of believers whose life is the law of God. Basic to true order therefore is grace. Without grace, man lacks the character to develop his potentialities, capitalize his activities, and order his life.

The extent to which a doctrine of grace permeates all society is apparent in executions. It was once commonplace at executions in the United States for public officials to make a plea to the criminal to receive God's saving grace before dying, and more than a few criminals died acknowledging themselves to be sinners in need of Christ's saving grace. In the mid-20th century, the situation was radically different although prison chaplains survived as a remnant of Christian order. To cite an example, Aaron Charles Mitchell was sentenced to death in California for murdering a police officer while committing a felony. His attorney pleaded before Governor Edmund G. Brown in May, 1967, "Had this man been fortunate enough to have been given white skin, he undoubtedly could have wound up in the seat now occupied by your honor." Mitchell, aged 37, had spent all but five years in prison since his 17th birthday. Mitchell declared to the press, "What people ought to be trying to find out about me is what it was in my environment that caused me to go bad." Mitchell then pointed out that he was born in Mississippi and moved to Memphis, Tennessee when five years old. His parents "broke up when I was 14 or 15." He was thus environmentally justified in his criminality![2]

Another telling illustration of this new creed was the Citizens Housing and Planning Council. Convinced that the problem of the slum dwellers was a bad environment, notably the evil landlords, the Council secured a quarter of a million dollars from Laurence Rockefeller to buy a slum apartment building, renovate it, and thereby rehabilitate the dwellers and demonstrate to the world that a decent profit could be made by providing a decent dwelling place for slum dwellers. The group had an advantage over slum landlords, in that its properties, as a non-profit corporation, enjoyed a tax abatement. The turnover of tenants in the project proved to be 80%. The repairs necessitated tripling the rent. But, instead of an 8% profit as expected, the result was a 3% loss. After four years of failure, they conceded it was impossible to maintain decent living conditions and make a profit.

[2.] Los Angeles *Herald-Examiner,* Sunday, April 9, 1967, CC, A-5, "Death on Wednesday."

The cost of maintenance proved very high, because slum dwellers were abusive of their quarters. The "answer" according to the Council, was Public Housing! [3]

In brief, many people in the slums deserve the slums and belong there; they make a slum out of the newest building, because such is their nature. A free economy allows the deserving to get out of the slums, and there has always been an exodus of those with character. But the socialist and environmental answer is so powerful today that it came naturally to the Council even when their experiment demonstrated its failure. By penalizing the hard-working to provide good housing for slum dwellers to pollute and destroy, these environmentalists are destroying freedom for all. By the progressively heavier taxation of all, they are preparing the way for a universal slum, the destruction of wealth and the repression of initiative in all.

The creed implicit in the Council's action is humanism, statist humanism. As a result, its actions followed the logic of their faith, and its answer was messianic. Salvation is in statist action, and hence it is the essential resort in every time of testing and trial.

Every social order has an implicit creed, and this creed defines the order and informs it. When a social order begins to crumble, it is because the basic faith, its creed, has been undermined. But the political defense of that order is usually made the first line of defense: it becomes the conservative position. But, because the defense is politically rather than creedally informed, it is a superficial defense and crumbles steadily under a highly doctrinaire and creedal opposition. Thus, Cicero's defense of the Roman republic was a spirited and heroic effort, but it was also the epitome of impotence. The republic was already dead; Cicero himself did not believe in the religion on which the republic had been based. When Cicero could not accept the religious foundations which made an aristocracy sovereign, how could he expect the rebellious masses to accept it? Cicero's position was essentially personal, and the various defenders of the republic were more linked by purely personal tastes and interests than a creedal position. Julius Caesar was able to capitalize on the new creedalism and make himself the religious and civil head of the new movement. Similarly, today humanism is the creedal basis of the various democratic and socialistic movements. The clearer the humanism, as in Marxism, the more direct its use of power, because it operates in terms of a consistency of principle. The conservatives attempt to retain the political forms of the Christian West with no belief in Biblical Christianity. Apart from vague affirmations of liberty, they cannot defend their position philosophically. The con-

---

3. William Buckley, Jr., "Failure in the Slums," in *National Review*, vol. XIX, no. 13, April 4, 1967, 341.

servatives therefore become *fact-finders:* they try to oppose the humanists by documenting their cruelty, corruption, and abuse of office. If the facts carry any conviction to the people, they lead them only to exchange one set of radical humanists for reforming radical humanists. It is never their faith in the system which is shaken, but only in a form or representative of that system. The success of the subversives rests on their attack on the creed of the establishment, and its replacement by a new creed. When the foundations are provided, the general form of the building is determined. When the creed is accepted, the social order is determined. There can therefore be no reconstruction of the Christian civilization of the west except on Christian creedal foundations.

INDEX

The Author

Rousas John Rushdoony is a well-known American scholar, writer, and author of over thirty books. He holds B.A. and M.A. degrees from the University of California and received his theological training at the Pacific School of Religion. An ordained minister, he has been a missionary among Paiute and Shoshone Indians as well as pastor of two California churches. He is founder of Chalcedon Foundation, an educational organization devoted to research, publishing, and cogent communication of a distinctively Christian scholarship to the world at large. His writing in the *Chalcedon Report* and his numerous books have spawned a generation of believers active in reconstructing the world to the glory of Jesus Christ. He resides in Vallecito, California and is currently engaged in research, lecturing, and assisting others in developing programs to put the Christian faith into action.

The Ministry of Chalcedon

CHALCEDON (kal•see•don) is a Christian educational organization devoted exclusively to research, publishing, and cogent communication of a distinctively Christian scholarship to the world at large. It makes available a variety of services and programs, all geared to the needs of interested ministers, scholars, and laymen who understand the propositions that Jesus Christ speaks to the mind as well as the heart, and that His claims extend beyond the narrow confines of the various institutional churches. We exist in order to support the efforts of all orthodox denominations and churches. Chalcedon derives its name from the great ecclesiastical Council of Chalcedon (A.D. 451), which produced the crucial Christological definition: "Therefore, following the holy Fathers, we all with one accord teach men to acknowledge one and the same Son, our Lord Jesus Christ, at once complete in Godhead and complete in manhood, truly God and truly man ...." This formula directly challenges every false claim of divinity by any human institution: state, church, cult, school, or human assembly. Christ alone is both God and man, the unique link between heaven and earth. All human power is therefore derivative: Christ alone can announce that "All power is given unto me in heaven and in earth" (Matthew 28:18). Historically, the Chalcedonian creed is therefore the foundation of Western liberty, for it sets limits on all authoritarian human institutions by acknowledging the validity of the claims of the One who is the source of true human freedom (Galatians 5:1).

The *Chalcedon Report* is published monthly and is sent to all who request it. All gifts to Chalcedon are tax deductible.

Chalcedon
Box 158
Vallecito, CA 95251 U.S.A.